Google SketchUp Cookbook
Practical Recipes and Essential Techniques

Bonnie Roskes

O'REILLY®

Beijing · Cambridge · Farnham · Köln · Sebastopol · Taipei · Tokyo

Google SketchUp Cookbook

by Bonnie Roskes

Published by O'Reilly Media, Inc., 1005 Gravenstein Highway North, Sebastopol, CA 95472.

O'Reilly books may be purchased for educational, business, or sales promotional use. Online editions are also available for most titles (*safari.oreilly.com*). For more information, contact our corporate/institutional sales department: 800-998-9938 or *corporate@oreilly.com*.

Editor: Steve Weiss

Developmental Editor: Linda Laflamme

Production Editors: Michele Filshie and Rachel Monaghan

Copyeditor: Sharon Wilkey

Proofreader: Nancy Reinhardt

Indexer: Julie Hawks

Technical Editors: Susan Sorger and Bill Eberle

Cover Designer: Karen Montgomery

Interior Designer: Ron Bilodeau

Illustrator: Robert Romano

Printing History:

March 2009: First Edition.

RepKover. This book uses Repkover,™ a durable and flexible lay-flat binding.

ISBN: 978-0-596-15511-7

[C]

Contents

Preface

If you're reading this book, you know a bit about Google SketchUp and probably have used it to create some great models. You love SketchUp's price (free, or about $500 for the Pro version) and you certainly love SketchUp's intuitive user interface. Dig beneath SketchUp's deceptively simple surface, however, and you can unearth techniques that enable you to create stunning models and presentations that you thought only pricey modeling applications could produce.

This book will teach you how to tap into that power. Through illustrated, step-by-step tutorials, the *Google SketchUp Cookbook* will show you features of SketchUp you should use (but haven't yet), or always wanted to try, or didn't even know existed.

This book will teach you all about groups, components, model intersection, materials and textures, presentation, animation, and styles. You will learn how to find your way around Google's vast model repository (the 3D Warehouse), and see how SketchUp models integrate seamlessly with Google Earth. You'll also learn about SketchUp 7's exciting new feature: dynamic components.

By the time you complete the *Google SketchUp Cookbook*, you will be able to create models you never thought you could and share them with the world (if you choose).

Who This Book Is For

This book is for intermediate and advanced users of SketchUp who want to go beyond the basic uses of drawing and editing tools. You should have a good working knowledge of SketchUp's 2D drawing tools (Line, Rectangle, Circle, and so on) as well as editing tools (Move, Push/Pull, Rotate, and so on). It also doesn't hurt if you already know how to use Intersect and Follow Me, how to create a group or component, and how to paint a face with colors or materials, although the basics of those topics are reviewed in this book. If you've never used texture positioning, Photo Match, scenes, layers, or styles before, don't worry; you'll learn all about those topics and many more in this book.

Who This Book Is Not For

If you haven't used SketchUp before or have used it only for simple models, you might want to practice the basics before continuing with this book. The SketchUp website has lots of online videos and self-paced tutorials to get everyone up and running rather quickly (go to *http://sketchup.google.com/training*). Another helpful resource that's appropriate for users of all levels is O'Reilly's *Google SketchUp: The Missing Manual* by Chris Grover.

After you understand all of the geometry creation and editing tools, can make a group and component, and can paint faces by using different textures, then you'll be ready to jump into this book.

How This Book Is Organized

The techniques in this book are grouped by topic. Here's a preview:

Chapter 1, "Making Multiple Copies," covers the various ways you can make linear or rotated arrays of objects.

Chapter 2, "Following Paths with Follow Me," describes how to use the Follow Me tool to extrude faces along paths, in order to remove volume from or add it to your model. You'll also learn what happens when Follow Me is used within the context of a group or component, how to use round paths to make round objects, and how to construct 3D paths.

Chapter 3, "Intersection Edges: Cutting and Trimming," describes how to generate intersection edges that enable you to cut and trim objects against one another. You'll also learn how to take advantage of groups and components while intersecting, and how to control exactly where intersection edges are generated.

Chapter 4, "Advanced Intersect and Follow Me Techniques," is dedicated to the most efficient and sophisticated ways of working with both tools, because the Intersect and Follow Me tools are used so often in tandem.

Chapter 5, "Roofs: Constraints and Inferences," uses mostly roofing examples to demonstrate the various ways you can constrain objects to other objects, constrain objects to specific directions, and use Autofold to force objects to move a specific way.

Chapter 6, "Groups: Protect and Defend," covers all the reasons to use groups, including protecting objects from changes, preventing stickiness with other objects, creating intersection slices, and two-sided painting.

Chapter 7, "Components: Efficiency in Repetition," describes how to create, import, replace, and reload components, as well as set alignment and gluing properties, because a true SketchUp expert must also be an expert in components. Special attention is given to the common problem of using window components to cut through 3D walls, as well as to the Outliner.

Chapter 8, "Painting, Materials, and Textures," explains how to find and import materials, as well as how to edit and position textured images, and to use translucent and alpha-transparent materials.

Chapter 9, "Modeling with Digital Photos," describes how to paint faces by using digital images, in order to produce photorealistic models with low file sizes. You'll learn how to position images in 2D and 3D, make minor changes to an image, and build 3D models from a single image by using texture positioning and Photo Match.

Chapter 10, "Modeling with Exact Dimensions," covers all of the ways you can enter and calculate exact dimensions while using drawing and editing tools. You'll also learn about resizing entire models, and resizing models that include groups and components.

Chapter 11, "Presentation: Showing off Your Model," demonstrates how to combine layers, scenes, shadows, section planes, and walk-through tools to explore multiple design scenarios, and to create impressive presentations and animations of your model.

Chapter 12, "Displaying Your Model," covers all aspects of how your model looks, including edge display, templates, and styles. You'll learn how to build your own custom edge style and how to include different styles in your model presentation.

Chapter 13, "3D Warehouse and Google Earth," describes how to navigate Google's 3D Warehouse to find exactly the model or collection you want, how to place your own models and collections in the 3D Warehouse, how to georeference your model, and how to place models in Google Earth.

Chapter 14, "Dynamic Components," discusses what makes a component dynamic, demonstrates what dynamic components can do, and explains how to find dynamic components in the 3D Warehouse.

How to Get the Models Used in This Book

You may be tempted to jump right into Chapter 1 and get started, but read this important section first! Without these details about downloading this book's model files, you won't get very far.

Although some examples in this book start from scratch, most start with a specific model you'll need to download. All of these starter models, and many of the completed ones, reside in Google's 3D Warehouse, in collections created specifically for the *Google SketchUp Cookbook*.

There are a few different ways to find and download models in the 3D Warehouse, either from within SketchUp or from your Internet browser. These methods are all detailed in Recipe 13.1, but this section explains how to find models by using your Internet browser. Downloading this way ensures that you will open each model in a new SketchUp window. This will prevent any problems relating to the following two issues:

- Many of these models have scenes, which are tabs at the top of the SketchUp window. Click a tab, and you go to the associated saved view. Some models have only two scenes for the start and end cases, others have numerous scenes in which each step is explained, and still others have scenes used for animation. (You'll learn all about scenes in Chapter 11.) If a model with scenes is downloaded directly into your SketchUp model, as opposed to opening it in a new SketchUp window, its scenes will not appear.

- When you import a model directly into a SketchUp model, the imported model is brought in as a component. Before you can do anything with this imported component, you have to explode it. This is not very difficult, but it is "cleaner" to start with an unexploded model that has no objects from other files in it.

To enter the 3D Warehouse, point your browser to *http://sketchup.google.com/3dwarehouse*. The opening page has a search field at the top, in which you can enter *cookbook*. Because you are searching for a collection, and not an individual model, select the Collections radio button (Figure P-1).

Figure P-1

At the time of this writing, there is only one cookbook collection, whose full name is *Google SketchUp Cookbook* (Figure P-2). Click this link, or click the collection's thumbnail.

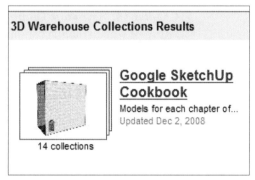

Figure P-2

Within the Cookbook collection, there is a separate collection for each chapter (Figure P-3). Find the collection for the chapter you are reading, and click its name or thumbnail to open the collection. Keep in mind that only 12 items are listed at a time in the 3D Warehouse. So if you don't see the model or collection you want, use the scroll arrows at the bottom of the web page.

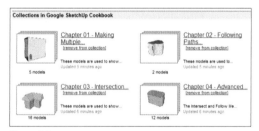

Figure P-3

Figure P-4 shows the models inside Chapter 1's collection. If you want to download a model straightaway, without seeing its description, click Download to Google SketchUp 7. You can either save the model or open it in SketchUp. If you already have a SketchUp model open, clicking Open will open a new SketchUp window; you will not close the existing model.

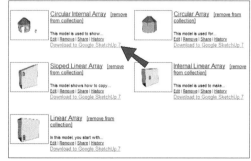

Figure P-4

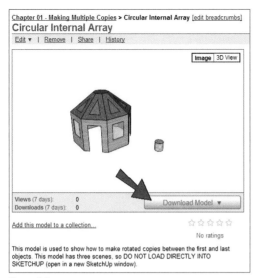

Figure P-5

If you want to see a larger view of a 3D Warehouse model, or read its description or check its reviews, click the model's name or thumbnail. Figure P-5 shows the 3D Warehouse page for the Circular Internal Array model in Chapter 1's collection. (It's not rated yet, but feel free to give all of my models five stars.) Any model for this book that has scenes comes with a warning in its description about how to download it. (This warning is not relevant when using the 3D Warehouse in your Internet browser.)

You do not have to page through these collections each time you want to find a model; you can search for a model name directly. In the Search field of the main page of the 3D Warehouse, make sure Models is selected instead of Collections, and enter the model name in the Search field. If you get too many models in your search results, you can add *roskes* to whittle down the search to ones I've uploaded. For example, you'll need a model called Dresser in Chapter 7. Entering *dresser* will result in hundreds of models, but entering *dresser roskes* should turn up just one model. (Good thing I have an unusual last name.) You could also enter *cookbook dresser* and get to the same model.

Conventions Used in This Book

The following typographical conventions are used in this book:

Menu options

Menu options are shown using the → character, such as File→Open.

Italic

Indicates new terms, emphasis, and text that should be typed literally by the user.

How to Use This Book

This isn't a book to take to bed (or the bathroom). It is meant to sit next to your keyboard while you have SketchUp up and running. SketchUp is the kind of application you can learn only by doing, so work through the steps of each example, checking the accompanying illustrations to compare your results to mine.

The chapters proceed in a logical, progressive order, but if you are already familiar with the concepts of a particular chapter or recipe, you won't get lost if you skip around. Some recipes refer to concepts in other recipes, so you may find yourself flipping pages back and forth.

O'Reilly Cookbooks

Looking for the right ingredients to solve a problem? Look no further than O'Reilly Cookbooks. Each Cookbook contains hundreds of recipes, and includes hundreds of techniques you can use to solve specific problems.

The recipes you'll find in an O'Reilly Cookbook follow a simple formula:

Problem
> Each Problem addressed in an O'Reilly Cookbook is clearly stated, specific, and practical.

Solution
> The Solution is easy to understand and implement.

Discussion
> The Discussion clarifies and explains the context of the Problem and the Solution.

To learn more about the O'Reilly Cookbook series, or to find other Cookbooks that are up your alley, visit the website at *http://cookbooks.oreilly.com*.

How to Contact Us

Please address comments and questions concerning this book to the publisher:

> O'Reilly Media, Inc.
> 1005 Gravenstein Highway North
> Sebastopol, CA 95472
> 800-998-9938 (in the United States or Canada)
> 707-829-0515 (international or local)
> 707-829-0104 (fax)

We have a web page for this book, where we list errata, examples, and any additional information. You can access this page at *http://oreilly.com/catalog/9780596155117*.

Safari® Books Online

 When you see a Safari® Books Online icon on the cover of your favorite technology book, that means the book is available online through the O'Reilly Network Safari Bookshelf.

Safari offers a solution that's better than e-books. It's a virtual library that lets you easily search thousands of top tech books, cut and paste code samples, download chapters, and find quick answers when you need the most accurate, current information. Try it for free at *http://my.safaribooksonline.com*.

Acknowledgments

I am honored to be part of the O'Reilly author community, and I'd like to thank Steve, Linda, Michele, Sharon, and Dennis from the O'Reilly team; their support made this book project so much fun. Susan Sorger and Bil Eberle are eagle-eyed with their technical editing, and Bryce Stout from Google never failed to quickly answer my technical questions. Finally, thanks to Sandy and the kids, who put up with my late nights working.

CHAPTER 1

Making Multiple Copies

This chapter covers the various ways you can make linear and rotated copies by using the Move and Rotate tools. If you've done any basic work with Sketch-Up, you might already be familiar with the concepts in this chapter. Keep reading, however. Even some experienced users don't know all there is about how to copy, which is a fundamental and important concept. (Plus it never hurts to review some basics.)

As you probably know, the Move tool is used to move objects, and the Rotate tool is used to rotate objects. For both tools, when you press the Ctrl/Option key, you will make copies. For linear copies, you can adjust the spacing and number of copies, and for rotated copies, you can adjust the angle between copies and the number of copies. For both kinds of copying, you can make these adjustments as many times as needed while the tool is still active. Keep in mind, however, that after you start a new Move or Rotate action, or activate a new tool, you can no longer adjust the spacing, angles, and so on.

1.1 Copying in Linear Arrays

Problem

You want to copy an object in a linear pattern (rows and columns).

Solution

Use the Move tool to make one copy and then adjust the number of copies and spacing between copies.

Discussion

To make copies, activate the Move tool and press the Ctrl key (Option on the Mac). SketchUp is very flexible in how you can set the spacing and number of copies: After the first copy is made, you can enter the number of copies you want and set the spacing between them. Until you activate a new tool or start a new Move operation, you can continue to adjust both the spacing and numbers.

Most often, you need to make several copies of something in the horizontal (red or green) or vertical (blue) direction. In this example, you will practice this scenario by placing rows of windows along a wall. In the "Other Uses" section, you'll see other examples of linear arrays: placing desks in a classroom, creating a neighborhood of identical houses, and arranging keys in a musical keyboard.

1. Start with a building like the one shown in Figure 1-1, which has one small window at the lower-left corner of the front face. You can create your model from scratch, or download my Linear Array model from the 3D Warehouse. Because the window will be copied, it should be a component. Why a component? A component is easy to select and will keep the file size small.

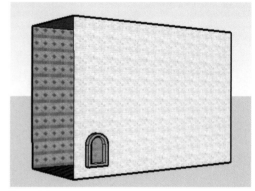

Figure 1-1

Note ───────────────────────────

Aside from the reasons already mentioned, components are an extremely powerful feature of SketchUp, and you should take advantage of them wherever you can. Components are covered in detail in Chapter 7.

Want to Create this Model Yourself?

1. Draw a rectangle and use Push/Pull to pull it up.
2. Erase a side wall so that you can see inside (right-click on the face and choose Erase).
3. Paint the front and back faces, if you want.
4. In the lower-left corner of the front wall, draw the basic window shape by using a rectangle and an · arc, erasing the dividing line between them. Make it small enough so that several rows and columns of windows can fit in the wall.
5. Use Offset to make the window frame.

6. To pull out the window frame, activate Push/Pull and press Ctrl (Option on the Mac) and pull out the frame face. (Ctrl/Option ensures that you will leave a flat face on the back of the frame, and not make a hollow shell.)
7. Select the entire window, including all edges and faces, taking care not to select any edges or faces of the building itself. Right-click on a selected face and choose Make Component.
8. Assign a component name, and be sure to select "Replace selection with component."

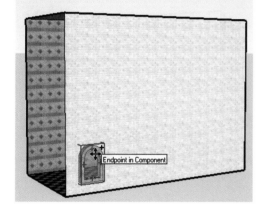

Figure 1-2

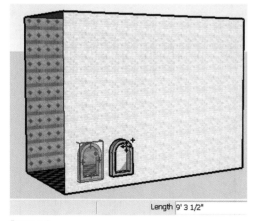

Figure 1-3

2. Activate Move and press the Ctrl/Option key. (You need to only tap the key; you don't have to keep it pressed.) You should see a + sign on the cursor symbol.

— **Note** —————————————

When you use the Ctrl/Option key to make a copy, you can tap the key either before or after clicking move points. You can also tap Ctrl/Option repeatedly to toggle copying on and off.

3. Move the cursor over the window, which becomes highlighted in a bounding box (Figure 1-2). Click anywhere on the window, but do not click on one of the red + signs, as these will switch you from Move to Rotate mode.
4. The second point places the copy. Move the mouse directly to the right, in the green or red axis direction, as shown in Figure 1-3. (Whether the direction is green or red depends on how you oriented your model.) While you're moving the mouse, look at the Length box, which indicates the distance between copies.

— **Note** —————————————

The length is indicated in the units of your model, which are set in the template you chose when you opened the file. If you want to change the units, open the Model Info window (Window→Model Info) to the Units page.

5. Click to place the copy. After the copy is placed, the window glass cuts the wall, and you can see through it.

6. Making an external linear array in SketchUp is easy: Type the number of copies you want, followed by an *x*, and then press Enter. Type *3x* and press Enter, for a total of four windows (Figure 1-4).

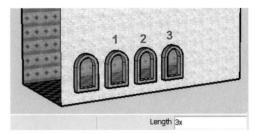
Figure 1-4

—— **Note** ——————————————————————

Do not click in the Length field; just type and press Enter. If you click to enter the Length field, SketchUp will think you are ending the current action.

_____

As long as you don't start another Move operation or activate another tool, you can change your mind about numbers and spacing. For example, entering *6x* yields seven windows, which is too many (Figure 1-5).

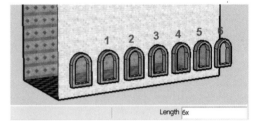
Figure 1-5

7. Enter *5x* to produce six copies (Figure 1-6). This is better, but the spacing isn't quite right. The windows should be closer together.

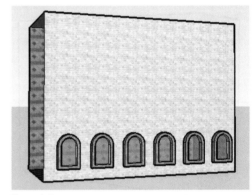
Figure 1-6

8. To make the windows 8 feet apart, type *8'* and press Enter. (If your units are Architectural, you need to include the apostrophe for the foot symbol.) As you can see in Figure 1-7, this looks too crowded.

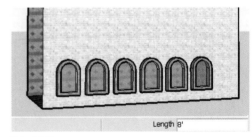
Figure 1-7

9. Try 8' 6" (Architectural format for 8 feet and 6 inches). You can enter this dimension most easily as *8.5'*. This still looks too crowded (Figure 1-8).

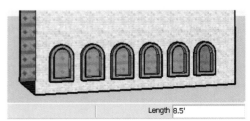
Figure 1-8

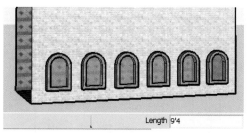

Figure 1-9

10. Keep trying out new numbers until your spacing looks right. As shown in Figure 1-9, I settled on spacing of 9' 4", which can be entered like this: *9'4*. (The inch symbol is not needed because that is the default unit.)

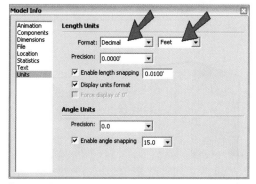

Figure 1-10

Entering Numbers

SketchUp is flexible in how you can enter numbers for lengths. If your units are Architectural, the default unit is inches. So for 7' 4" you could enter 88 (for 88 inches), 7.33', or 7'4. If you want precision to fractions of an inch, you can enter 5'8 7/16. If your units are Imperial (feet or inches), you can still enter values with metric units, such as 440cm, 4400m, or 4.4m. (Conversely, you can enter Imperial units in a metric unit model.) If you want to stick with Architectural units but have your default unit be feet, switch your units to Decimal and Feet (Figure 1-10).

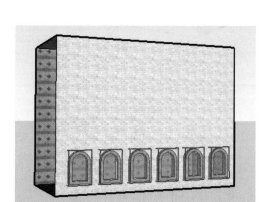

Figure 1-11

11. When your row of windows looks right, you can copy the entire row. The Move tool will actively select only one object at a time, so when you want to copy multiple objects, you must first preselect the objects. Activate Select and select all of the windows in the row, as shown in Figure 1-11. (Holding the Shift key enables you to select multiple objects.)

Figure 1-12

12. Activate Move and press Ctrl/Option. Click anywhere for the first move point—on a face, edge, or in blank space. Then click the second move point straight above the first move point, in the blue direction (Figure 1-12).

SketchUp moves the selected objects by the distance and direction between the two move points.

13. Enter *2x* (or whatever number works for you) and adjust the spacing to fill the wall with windows (Figure 1-13).

Figure 1-13

14. Now you can copy all of these windows to the back of the building. Select them all, activate Move with Ctrl/Option, and for the first move point, click the midpoint shown in Figure 1-14. This midpoint is used so that the position of the windows relative to the front wall will be the same for the windows copied to the back wall.

Figure 1-14

15. Orbit to face the back wall, and click the same midpoint on this wall. The finished building is shown in Figure 1-15.

Figure 1-15

Other Uses

There are endless possibilities for external linear array copies, but here are just a few:

Figure 1-16 shows repeated chair-and-desk components that fill a classroom.

Figure 1-16

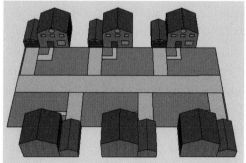

Figure 1-17

Figure 1-17 shows houses copied to make a neighborhood. (To copy the houses from one side of the street to the other, you can turn them to face the right way with the Flip option on the pop-up menu.)

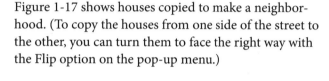

Note

To make a neighborhood with houses of different colors, see Recipe 7.8.

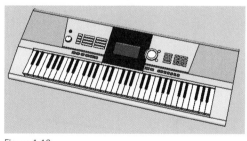

Figure 1-18

Figure 1-18 shows a set of piano keys copied to make a keyboard. The buttons at the top are also copied components.

1.2 Creating Linear Internal Arrays

Problem

You want to place your first and last copies, and space additional objects between them.

Solution

Use construction lines for exact placement, and use the "forward slash" format for the number of copies.

Discussion

In this scenario, you know where the first and last objects are located, and want to space objects evenly between them. The format for placing a specific number of copies between two objects is to enter the desired number of copies, followed by the / (forward slash) symbol. (The forward slash symbol denotes division.) For example, if you make a copy of an object 20 feet away, and then type 4/ and press Enter, you will have five objects (four copies plus one original), with four equal spaces of 5 feet each in between copies.

To help you align your copies, you can use construction lines, which are temporary guide lines that can easily be erased or hidden when you're finished with them. Construction lines are created with the Tape Measure tool.

In this example, you'll use construction lines to place the first and last windows in a row, and then use the forward slash format to place more windows in between. In the "Other Uses" section, you'll see how an internal array can be used to space pickets of a fence.

1. Start with a model like the one shown in Figure 1-19, which has one window in the middle of the front wall. You can create your model from scratch, or download my Internal Linear Array model from the 3D Warehouse. The window should be a component.

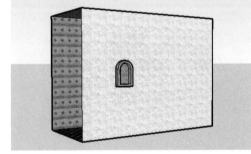

Figure 1-19

--- **Note** ---------------------------------

If you want to create this model from scratch, see the sidebar "Want to Create This Model Yourself?" in Recipe 1.1.

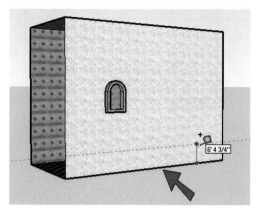

Figure 1-20

2. In addition to measuring, the Tape Measure tool can be used for creating construction lines. Activate Tape Measure. You should see a + sign attached to your cursor, but if not, press the Ctrl/Option key (otherwise, you will only be taking a measurement). Click anywhere on the lower edge of the wall (don't click on an endpoint), and move the cursor straight up, creating an offset construction line as shown in Figure 1-20. The offset distance appears next to the cursor.

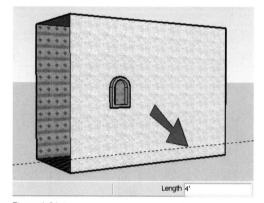

Figure 1-21

3. To make the offset exact, type the offset distance and press Enter. For this example, type *4'* for 4 feet (Figure 1-21).

Note

You can use the Tape Measure to resize an entire model, group, or component. This is shown in Recipes 10.10, 10.11, and 10.12.

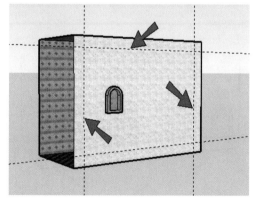

Figure 1-22

4. Create construction lines at the same offset distance from the other three edges of this wall (Figure 1-22).

Note

When you need to create angled construction lines, use the Protractor tool (not to be confused with the Rotate tool).

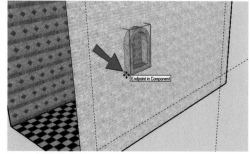

Figure 1-23

5. You can now move the window into place. Select it, activate Move, and for the first move point, click the window's lower-left corner, where the back of the window meets the wall (Figure 1-23).

6. Place this corner at the intersection point of the bottom and left construction lines, as shown in Figure 1-24 (make sure you see the *Intersection* inference, which is a snap point).

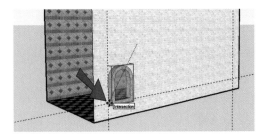

Figure 1-24

7. To place a copy on the other side, click the first move point on the lower-right back corner of the window (Figure 1-25).

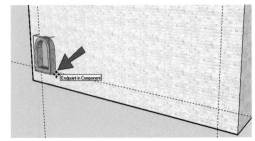

Figure 1-25

8. Press Ctrl/Option, and click the second move point at the intersection of the right and bottom construction lines (Figure 1-26).

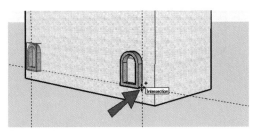

Figure 1-26

9. Type *3/* and press Enter (don't forget the forward slash symbol after the number). This gives you four windows (three copies plus the original), with three equal spaces in between (Figure 1-27).

You can still change your mind; in Figure 1-28, for example, I switched to five copied windows (*5/*).

Figure 1-27

Figure 1-28

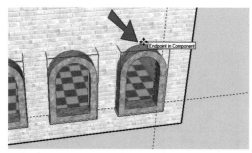

Figure 1-29

10. To make additional evenly spaced rows, select all of the windows, and for the first move point, click any one of the windows at its top point (Figure 1-29).

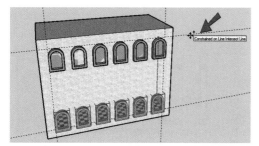

Figure 1-30

11. Start to move the copy up vertically (blue direction), and press and hold the Shift key to lock in the blue direction. With Shift pressed, click anywhere on the top construction line (Figure 1-30).

    You could also tap (but not hold) the up arrow key to lock the blue direction, which saves you from having to keep Shift pressed. How you lock directions is a personal preference. Locking directions and other constraints are covered in depth in Chapter 5.

12. Enter *2/* to get three rows, and you're finished.

13. To erase the construction lines, you can use the Eraser tool and click each one, or choose Edit→Delete Guides. (You can also hide construction lines by choosing View→Hide Guides.) The completed model is shown in Figure 1-31.

Figure 1-31

Other Uses

An internal linear array can be used to space pickets of a fence. Figure 1-32 shows a fence in which the first picket is copied to the end of the fence.

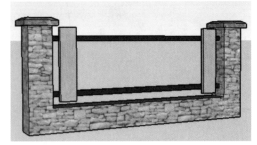

Figure 1-32

In Figure 1-33, the 4/ spacing creates four copies of the picket.

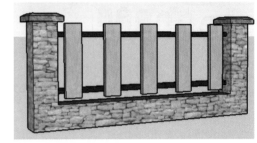

Figure 1-33

In Figure 1-34, the 7/ spacing creates seven copies, producing a denser fence.

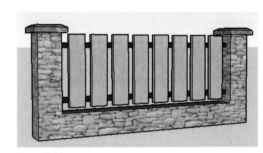

Figure 1-34

1.3 Building a Nonorthogonal Linear Array

Problem

You want to make linear copies along a slope, in a nonorthogonal direction.

Solution

When defining the move points, use reference geometry that defines the move direction.

Discussion

In the previous recipes, the copies have followed the red, green, or blue directions. When you want to move in another direction, first be sure that you have objects in your model that define the direction you want to use. In this example, the model has an edge that defines the move direction, and both move points will be clicked along this edge.

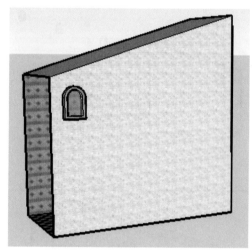

Figure 1-35

1. Start with a building like the one shown in Figure 1-35, with a sloped top and one window in the top-left corner of the front wall. You can create your model from scratch, or download my Sloped Linear Array model from the 3D Warehouse. The window should be a component.

> **Note**
>
> If you want to create this model from scratch, see the sidebar "Want to Create This Model Yourself?" in Recipe 1.1. To slope the roof, select one of the top side edges and move it straight up.

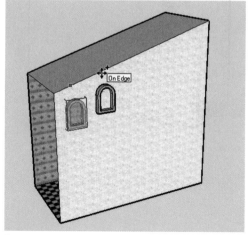

Figure 1-36

2. Select the window and activate Move. Press Ctrl/ Option. For the move distance and direction, click two points along the sloped edge, as shown in Figure 1-36. (If your window jumps to the wrong face, wiggle the mouse to tweak it into place.)

3. Using the method demonstrated in Recipe 1.1, enter the number of copies you want (say, *4x*) and adjust the spacing to get a line of sloped windows (Figure 1-37). The spacing is the distance measured along the diagonal edge.

Figure 1-37

4. You can change your mind and use an internal array as shown in Recipe 1.2. Just enter the distance between the first and last windows. The distance in this example is 50 feet. You will still have the same number of windows as before, but they will be spaced so that only two appear on the building (Figure 1-38). You may have to zoom out to see the rest of the windows.

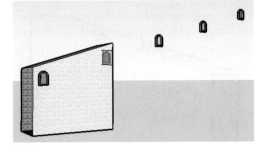

Figure 1-38

5. Enter *6/*, or whatever number works for you, to get your internal array of windows (Figure 1-39). All of the copies now appear between the first and last windows.

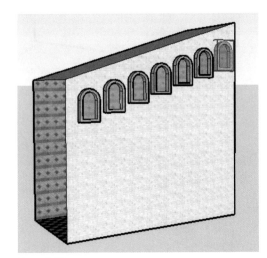

Figure 1-39

1.4 Copying in Circular Arrays

Problem

You want to make copies of an object in a circular pattern.

Solution

Use the Rotate tool to make copies, adjusting the number of copies and the angle between copies.

Discussion

To make copies with the Rotate tool, you must first preselect the objects to be copied. Then activate the Rotate tool and press the Ctrl key (Option on the Mac). You can enter the angle between copies before or after you place the copy. After the first copy is made, you can enter the number of copies you want. Until you activate a new tool or start a new Rotate operation, you can continue to adjust both the angle and numbers.

This example is an octagonal-shaped building, in which windows and doors will be copied in a circular pattern, to fit on the walls.

In "Other Uses," you'll see how rotated copies can be used to make a jewel-studded bracelet, a dining room set, a Ferris wheel, and a circular group of columns.

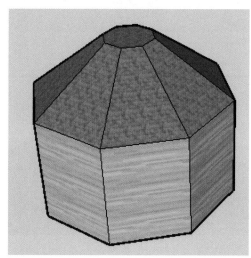

Figure 1-40

1. Start with an octagon-shaped building as shown in Figure 1-40, with a sloped octagonal roof. You can create your model from scratch, or download my Circular Array model from the 3D Warehouse.

Want to Create This Model Yourself?

1. To create the base, activate Polygon and enter *8* to set the number of sides. Draw the polygon on the flat (red-green) plane.
2. Paint the octagon the color you want for the vertical walls.
3. Pull the octagon up.
4. Paint the top face a different color.
5. Activate Push/Pull again, and press Ctrl/Option so that new faces will be created. Pull the top face up.
6. Select the top face and use Scale to shrink it. While scaling, press Ctrl/Option to scale about the center.

2. To create one of the roof windows, use the Offset tool to make a triangle inside one of the roof faces. Trim any extra edges, and paint the window with glass.

3. Select this new window face (Figure 1-41).

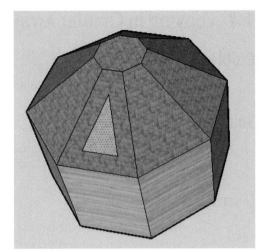

Figure 1-41

4. Activate Rotate. The first click places the center of rotation, which should be the center of the top octagonal face. Before you can find this point, you need to remind SketchUp of that inference point, so hover over one of the corner points of the top octagon (Figure 1-42).

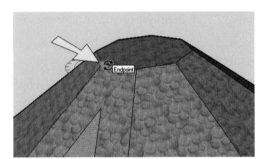

Figure 1-42

5. Having found the circumference of the octagon, SketchUp can now find its center point. Move the cursor to the center and click the center point, as shown in Figure 1-43.

> **Note**
>
> SketchUp always keeps the last five defined points in its immediate memory buffer. If you are looking for an object created more than five clicks ago, you need to move that object up into the buffer. Hovering over a point or edge does just this.

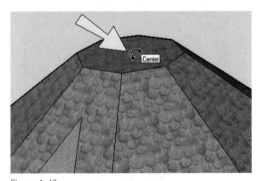

Figure 1-43

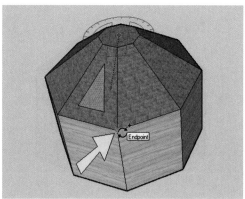

Figure 1-44

6. The next two clicks define the rotation angle. The first click defines the angle's baseline, and the second click defines the rotation angle relative to the baseline. Press Ctrl/Option to make a copy (look for the + sign on the cursor), and click any corner of any octagon (top, middle, or bottom of the building), as shown in Figure 1-44.

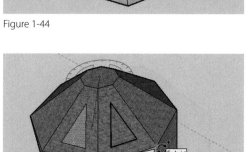

Figure 1-45

7. Click an adjacent octagon corner, and the Angle field informs you that the angle is 45 degrees (Figure 1-45).

   In this example, 45 degrees is the correct angle (360 / 8 = 45). If you wanted to try out a different angle, you would just type it and press Enter. (You can also simply enter an angle value instead of clicking the second rotation point.)

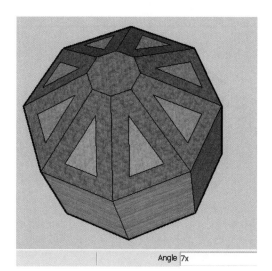

Figure 1-46

8. Enter 7x, and you have eight total windows (Figure 1-46).

9. Now you'll make alternating windows and doors on the vertical faces. Activate Offset again, and place your cursor inside one of the faces, as shown in Figure 1-47 (don't click yet).

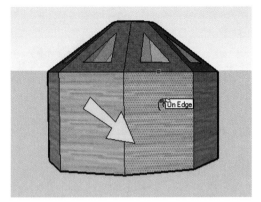

Figure 1-47

10. While the face is highlighted, double-click on it. This offsets the face by the same offset distance you used to make the triangular roof window (Figure 1-48).

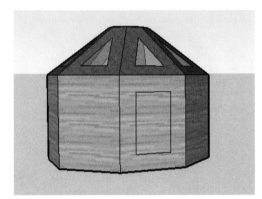

Figure 1-48

11. Make the same offset on an adjacent face (Figure 1-49).

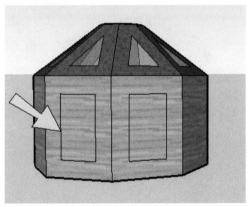

Figure 1-49

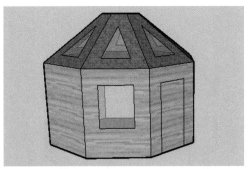

Figure 1-50

12. One offset rectangle will become a door, and the other will become a window. To make the door, move the bottom edge straight down to meet the ground. The door faces will eventually be erased, but it's hard to copy what isn't there, so leave the door face there for now. To make the window, move the bottom edge up and paint the face. The window and door are shown in Figure 1-50.

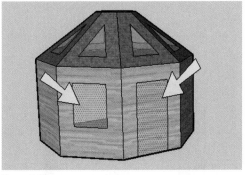

Figure 1-51

13. Select both of these faces (Figure 1-51).

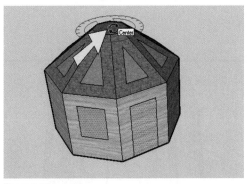

Figure 1-52

14. Activate Rotate and click the same center point as before, at the center of the top octagon (Figure 1-52).

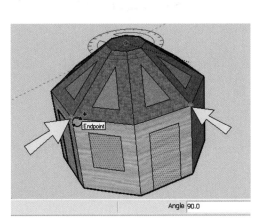

Figure 1-53

15. Because you are copying both faces at once, the rotation will be double what it was previously. Click two corner points that are 90 degrees apart (Figure 1-53).

16. Enter *3x*, and every face should have either a window or a door (Figure 1-54).

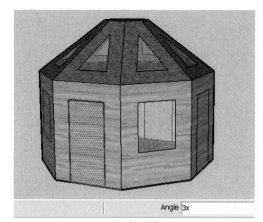

Figure 1-54

17. To remove the door face, use the Eraser tool on the edge shown in Figure 1-55.

18. Repeat this step for the other three doors.

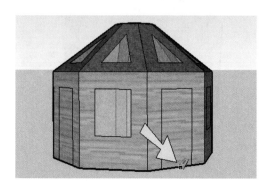

Figure 1-55

19. If any window faces aren't painted correctly, fix them with the Paint tool. Figure 1-56 shows the building viewed from below.

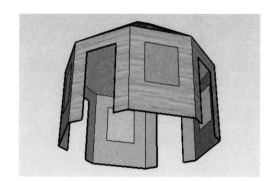

Figure 1-56

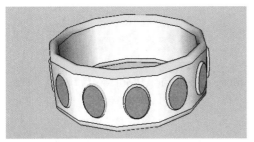

Figure 1-57

Other Uses

Here are a few examples of where rotated copies are used.

You can copy emeralds around a ring or bracelet (Figure 1-57).

Figure 1-58

You can arrange chairs around a circular table (Figure 1-58).

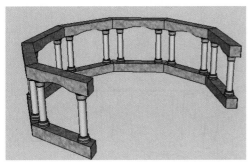

Figure 1-59

You can arrange pairs of columns in an open, circular pattern (Figure 1-59), perhaps for a hotel lobby or ballroom.

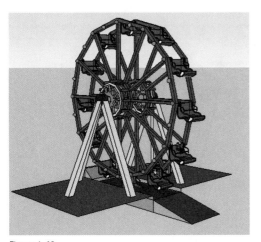

Figure 1-60

Finally, you can create supports and seats for a Ferris wheel (Figure 1-60).

1.5 Creating Circular Internal Arrays

Problem

You want to place your first and last rotated copies, and space additional objects between them.

Solution

Use the Rotate tool to make the last copy, and specify the number of internal copies in between using the forward slash format.

Discussion

In this scenario, you know where the first and last objects are located, and want to space objects evenly between them. The format for placing a specific number of copies between two rotate-copied objects is to enter the desired number of copies, followed by the / (forward slash) symbol, which denotes division. For example, if you make a copy of an object 90 degrees away, and then type *3/* and press Enter, you will have four objects (three copies plus one original), with three equal spaces of 30 degrees between copies.

In this example, you'll place a ring of planters around the model you created in Recipe 1.4. In the "Other Uses" section, you'll see how a circular internal array can be used to place chairs around a lecture podium.

1. Start with the model you completed in Recipe 1.4. Instead of making an actual planter with a plant in it, or taking the trouble to find a component for it, use a simplified cylinder instead. Somewhere outside the building, draw a circle and pull it up to represent a planter (Figure 1-61). Because it will be copied, make this cylinder a component. (If you don't have this model, you can download my Circular Internal Array model from the 3D Warehouse.)

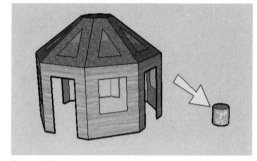

Figure 1-61

2. Select the planter, activate Rotate, and place the center of rotation at the center of the building (Figure 1-62).

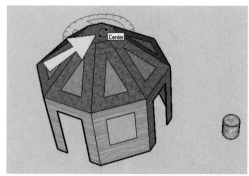

Figure 1-62

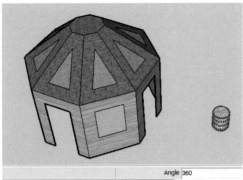

Figure 1-63

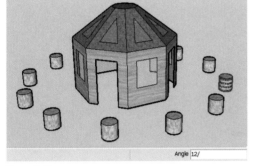

Figure 1-64

Figure 1-65

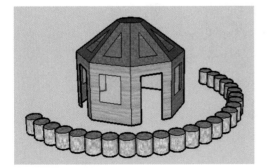

Figure 1-66

3. Create a copy 360 degrees away. This is a full turn around the circle, which means the copy is placed exactly on top of the original (Figure 1-63).

4. Enter *12/* (use the slash symbol) to get a total of 13 planters evenly spaced around the circle, as shown in Figure 1-64. (The last planter shares the same space as the first copy, so it appears that you have 12 planters.)

5. To get more planters, enter *24/* (Figure 1-65).

6. You can adjust the total rotation angle as well. Enter *180* to set 25 planters spaced within a 180-degree angle. This time there is no overlap between the first and last planters, so you can see all 25 planters (Figure 1-66).

Component Placeholders

When creating large object arrays, use the file-size-saving technique of component place-holding. Say the actual planter you need is very complex or contains a 3D tree with a great many faces and edges. Keeping 25 of these in your model would slow things down considerably, because each time you orbit to a new view, SketchUp has to redraw every edge and every face. To keep things small and smooth, use a simple object, such as a cylinder, as a temporary placeholder. Then when you're ready to switch, you can easily select all components and reload them as the "real thing." This technique is shown in Recipe 7.13.

Other Uses

A circular internal array can be used to place chairs in a circular pattern around a lecture podium.

Figure 1-67 shows the first and last chair in the room. Their location is determined by the maximum viewing angle from the chair to the lecture podium.

For four copies of the chair, use 4/ spacing (Figure 1-68).

The 8/ spacing shown Figure 1-69 can be used for a more crowded lecture.

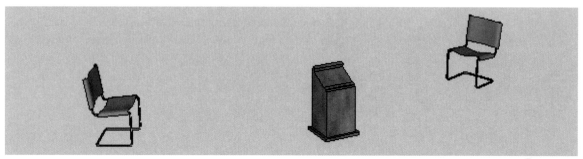

Figure 1-67

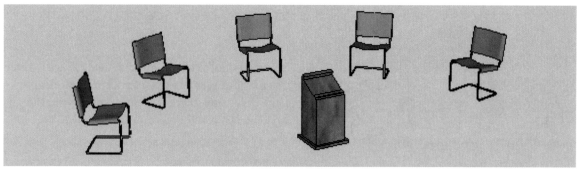

Figure 1-68

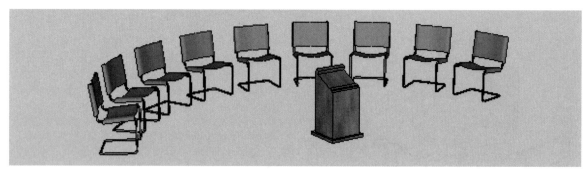

Figure 1-69

CHAPTER 2

Following Paths with Follow Me

The Follow Me tool is used to extrude a 2D face along a 2D or 3D path. In other design applications, this is sometimes called *sweeping* or *driving*. Follow Me is an incredibly useful tool for making such architectural details as moldings, parapets, railings, and fences, as well as circular objects such as cups, vases, and spheres. (It's also quite fun to watch Follow Me in action.)

The basics of Follow Me are pretty easy to understand, but there are some little-known tricks you can use to make your designing easier. In this chapter, you'll learn the best ways to use Follow Me, how to set up Follow Me paths relative to Follow Me faces, and how to take advantage of groups and components in order to prevent changes to other objects. You'll also learn how you can use a circular path to lathe all sorts of round objects, and how to create 3D Follow Me paths.

Before using Follow Me, you need to have these two things in your model:

- A Follow Me face, which will be extruded along the path. This must be a single face (not divided by edges) and must be 2D.

- A Follow Me path, which the Follow Me face will follow. The path must be continuous and can be 2D or 3D.

Follow Me is available on the Tools menu and as an icon on the Large Tool Set toolbar (Figure 2-1).

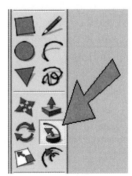

Figure 2-1

Note

To display the Large Tool Set toolbar, choose View→Toolbars→Large Tool Set (Windows) or View→Tool Palettes→Large Tool Set (Mac).

2.1 Extruding a Follow Me Face to Cut Volume Along a Path

Problem

You want to extrude a face along a path that will cut volume along the path.

Solution

Choose one of the three best methods to use Follow Me: preselect a face as a path, use the Alt/ Cmd key to define a path around a face, or preselect edges of a path.

Discussion

The three methods for using Follow Me are the following:

- Preselect a face as a path.

- Use the Alt/Cmd key to define a path around a face.

- Preselect edges of a path.

These can all be demonstrated by using a model of a building with a face drawn on one wall.

Start with a building like the one shown in Figure 2-2, which has at least one curved wall. You can create your model from scratch, or download my Paths and Faces model from the 3D Warehouse. The top face is a single face; it has no dividing edges. There is an arc face drawn on one wall, located along a vertical corner. This face, indicated in Figure 2-2, is the Follow Me face, which you will extrude all around the building.

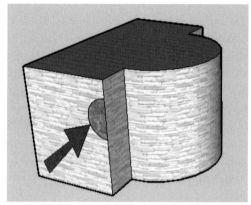

Figure 2-2

--- Note --

A Follow Me face is sometimes also called a shape profile. The only requirements for a face to be used as a Follow Me face is that it be planar (not curved or folded) and it must a single face, not divided with internal edges.

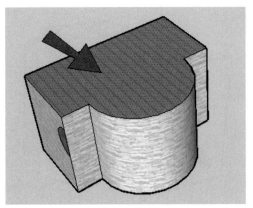
Figure 2-3

Method 1: Use a Face As the Follow Me Path

Method 1 is a fast way to use Follow Me when the path forms a closed loop all the way around a single face.

1. The path will go around the entire building, so select the top face (Figure 2-3). The edges surrounding this face compose the Follow Me path.

2. With the top face selected, activate Follow Me.

3. Click the Follow Me face (Figure 2-4).

Figure 2-4

The Follow Me face goes around the Follow Me path, removing volume all around the building, as shown in Figure 2-5.

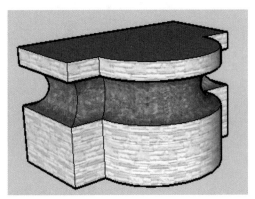
Figure 2-5

Method 2: Use the Alt or Cmd Key

This method produces the same results as Method 1, but you don't have to select the path face in advance.

1. Choose Undo to return to the intact building with the Follow Me face.

2. With nothing selected in advance, activate Follow Me.

3. Click the arc face (Figure 2-6).

Figure 2-6

4. Move the cursor to the top face of the building (don't click yet), and press and hold the Alt key (Cmd on the Mac). You'll see preview edges of the completed extrusion all around the building, as shown in Figure 2-7.

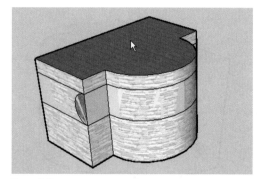
Figure 2-7

5. Click the top face, and the same volume is removed (Figure 2-8).

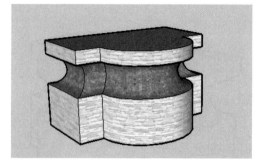
Figure 2-8

Method 3: Select the Path Edges

This is the method you use when you have an open path (not a closed loop) or if there is no single face you can click for the path.

1. Choose Undo again to undo the Follow Me.

2. Select the three edges shown in Figure 2-9.

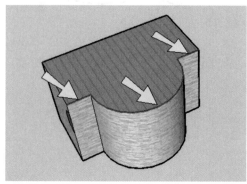
Figure 2-9

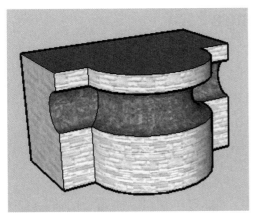

Figure 2-10

3. Activate Follow Me and click the arc face. The volume is removed only along the predefined path, as shown in Figure 2-10.

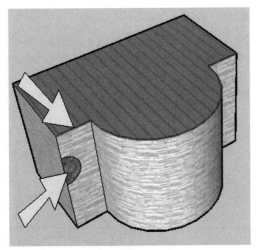

Figure 2-11

Faces and Open Paths

For a closed Follow Me path, the orientation and location of the Follow Me face aren't important. But orientation and location **are** important when using an open path. Be sure that the Follow Me face meets one endpoint of the path (or is directly above or below it), and has a different orientation at that endpoint. Otherwise, you'll get some strange results, or the tool won't work at all.

In Figure 2-11, Follow Me won't work, because the face and the path are in the same plane.

Follow Me won't work in Figure 2-12 either; the face is too far from the path.

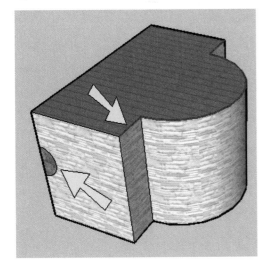

Figure 2-12

Manual Path

There is another way to use Follow Me that I didn't show here. You can activate Follow Me, click the Follow Me face, and manually move the face along the path. I don't like using this method, because it's sometimes hard to get the face to follow the exact path you want. And if you're using a closed face, you can end up with a tiny segment at the end of the path, making the path hard to close. Feel free to try this method, but you'll probably find that preselecting the path is a better way to go.

2.2   Using Follow Me to Add Volume Along a Path

Problem

You want to add volume to an object along a path.

Solution

Draw the Follow Me face projecting outward from the path.

Discussion

In the previous example, the Follow Me face was "inside" the path, drawn within a face of the building, so volume was removed. If the Follow Me face is "outside" the path, and projecting outward from the object, volume will be added. This generally means adding a Follow Me face to the model, rather than placing it within an existing face.

You'll see two examples of how to do this. First, you'll add a mantel to the top of a fireplace by adding a larger face from which the Follow Me face will be cut. The second example will add a base to the bottom of a column. In this case, you'll create a Follow Me face within an existing face, and then move it into place so that it's outside the Follow Me path.

Example 1: Fireplace Mantel

In this example, you will add a face adjacent to a fireplace on which to draw the mantel section. Then you'll use Follow Me to create the mantel.

1. Draw a basic model of a fireplace. (The model shown in Figure 2-13 is a simple box with a pushed-in rectangle on the front face.)

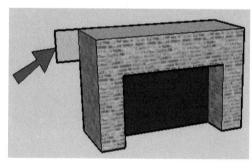

Figure 2-13

2. Add a small vertical rectangle along the top-back corner (Figure 2-13). If you can't get the rectangle oriented correctly, try switching to Front view, or use the Line tool instead. The Follow Me face will be drawn on this rectangle.

Why not just draw the Follow Me face from the top-back corner? You could try this, but it's rather difficult to orient lines correctly when they don't follow the red, green, or blue direction. It's much easier to draw lines and arcs on an existing face.

Figure 2-14

3. Draw the mantel cross-section for the Follow Me face. Be careful when you draw lines on this face: If you don't see the *On Face* inference, you might be drawing lines in the wrong plane. Then use the Eraser tool to trim away the rest of the rectangle. If you want to paint the mantel face, it's the color of the *back* side of the face that will be used for the completed mantel. The finished mantel Follow Me face is shown in Figure 2-14.

Note

It's not always easy to know which side of a face will have its color used during a Follow Me or Push/Pull action. My rule is simply to paint both sides of a face to cover all bases.

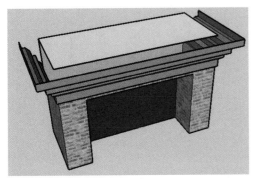

Figure 2-15

4. Preselect the Follow Me path by selecting the front and side edges of the fireplace. Then activate Follow Me and click the mantel face. The faces of the completed mantel shape are correct, but the top face of the fireplace is cut, and the mantel is hollow (Figure 2-15).

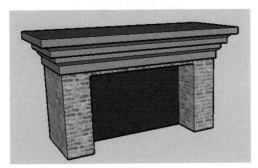

Figure 2-16

5. Add some lines and erase any extra lines, to fix the mantel top (Figure 2-16).

Note

Recipe 2.3 shows how to use groups to prevent the original object from being broken by Follow Me, as happened to the fireplace in this example when you extruded the mantel section around it.

Example 2: Column Base

In this example, you'll use an existing face to draw the Follow Me face. Then you'll move that face so that it's outside the Follow Me path.

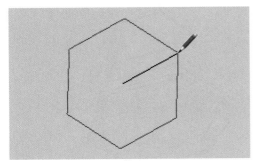

Figure 2-17

1. Use the Polygon tool (Draw→Polygon) to draw a hexagon on the flat (red-green) plane, with corners that are not in the red or green direction, as shown in Figure 2-17. (The Polygon tool is also available on the Large Tool Set toolbar.)

— **Note** —————————————————

The default number of sides for a Polygon tool is six (even though the Polygon icon is a triangle). If you have changed this value previously, here's how to change it back: Activate Polygon, type *6*, and press Enter. You can also change the number of sides of a polygon you are in the middle of creating, or have just finished creating: Just type *6s* and press Enter.

2. Pull up the hexagon face to make the column.

3. For the Follow Me face, you could add a vertical rectangle next to this column, as you did for the fireplace, but this is not so easy when none of the vertical faces is in a standard plane. So instead, draw the Follow Me face right on one of the vertical faces (Figure 2-18).

4. This face is "inside" the Follow Me path, so it must be moved to the outside of the column. But because the face is attached to an edge of the column, you can't move it without changing the column itself. So make a copy of it (Figure 2-19).

— **Note** —————————————————

If you drew the Follow Me face entirely within the vertical face, not attached to any edges, you could move it and not copy it.

5. Erase the original Follow Me face and use the top of the column as the Follow Me path. The column base is shown in Figure 2-20.

6. Look at the underside; as you can see in Figure 2-21, the column and base are a hollow shell. This is like what happened to the fireplace, which had its top face cut. You can trace any edge of the bottom hexagon to add a bottom face.

In both of these examples, the original objects (fireplace and column) were changed after Follow Me. The next recipe shows you how to use groups to keep these objects intact.

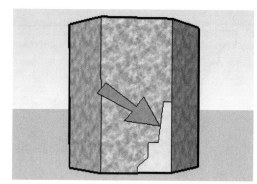

Figure 2-18

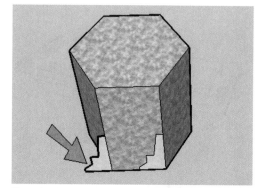

Figure 2-19

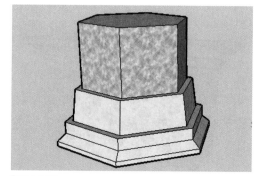

Figure 2-20

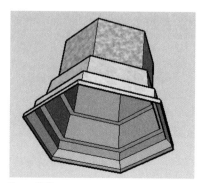

Figure 2-21

2.3   Keeping Original Objects Intact During Follow Me

Problem

You want to use Follow Me but keep your original object intact.

Solution

Make your Follow Me face a group or component.

Discussion

As you saw in Recipes 2.1 and 2.2, if the Follow Me face is attached to an object's edge, either inside or outside the Follow Me path, using Follow Me breaks faces of the original object. For another example, consider the model of a blue box with the magenta Follow Me face in the corner (Figure 2-22).

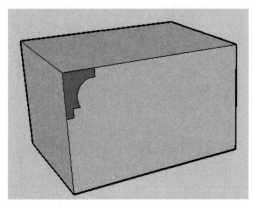

Figure 2-22

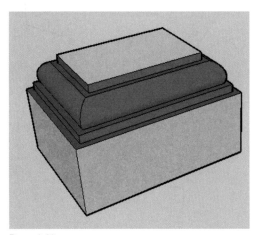

Figure 2-23

When you select the yellow-green top face as the Follow Me path, the result is shown in Figure 2-23; the side and top walls are broken.

Among the many reasons to use groups and components, the main benefit is to prevent objects within the group or component from affecting other objects. When a Follow Me face is made into a group or component, the other objects in your model will remain intact after Follow Me.

Use a group if you want to use Follow Me just once, which is the most common scenario. Use a component if you want to use Follow Me simultaneously on more than one copy of a Follow Me face.

In the main example, you'll use this technique to create a molding around a ceiling. In the "Other Uses" section, you'll see how to apply this technique to the fireplace and column models from Recipe 2.2. You'll also see how to use components to make a tower with repeating rows of windows.

1. Make a box with a Follow Me face in a top corner. This face will be made into a group. But if you select just the face, and not its edges, Make Group won't appear in the pop-up menu. However, you *can* choose Edit→Make Group from the main menu.

Another way to make this face a group (which I prefer) is to activate the Select tool, and double-click the Follow Me face. This selects both the face and its edges, and then Make Group will appear in the pop-up menu. Figure 2-24 shows the model with the grouped Follow Me face.

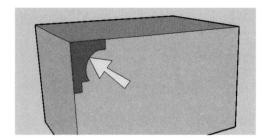

Figure 2-24

2. To define the Follow Me path, select the top face of the box, as shown in Figure 2-25.

3. Activate Follow Me.

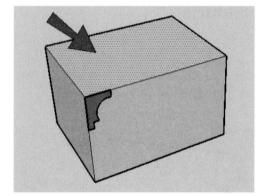

Figure 2-25

4. Right-click on the Follow Me face (now a group), and choose Edit Group from the pop-up menu (Figure 2-26).

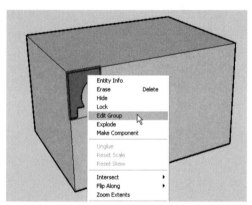

Figure 2-26

5. Click the Follow Me face (Figure 2-27).

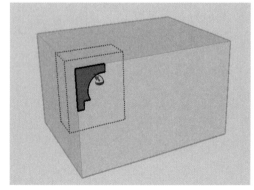

Figure 2-27

Figure 2-28

The face goes around the path, still within the group (Figure 2-28).

Figure 2-29

6. To close the group, right-click anywhere in blank space and choose Close Group. Or you can activate Select and click anywhere outside the group.

The Follow Me operation is finished, and the original walls are intact, as shown in Figure 2-29. Because the original walls have zero thickness, the new Follow Me faces share space with the original faces, which is why the molding looks a little messy.

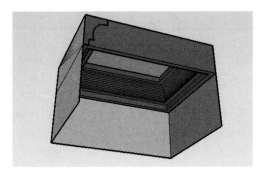

Figure 2-30

7. Hide or erase the floor and some walls, and look up into the room. In Figure 2-30, you can see the intact walls and ceiling, and the Follow Me faces creating a molding.

Other Uses

Here are three more examples of how you can apply the group/component technique with Follow Me.

Fireplace mantel

Create the same model of a fireplace and mantel cross-section from "Example 1: Fireplace Mantel" in Recipe 2.2. Make the mantel cross-section a group (Figure 2-31).

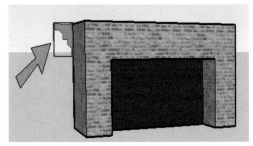

Figure 2-31

When you use the group technique (select the path, activate Follow Me, edit the group, click the mantel section), Figure 2-32 shows the result. The top of the fireplace is intact, and the mantel appears solid.

Figure 2-32

Column base

Create the same model of a column and base cross-section from "Example 2: Column Base" in Recipe 2.2. Make the base section into a group (Figure 2-33).

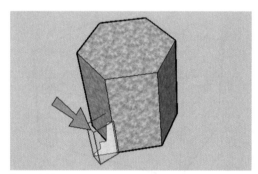
Figure 2-33

When you use the group technique, the column remains whole and the base is solid, as shown in Figure 2-34.

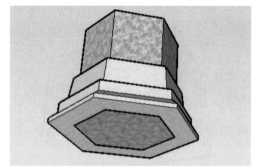
Figure 2-34

Tower with repeating window rows

This example uses components instead of groups. Components are great to use if they will repeat, because if you edit one, all others get the same changes.

Start with a building like the one in Figure 2-35, and draw one window face within a vertical wall. Make this face a component. (A component is made the same way as a group, with the added step of assigning it a name. Also, make sure that "Replace selection with component" is selected.)

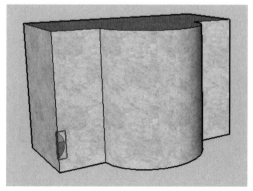
Figure 2-35

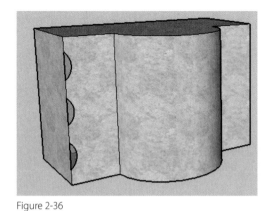

Figure 2-36

Make a few copies of this component along the vertical wall (Figure 2-36).

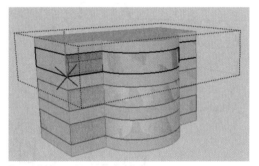

Figure 2-37

Use the group technique, right-clicking on any window component and choosing Edit Component. When one window is extruded around the building, all others are too, as shown in Figure 2-37.

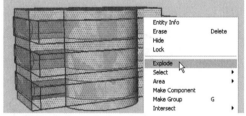

Figure 2-38

To cut faces from the building so that you can see the window, you need to explode, or *ungroup* the components. To do this, select everything, right-click on any selected object, and choose Explode from the pop-up menu, shown in Figure 2-38. (You could also start by just selecting each component, but it is not so easy to select components that are inside other objects.)

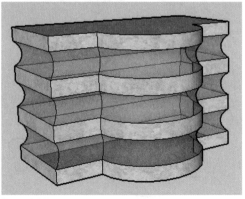

Figure 2-39

Now you can erase the faces and edges that cover the windows. The finished building is shown in Figure 2-39.

2.4 Using Follow Me When Faces and Paths Are Not Adjacent

Problem

You want to use Follow Me on a path that's not adjacent to the Follow Me face.

Solution

In some cases, a nonadjacent path will give you the results you want. But if not, you can create a new path by offsetting the original one and making the necessary changes.

Discussion

When a Follow Me path is not adjacent to the Follow Me face, an offset of the path is used. The offset path can sometimes give you the Follow Me results you want, such as for the model in Figure 2-40. In this example, the building footprint is selected as the Follow Me path, and the blue face is the Follow Me face.

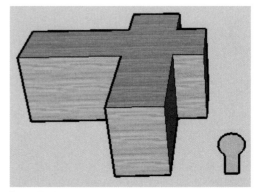

Figure 2-40

Figure 2-41 shows the Follow Me result: the face is extruded around a path offset from the building footprint, and the resulting fence is what you would expect.

But sometimes the results are not what you want, particularly when parts of the path are curved. In cases like these, you can use the Offset tool to create the new path manually, and trim and erase as needed to get the path you want.

The following example demonstrates this technique on a building with round edges. In "Other Uses," you'll use the same technique to create decorative trim around a group of windows.

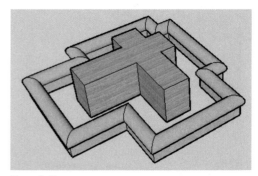

Figure 2-41

1. Start with a building like the one in Figure 2-42, with at least one round wall and with no dividing edges on the top face. Add a Follow Me face next to, but not touching, the building. You can create your model from scratch, or download my Nonadjacent Path model from the 3D Warehouse.

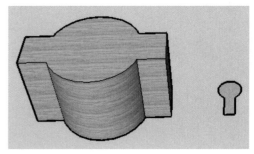

Figure 2-42

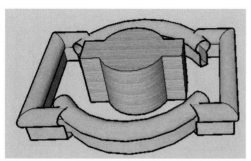

Figure 2-43

2. Use the top face as the Follow Me path and extrude the Follow Me face around. The result is shown in Figure 2-43: the offset path is not smooth.

3. Choose Undo.

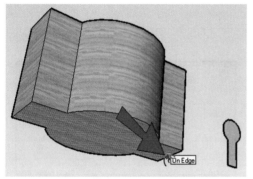

Figure 2-44

4. To see how the offset path is created, activate Offset. You'll create the offset from the bottom of the building, which should also be a single face (no dividing edges). When you click this face, click somewhere on the edge closest to the Follow Me face (Figure 2-44).

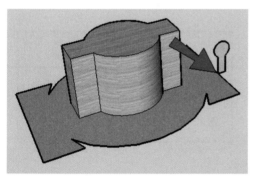

Figure 2-45

5. End the offset at the closest point on the Follow Me face (Figure 2-45).

   Now you can see why the previous Follow Me operation had such a messy result; there are sharp corners between the straight and round edges.

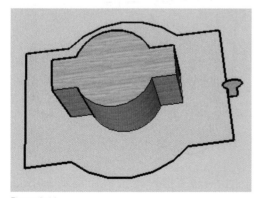

Figure 2-46

6. To correct the offset shape, add some straight lines to eliminate the sharp corners, and erase extra edges so that there is a single face (Figure 2-46).

7. Use the new offset face for the Follow Me path, and try Follow Me again. This time, the results look great (Figure 2-47).

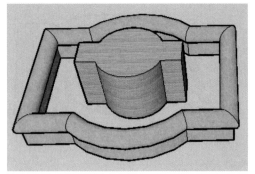
Figure 2-47

Other Uses

The offset path technique can also be used to create decorative trim around a set of windows.

On one wall of a building, draw a shape for one window. Create one offset for the window frame and then a slightly larger offset for the decorative trim. Copy all three faces a few times, so that the trim offset faces overlap (Figure 2-48).

Figure 2-48

Clean up the overlapping segments of the trim offset edges, so that you have one, clean border for the trim. Figure 2-49 shows the window frames in red, and the single border surrounding all three frames.

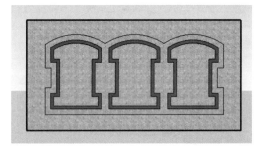
Figure 2-49

Figure 2-50 shows the result after placing an actual window in each window frame and using the outer border as the Follow Me path for a round Follow Me face.

If you try this example and your Follow Me operation causes any faces of the building to disappear, use the group technique described in Recipe 2.3.

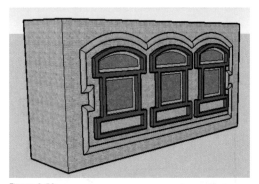
Figure 2-50

2.5 Creating Objects in the Round

Problem

You want to create round, or lathed, objects.

Solution

Use a circle for the Follow Me path.

Discussion

When you extrude a face around a circle, you create a lathed object. In other design applications, this action is sometimes called *revolving*. The circular Follow Me path is basically a temporary object, which you can remove after the round object is created.

This example shows how to use the circle-path technique to create a cup. In "Other Uses," you'll see how to use different Follow Me faces to create vases, how to adjust the location of the Follow Me circle to make a ring, and how to modify the circular path to create interesting objects that aren't purely round.

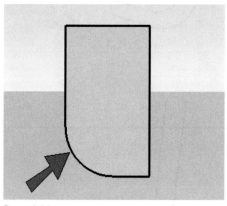

Figure 2-51

1. To start the cup, you need to make the face that will be extruded along the circle. This is actually half of the cup's cross-section. In Front view, make a rectangle with an arc cutout at one corner (Figure 2-51).

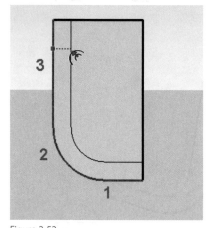

Figure 2-52

2. Select edges 1, 2, and 3, and use Offset to make the inner curves, as shown in Figure 2-52.

3. Use the Eraser tool to remove the rest of the rectangle, and paint your half-section (Figure 2-53).

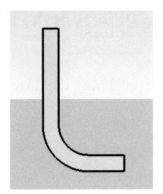
Figure 2-53

4. Activate Circle. Because the circle needs to be flat (red-green plane), keep the cursor away from other objects, so that the preview circle stays blue (Figure 2-54). Press and hold Shift to lock this orientation.

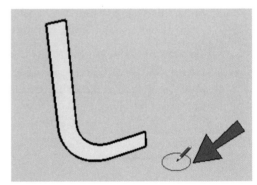
Figure 2-54

5. With Shift pressed, hover over the corner shown in Figure 2-55, but don't click. You want to use this point as a placement inference.

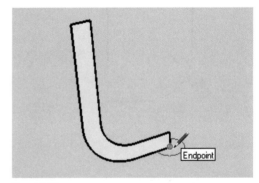
Figure 2-55

6. Follow Me sometimes breaks faces (unless the Follow Me face is a group or component), but this won't happen if the path and face are not touching. So move the mouse straight down from the inference point, and click to place the center of the circle below the Follow Me face (Figure 2-56).

7. Make the circle any size.

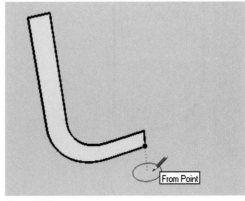
Figure 2-56

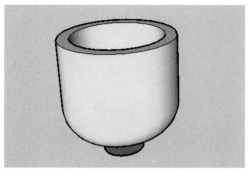

Figure 2-57

8. Select the circle (you can select either the face or edge), activate Follow Me, and click the half-section face. The face is extruded around the circle to make the cup (Figure 2-57).

9. Erase the Follow Me circle, and you're finished.

Figure 2-58

Figure 2-59

Other Uses

When you vary the Follow Me face, adjust the location of the Follow Me circle, or even change the Follow Me circle itself, you can make some wonderful models. Here are a few examples.

When the face made of tangent arcs in Figure 2-58 is extruded around a circle, the result is the smooth vase in Figure 2-59. This vase is painted with translucent glass.

Figure 2-60

Figure 2-61

The face with arcs sticking out shown in Figure 2-60 (which has to be a single face) produces the bumpy vase shown in Figure 2-61 when extruded along a circle. The bumpy bits can be painted after the Follow Me is complete.

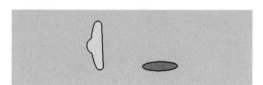

Figure 2-62

The Follow Me face in Figure 2-62, when extruded around a circle that's placed far away, will produce the ring in Figure 2-63.

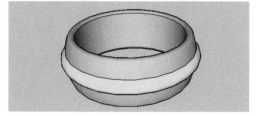

Figure 2-63

If you extrude a vertical circle (Figure 2-64) around a far-off horizontal circle, you will get a torus, or a donut shape (Figure 2-65).

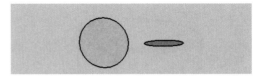

Figure 2-64

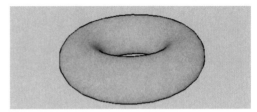

Figure 2-65

If you change the Follow Me circle to an oval, you can make something that looks like an oval-shaped trash bin. (Use the Scale tool to change a circle to an oval.) Figure 2-66 shows the Follow Me face that will be extruded along the oval, and Figure 2-67 shows the resulting trash bin.

Figure 2-66   Figure 2-67

Lastly, Figure 2-68 shows a Follow Me path with a cloudlike shape. The result, shown in Figure 2-69, is an interesting model—perhaps a candy dish.

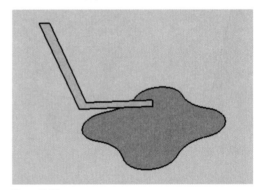

Figure 2-68

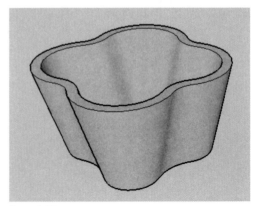

Figure 2-69

2.6 Creating Spheres

Problem

You want to create a sphere.

Solution

Use Follow Me on two concentric, perpendicular circles.

Discussion

When the Follow Me path and face are concentric circles, one perpendicular to the other, you will get a sphere.

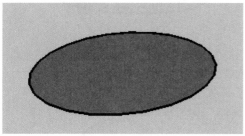

Figure 2-70

1. Start with a circle in the red-green plane (Figure 2-70). This will be the Follow Me path.

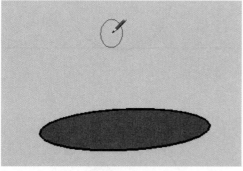

Figure 2-71

2. The next circle, which will be the Follow Me face, must be vertical. So move the mouse up until the preview circle is either red or green (Figure 2-71), and press and hold Shift to lock the orientation.

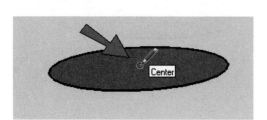

Figure 2-72

3. Place the center of the new circle at the center of the first circle (Figure 2-72).

4. Make the new circle smaller than the first one (Figure 2-73).

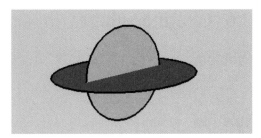

Figure 2-73

5. Select the larger circle as the path, and use Follow Me on the smaller circle. The resulting sphere is shown in Figure 2-74.

Figure 2-74

6. Erase the larger circle, leaving only the sphere (Figure 2-75).

Note ───────────────────────

You could have selected the smaller circle as the path, but then the smaller circle would have ended up inside the sphere, and therefore would have been harder to erase. (But you wouldn't see it.) Or you could have made both circles the same size.

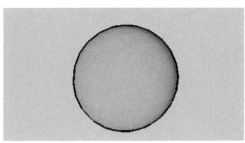

Figure 2-75

You can use the same technique to make a half-sphere.

1. Make the same two circles as before, and use Line to divide the vertical circle in half (Figure 2-76).

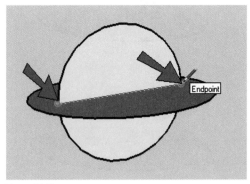

Figure 2-76

Figure 2-77

2. Remove the lower half (Figure 2-77).

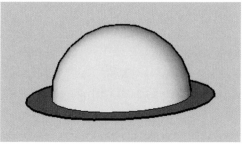
Figure 2-78

3. Select the circle, and use Follow Me on the half-circle. This produces the half-sphere shown in Figure 2-78.

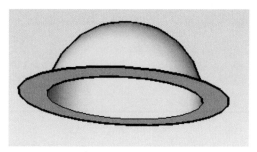
Figure 2-79

4. Look at the bottom. As you can see in Figure 2-79, the dome is hollow.

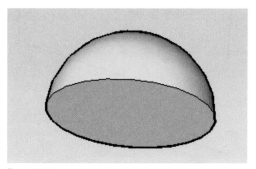
Figure 2-80

5. Remove the larger circle. Then you can easily cover the hole by tracing any edge of the bottom circle. The final half-sphere is shown in Figure 2-80.

2.7 Using a Follow Me Path in 3D

Problem

You want to extrude a Follow Me face along a 3D path, but the path is difficult to draw.

Solution

Create reference objects first, group these objects, and then draw the path by using inference points that are inside the group.

Discussion

Without reference geometry, creating a 3D path from scratch can be difficult. If you instead create a grouped set of reference geometry, the process becomes much easier because of the following:

- You can use points or edges of the reference group for drawing the 3D path, and the new geometry you create will not stick to the group.
- When the path is complete and you no longer need the reference geometry, you can easily erase the group.

The first example shows how to make a 3D path for a bike handlebar. The second example uses the same technique to make a spiral, which can be rotate-copied to make into a rope coil.

Example 1: Bike Handlebar

In this example, you will create a curvy, 3D path that will be used to extrude a hexagon, resulting in a bike handlebar.

1. The first step is to make the reference geometry. Start with a simple box. Use Push/Pull with the Ctrl/Option key to pull out another, smaller box from the side, as in Figure 2-81.

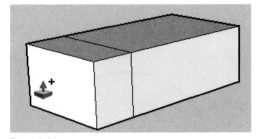

Figure 2-81

2. Using Push/Pull with Ctrl/Option again, double-click the other side of the box to pull out an identical box (Figure 2-82).

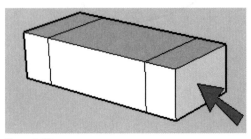

Figure 2-82

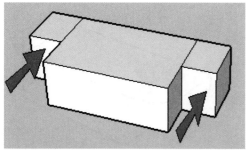

Figure 2-83

3. Push in the two side boxes by the same distance (Figure 2-83).

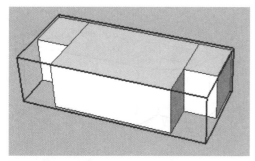

Figure 2-84

4. Make these three boxes into a group (select them all, right-click on any face, and choose Make Group from the pop-up menu). The resulting group is surrounded by a bounding box (Figure 2-84).

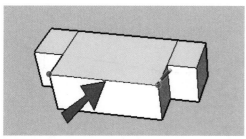

Figure 2-85

5. Now you can start making the 3D path. Activate Line and click the two endpoints of the line indicated in Figure 2-85. Because the boxes are grouped, the line does not stick to it and remains a separate object.

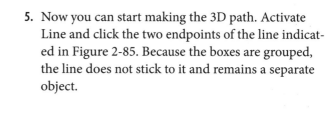

6. Next, make an arc tangent to the line you created in the previous step, ending at the smaller box, as shown in Figure 2-86. (The preview color of a tangent arc is cyan.)

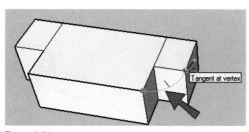

Figure 2-86

7. Add a vertical arc on the side of the smaller box (Figure 2-87).

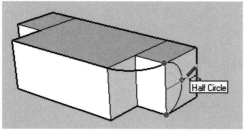

Figure 2-87

8. Draw the same two arcs on the other side (Figure 2-88). These five objects complete the 3D Follow Me path.

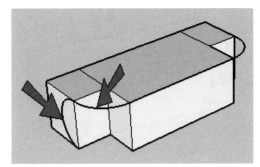

Figure 2-88

9. The reference geometry is needed for one more step: drawing the vertical Follow Me face at one end of the path. The face shown in Figure 2-89 is a hexagon, but you could draw a circle or rectangle. You could also draw this face without the reference group, but it's easier to draw geometry against an existing face than to draw it in empty space.

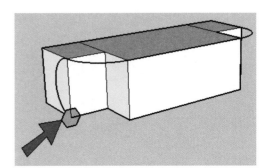

Figure 2-89

10. Erase the group, and you're left with the Follow Me face and path (Figure 2-90).

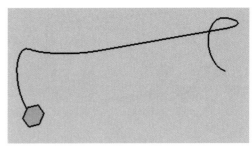

Figure 2-90

11. Select the entire path, activate Follow Me, and click the face. The result is the handlebar shown in Figure 2-91.

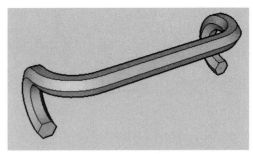

Figure 2-91

Example 2: Rope Coil

This example shows how to make a spiral, which can then be rotate-copied to make a rope coil.

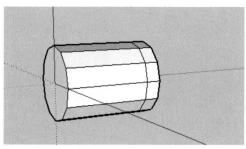

Figure 2-92

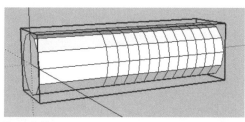

Figure 2-93

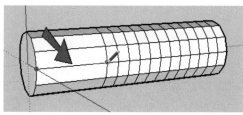

Figure 2-94

1. Start in Front view and use the Polygon tool (Draw→Polygon) to make a 12-sided polygon. Place the center at the origin. (If your axes are not displayed, you can turn them on by choosing View→Axes.)

2. Activate Push/Pull and pull the polygon out by a long distance. Then press Ctrl/Option and pull it out again by a short distance, as shown in Figure 2-92. One of the longer segments will be used to start the spiral, and the short segments will be copied to form the basis of the spiral path.

3. Copy the short section 11 times, for a total of 12 short sections. Because the polygon has 12 sides, you need 12 sets of faces to make one revolution of the spiral path.

4. This set of polygon faces forms the reference geometry, so make it into a group (Figure 2-93).

5. Now you can start drawing the spiral path. First, trace over any of the longer segments (Figure 2-94).

Perpendicular Follow Me Paths

The reason for starting the spiral path with a long, horizontal segment is that the Follow Me circle can easily be drawn perpendicular to the start of the path. Without this horizontal segment, you would be drawing the circle at the end of a diagonal line, and it would be difficult (though not impossible) to draw a Follow Me circle perpendicular to the path.

Follow Me will work on a face that is not perpendicular to the starting segment of the path, but the face will be distorted and the beginning of the extrusion will be cut off at an angle perpendicular to the starting segment.

The degree of distortion is dependent on various factors including the degree of tilt and how many planes it is tilting in. In some cases, the distortion may be small and not readily visible, but it will be there.

If the precise size and shape of your Follow Me face is important, you need to keep the Follow Me face perpendicular to the start of the Follow Me path. For a diagonal path, like the one used in this example for the spiral, this means you would need a Follow Me face that is not in a standard plane. The technique shown in this example, of drawing an extra path segment oriented in the desired axis direction, is a good solution to this problem.

6. Now draw the 12 short segments for the spiral. Starting from the end of the long segment you just traced, draw diagonals, one by one, in the small faces (Figure 2-95).

   When you complete the last spiral segment, you have completed one revolution of the spiral.

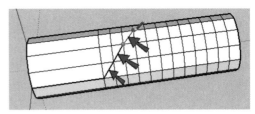

Figure 2-95

7. Orbit back to the beginning of the first, long segment you traced. Using the starting end of this segment as the center point, draw a vertical circle as your Follow Me face, as shown in Figure 2-96.

8. Erase the reference group.

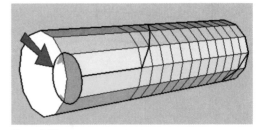

Figure 2-96

9. For a longer spiral, copy all of the diagonal spiral segments (not the horizontal segment) a few times, as shown in Figure 2-97.

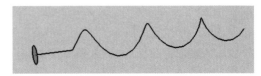

Figure 2-97

10. Extrude the Follow Me circle along the spiral path (Figure 2-98).

11. The long horizontal segment at the beginning is not needed, so erase it. (You could also use Push/Pull on the starting face, which would keep the starting face vertical.)

Figure 2-98

12. To smooth the spiral, select the entire thing, right-click on any selected face, and choose Soften/Smooth Edges. Adjust the sliders until the face is smooth, as shown in Figure 2-99.

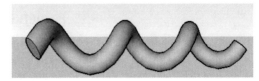

Figure 2-99

13. To complete the rope, make rotated copies of it. This is easiest to do in Front view, placing the protractor at the model origin. (You can set the protractor in the desired orientation, hold Shift to lock the orientation, and then click the origin to place it.) The resulting rope coil shown in Figure 2-100 shows two copies (three total spirals), each separated by 120 degrees.

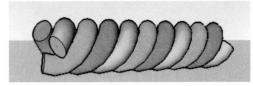

Figure 2-100

CHAPTER 3

Intersection Edges: Cutting and Trimming

When you want to use objects to trim or cut other objects, you use the Intersect tool. This tool calculates where two or more objects intersect or overlap one another, and draws edges along these intersections. These intersection edges define the area or volume to cut.

Along with the Follow Me tool, the Intersect tool was introduced back in version 5 to much fanfare. Prior to Intersect, users had to manually trace intersection edges. For example, if you needed to cut a roof to accommodate a chimney, you would use the Line tool to trace edges between intersection points (Figure 3-1).

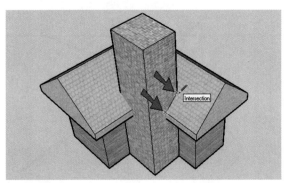

Figure 3-1

The problem with manual tracing is that, as in the preceding example, you sometimes have to orbit all the way around to find all the edges to draw. Missing or forgetting edges, such as the ones along the bottom of the roof, is easy too. Not to mention, for complex models, manual tracing can be quite tedious, particularly when you use round objects: "round" objects in SketchUp are actually composed of short linear segments, so you have to draw intersection edges along each small segment.

When you use Intersect, you can quickly get an entire set of accurate intersection edges, without changing your view or using your mouse to create dozens of edges.

Note

New to version 7 is the Break Edges function, which automatically breaks edges where they're intersected by other edges. This is relevant when drawing in 2D; for example, if you draw two overlapping circles, each circle's edge will be broken where it meets the other circle. Prior to version 7, you had to use the Intersect tool to break these edges, but now the Intersect tool is not necessary for breaking edges in 2D drawing. If you want to preserve edges of a face and ensure that the edges are not broken by other edges, make the face a group.

Available on the Edit menu, as well as on the local menu, Intersect has three suboptions:

- **Intersect with Model**. Considers the entire model in the calculation.

- **Intersect Selected**. Considers only selected objects in the calculation.

- **Intersect with Context**. Available when editing a group or component, this enables you to disregard geometry outside the group or component when calculating intersection edges.

This chapter demonstrates how to use the Intersect tool and its options. You will practice cutting just one object, as well as cutting all objects involved in an intersection. You'll also learn how to take advantage of groups and components to make trimming and cutting much easier.

3.1 Trimming an Object

Problem

You need to use one object to trim another object.

Solution

Use Intersect with Model to get quick and accurate intersection edges, which define the area to be trimmed.

Discussion

Whether you're cutting a roof to accommodate a chimney, cutting holes in a floor, trimming rails, or designing a deck, Intersect with Model makes the job easy by quickly defining the areas that need to be cut. Although this example focuses on cutting a roof to accommodate a chimney, you can easily adapt the technique to the other situations described in the "Other Uses" section.

1. Start with an L-shaped house and roof like the model shown in Figure 3-2. You can create your model from scratch or download my Chimney House model from the 3D Warehouse.

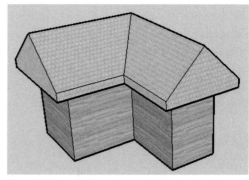

Figure 3-2

Want to Create This Model Yourself?

1. Start with an L-shaped box.
2. Make the roof by offsetting the top face outward and pulling both roof faces up by the same distance.
3. Erase the extra lines on the top face.
4. Draw the ridge lines on top of the roof, starting from the midpoints of both ends of the **L** face.
5. Select both ridge lines and use Move to move them straight up.

2. Draw the chimney footprint in the corner indicated in Figure 3-3.

3. Pull up the chimney so that it passes through the roof.

4. To cut the roof around the chimney, you need to know where it meets the roof. Select the entire model and right-click on any of the selected faces. From the pop-up menu, choose Intersect→Intersect with Model. (You could also choose Edit→Intersect→Intersect with Model from the main menu; I prefer using the pop-up menu, because it's faster than going up to the main menu.)

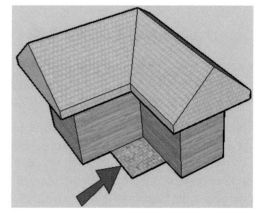

Figure 3-3

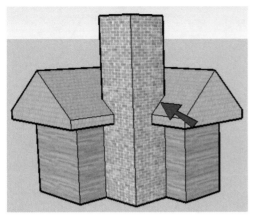

Figure 3-4

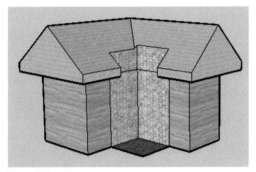

Figure 3-5

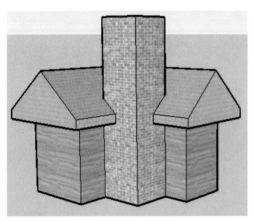

Figure 3-6

This creates edges all around the chimney, where it meets the roof (Figure 3-4).

5. To better see these edges, hide the chimney. To do this, you can select all of the vertical chimney faces, right-click one of the selected faces, and choose Hide from the pop-up menu. (You can also choose Edit→Hide from the main menu.)

6. Erase the extra roof edges to make space for the chimney (Figure 3-5).

7. To replace the chimney, choose Edit→Unhide→All or Unhide→Last. You can see that the roof is cleanly cut and that no faces are hidden inside the chimney (Figure 3-6).

Other Uses

Intersect with Model can be used for a wide range of designs. Here are a few examples.

Cutting a floor for columns

Figure 3-7 shows a floor plate with holes for columns. It was created by intersecting columns with the floor, then trimming away the columns and erasing the faces covering the holes.

To see how this was done, download my Plate with Holes model from the 3D Warehouse.

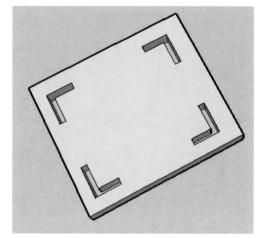

Figure 3-7

Trimming rails to meet a curved face

Rails are a common element in many designs. You can use Intersect with Model to trim a set of rails to meet a curved face, and the resulting model can be used for a headboard and footboard for a bed (Figure 3-8), or supports for a bridge (Figure 3-9).

To see how this was done, download my Trimmed Rails model from the 3D Warehouse.

Figure 3-8

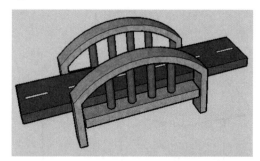

Figure 3-9

Designing a deck

Intersect with Model can help you quickly make a deck design. Figure 3-10 shows a deck of irregular shape, whose planks were trimmed using the Intersect tool.

To see how this was done, download my Irregular Deck Shape model from the 3D Warehouse.

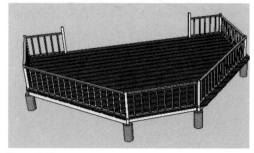

Figure 3-10

3.2 Cutting All Intersected Objects

Problem

You want to cut more than one intersected object.

Solution

Use Intersect with Model and decide which edges need to be cut.

Discussion

In the previous recipe, you cut only one object: the roof. The cutting object itself (the chimney) was not cut. What if all intersected objects need to be trimmed? This can occur when creating intersecting passageways, when engraving, or when cutting a skylight into a roof. This example demonstrates how to create a passageway between two intersecting arch sections. Engraving and skylight scenarios will be shown in the "Other Uses" section.

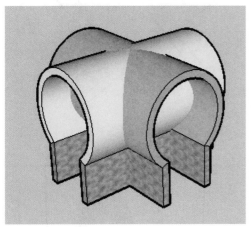

Figure 3-11

1. Start with a model like the one in Figure 3-11, with two arch forms that meet at their midpoints, at a 90-degree angle. You can create your model from scratch, or download my Intersecting Arches model from the 3D Warehouse.

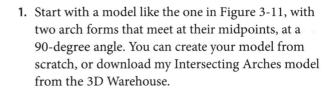

Want to Create This Model Yourself?

1. Create the basic arch shape in Front view and pull it back to get the first arch passageway.
2. Make a 90-degree rotated copy of the arch shape, approximately at the center of the original shape. Press Shift to lock the protractor in the red-green plane before moving the protractor to the arch.
3. Use a different color for the round part of the copy.

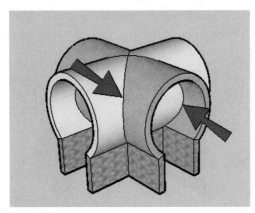

Figure 3-12

2. Select everything, right-click on any selected object, and choose Intersect→Intersect with Model from the pop-up menu. Intersection edges are created on the inside and outside faces of both arches (Figure 3-12).

3. To easily cut through the first passageway, orbit to a view like the one in Figure 3-13 and use a right-to-left selection window within the passageway to select all faces in and behind the selection window, going straight back. Then press the Delete key to erase the selected faces, and you can see straight through. Do the same for the passageway in the other direction.

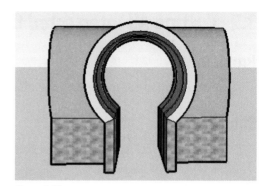

Figure 3-13

4. Orbit so that you are looking up at the ceiling. Erase all of the edges within areas of the same color (Figure 3-14).

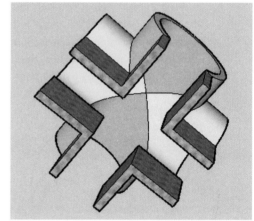

Figure 3-14

Other Uses

Here are two more examples in which both intersected objects are trimmed.

Engraving

Figure 3-15 shows a box that has a flower shape engraved into the front. The engraving was done by intersecting a 3D flower-shaped cutting object with the front of the box, and trimming faces and edges.

To see how this was done, download my Engraving model from the 3D Warehouse.

Figure 3-15

Skylight

Figure 3-16 shows a domed skylight that was cut into a sloped roof. The original skylight shape was a sphere and the sphere and the roof were used to trim each other.

To see how this was done, download my Domed Skylight model from the 3D Warehouse.

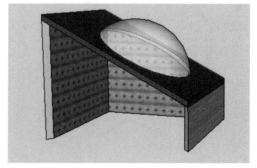

Figure 3-16

3.3   Using Groups or Components to Create Cutting Objects

Problem

You want to use an object to cut holes, but you can't get the cutting object through what you want to cut.

Solution

Make your cutting object into a group or component, move it where you want, and then run Intersect with Model.

Discussion

One great advantage of groups and components is that they can be used for cutting. Ungrouped objects can be limited in movement according to the objects to which they are attached. Because groups don't "stick" to other objects, they can be moved anywhere. For cutting and trimming purposes, components work the same way as groups. And because an entire group or component can be selected with one click, you can easily define what you want to intersect.

To demonstrate these advantages, the first example uses groups to cut identical passageways through each side of a hexagonal gazebo. In the "Other Uses" section, you'll see how groups can help create a keypad with a cover plate, and help engrave text.

Want to Create this Model Yourself?

1. Leave the axes displayed. If they are not already displayed, turn them on by choosing View→Axes from the main menu.

2. Use the Polygon tool to make a hexagon flat on the ground. Center it at the origin and draw one corner in the green direction. This makes the footprint of the building.

3. Use Push/Pull to pull it up, and then use the tool again with Ctrl/Option to pull up the top of the hexagon again. (This creates a new set of faces, rather than just stretching the top.)

4. Use Scale to shrink the top face of the roof. Be sure to press the Ctrl/Option key, which scales about the center.

5. On one of the vertical faces perpendicular to the red axis, draw the peaked doorway shape. The shape must be centered on the face, so use Offset and move the horizontal offset lines as needed. The peak point should be directly above the midpoint of the face.

6. Use Push/Pull with the Ctrl/Option key to pull out the peaked shape. This will be the cutting object. (If you don't use the Ctrl/Option key, the bottom hexagon face will extend into the bottom of the cutting shape, and then the face would need to be broken.) Make it rather long, which will make trimming easier later.

---

1. Start with a hexagonal gazebo with a sloped roof and add to one face a long cutting shape for the passageway (Figure 3-17). You can create your model from scratch, or download my Gazebo model from the 3D Warehouse.

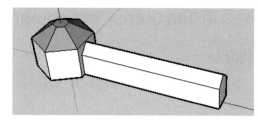

Figure 3-17

2. If you try to move the cutout object through the gazebo, you'll find that it won't go—the object is "glued" to the face on which it was drawn. To get rid of this stickiness, make the cutting object a group (Figure 3-18): Select its front and side faces with a right-to-left selection window, right-click on one of the selected faces, and choose Make Group.

   A group becomes "enclosed" as a single unit. This unit is protected from being changed, unless you open it for editing. It can be selected as one unit and does not stick to any other object.

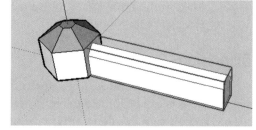

Figure 3-18

3. Move the group along the red axis so that it pokes all the way through the gazebo, as shown in Figure 3-19.

4. Make two rotated copies of the group, using the center of the top face for the protractor, with 60 degrees between copies. You should now have three groups.

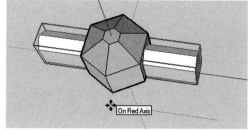

Figure 3-19

─── **Note** ───────────────────────────────

Making rotated copies is discussed in Recipe 1.4.

───

Because this cutting object is repeated, you might be wondering why it is a group and not a component. You certainly could use a component instead, but a group is quicker to create. (A component requires that you enter a name and specify a few parameters.) Because all three groups will eventually be exploded (ungrouped), however, it doesn't really matter whether they start out as groups or components.

5. Paint each group. You do not have to edit a group in order to paint it; just pick the color and click the group (Figure 3-20).

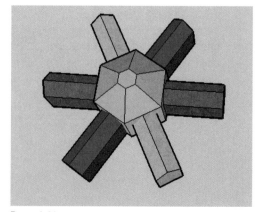

Figure 3-20

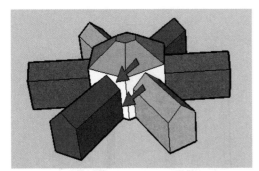

Figure 3-21

Painting Groups and Components

When you pick a color and click a group or component, you paint all faces of the group that have the *default color*. If any faces are already painted, either from before the group was created or when the group was edited, applying a global color to the whole group won't affect those faces.

Painting a group like this has two advantages: It's quick (one click), and both front and back faces get painted. This is helpful when using a group or component for cutting, because you can easily identify its faces after the cutting is complete.

All of this is shown in detail, in Recipe 6.5.

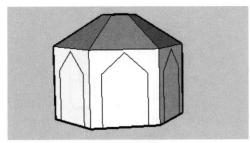

Figure 3-22

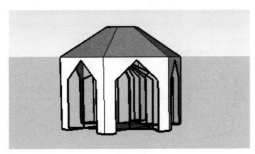

Figure 3-23

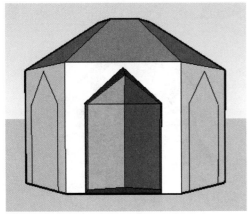

Figure 3-24

6. Select everything, right-click on any selected object, and choose Intersect→Intersect with Model. You now have edges along each vertical face (Figure 3-21).

7. Erase the groups, and your intersection edges remain, as shown in Figure 3-22.

8. Erase the peak face within each vertical face, and you have just holes and edges (Figure 3-23). Those edges are the where the cutout groups intersected each other.

   This looks nice, but there are no passageways. To make the passageways, you need to keep a portion of each cutting group, which will provide the necessary faces within the gazebo.

9. Choose Undo to bring back the three groups, and be sure to keep the intersection edges.

10. Because you need to keep portions of each group, the groups need to be exploded, or ungrouped. Select all three groups, right-click on one of them, and choose Explode from the pop-up menu.

11. You can't erase each group with one click anymore, but you can remove the parts that stick out. (Do this in Top view, using several right-to-left selection windows. This is easy when the faces protrude far enough from the gazebo.)

12. Erase one of the front peak faces, and this time you can see portions of the cutting groups running through the building (Figure 3-24).

13. Remove all of the faces inside the passageway so that you have a smooth, peaked opening straight through (Figure 3-25).

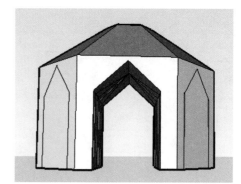

Figure 3-25

14. Remove faces inside the other two passageways. After some cleanup (you might have to trace edges to re-create some of the faces), the underside should look like Figure 3-26.

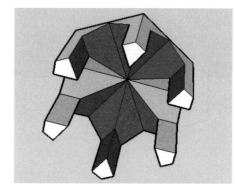

Figure 3-26

If you have some time, try this variation. Instead of a simple peaked opening, use something more complex. You can download my Complex Gazebo model from the 3D Warehouse (Figure 3-27), or make your own opening. The opening should be symmetric and centered horizontally within the face, so that the midpoints of all cutouts will meet at the center.

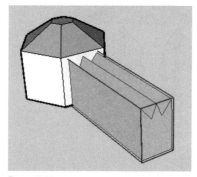

Figure 3-27

After following the same steps as before, the underside looks really impressive (Figure 3-28)!

Figure 3-28

Other Uses

Here are two more examples of using groups or components with Intersect with Model.

Keypad and cover

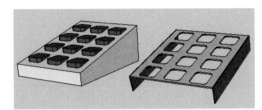

Figure 3-29

Figure 3-29 shows a model of a keypad with a matching cover. The model starts with the keypad box and one button, which is made into a group. An exploded copy of the button group is used to make one button hole, and the hole is copied to make room for more buttons. Each hole is filled a button, and the entire keypad is made into a group. To make the cover, start with a face drawn on the top of the keypad group, intersect it to make the holes, and then give it some thickness.

To see how this was done, download my Keypad and Cover model from the 3D Warehouse.

Text engraving

Figure 3-30

This example is similar to "Engraving" from Recipe 3.2, except that the 3D text is automatically created as a component. The interaction is the basically the same, with the added step of ungluing the text from the face on which it is created.

Create a box and use the 3D Text tool to write something on it (Figure 3-30). If the text is the wrong size, use the Scale tool to change it.

3D Text automatically produces a component. And when a text component is placed directly on a face, it becomes "glued" to that face. This means the text can be moved only within the plane of the face and therefore cannot be pushed inside the box. To change this, right-click on the text and choose Unglue from the pop-up menu. Now you can move the text slightly into the box.

Figure 3-31

Explode the text component and then intersect it. Trim the letters beyond the front of the box and then erase faces on the front of the box to uncover each letter (Figure 3-31). For letters that have internal shapes, such as the *B* and the *O* in Figure 3-31, you'll have to trace one edge of each shape before the outer shape can be removed.

3.4 Intersecting with Groups and Components, Without Exploding

Problem

You want to leave your cutting object intact and still get intersection edges, rather than exploding all groups and components after intersecting them.

Solution

Use Intersect with Model while a group or component is open for editing, to get intersection edges on it.

Discussion

There are several reasons to keep a group or component intact after intersecting it, including the following:

- You can continue to select it as one object.

- The group or component will not stick to other objects.

- You can easily repeat objects.

By using Intersect with Model within a group or component while it is open for editing, you can keep it intact after it is intersected and trimmed.

The best way to show this technique is with window components, because after you edit one window, all other windows update accordingly. (If you had to explode a window component, you would have to manually repeat the trimming for all other windows.) In the following example, you'll create rectangular windows along a curved wall, which would be hard to do without the Intersect tool. You'll use the window component to trim the building, and the building to trim the window component, without having to explode the component.

Make the Building and Window-Cutting Components

This section contains some helpful information about how to make cutting shapes. If you want to skip ahead to "Trim the Building, Trim the Windows," you can download my Wavy Windows model from the 3D Warehouse.

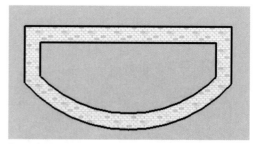

Figure 3-32

1. In Top view, start with a footprint like the one in Figure 3-32. Make the walls overly thick so that the window frame will be overly deep (and easy to see).

2. Pull up the building so that three large windows can fit top-to-bottom.

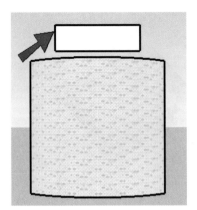

Figure 3-33

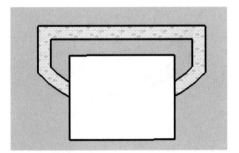

Figure 3-34

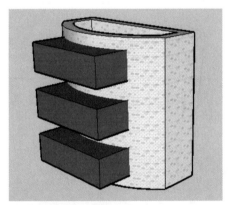

Figure 3-35

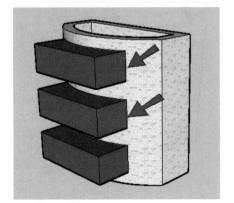

Figure 3-36

3. Now make the shape for the window. In Front view, make a rectangle like the one in Figure 3-33. Keep it above the building for two reasons: to prevent faces from sticking and to avoid having to draw a rectangle on a curved face. This rectangle will become the base shape for the window component.

4. Pull out the rectangle so that it extends over the curved wall. In Top view, the window shape should look like in Figure 3-34: covering the front, curved wall, but not the back wall.

Note

To see a true parallel view, without the distortion you get in the default Perspective view, choose Camera→Parallel Projection.

---

5. Make the window box into a component.

6. Paint the component and place three of them along the curved wall (Figure 3-35).

Trim the Building, Trim the Windows

1. Select everything and choose Intersect→Intersect with Model to get the intersection edges on the building (Figure 3-36).

These edges appear only on the building, not on the components. To get intersection edges on the windows themselves, the component must be open for editing first.

2. Open any of the windows for editing. Opening a component is like opening a group: You can activate Select and double-click the component, or you can right-click on the component and choose Edit Component.

3. The other components and the building are still visible, though faded in the background. It will be difficult to see intersection edges on this component while all the other objects are in view. So open the Model Info window (choose Window→Model Info) to the Components page. Select my Hide checkboxes for both similar components and the rest of the model. Now only the window cutout box is visible.

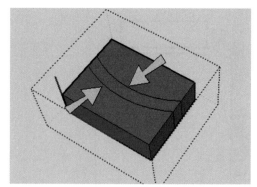

Figure 3-37

4. Select the whole box and run Intersect with Model. This creates the intersection edges where the box meets the building, even though the building is currently hidden (Figure 3-37).

5. Trim the box so that you're left with just the frame (Figure 3-38).

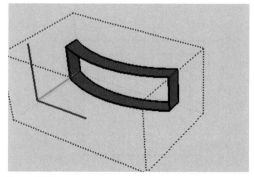

Figure 3-38

6. Close the component (right-click outside the component and choose Close Component). The building and the other window frames return to the view. Because each component is identical, each window is now a trimmed frame (Figure 3-39).

7. The intersection edges were previously created on the curved wall of the building. So erase the three faces covering the fronts of the windows. Then erase the two lower back window faces but leave the top one.

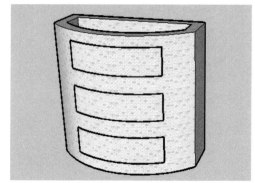

Figure 3-39

8. This top face will become the window glass, but first it should be removed from the building and made part of the window component. So select the face (do not select its edges) at the back of the window (Figure 3-40).

9. Cut this face (Ctrl+X / Cmd-X).

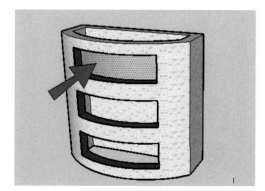

Figure 3-40

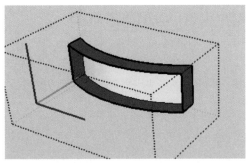

Figure 3-41

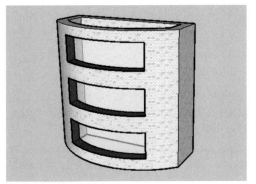

Figure 3-42

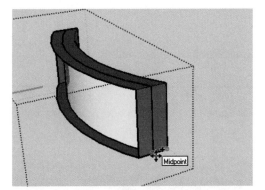

Figure 3-43

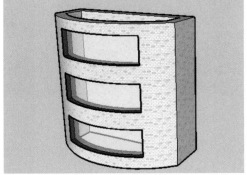

Figure 3-44

10. Open the top window component, and choose Edit→Paste in Place to replace the face in the exact spot from where it was removed. Paint both sides of this face with glass (Figure 3-41).

11. Close the component. Each window now has its own glass face, as shown in Figure 3-42.

12. What if you want the glass to sit in the middle of the frame, not all the way against the back? Open the component and copy the glass face to the midpoint of the frame, as indicated in Figure 3-43. (If you just move the glass instead of copy it, you'll move the limits of the frame, too.)

13. Erase the original glass in the back, and you're finished (Figure 3-44).

3.5 Intersecting with Both Intact and Exploded Components

Problem

You need to use an exploded component for trimming but also need to keep the component intact.

Solution

Place components where they need to go but keep one component aside. You can edit an in-place component to get its intersection edges, and those edges also appear on the set-aside component. After you explode and trim the in-place components, you can replace them with the component you set aside.

Discussion

This technique enables you to use exploded components to trim another object, while keeping an extra component on hand to replace what was exploded. To better understand how it works, you'll create a cabinet with handles. Each handle is the same component. The in-place handles are used to place intersection edges on the handle you set aside. Then you trim and explode the in-place handles to make the holes within the cabinet face. Finally, you'll copy the intact handle component into each hole.

There are three reasons to keep the handles as components:

- Using components keeps file size low.

- The handle component could be saved as its own file and could be manufactured as is, with no intersection edges.

- Keeping the handle as a component makes it easy to modify or easy to replace with another component. (Substituting components is discussed in Recipes 7.13 and 7.14.) However, if the new handle has a different shape, it will affect the shape of the holes.

1. Start with a cabinet that has one handle component off to the side and the rest of the handle components protruding slightly into the cabinet front. You can create your model from scratch, or download my Cabinet model from the 3D Warehouse (Figure 3-45).

Figure 3-45

--- Note ---------------------------------

The handle in this model was created using Follow Me, extruding the face along an arc path.

_____

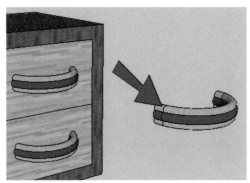

Figure 3-46

2. Open one of the cabinet handles for editing (not the handle off to the side). Run Intersect with Model on it to create intersection edges where the handle meets the cabinet.

Because Intersect affects all components, the intersection edges also appear on the handle off to the side (Figure 3-46). These edges will come in handy later, when we replace the handles in the cabinet holes.

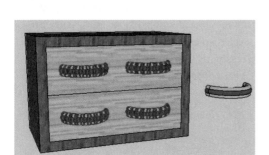

Figure 3-47

3. Explode and intersect the handles in the cabinet but leave intact the component off to the side (Figure 3-47).

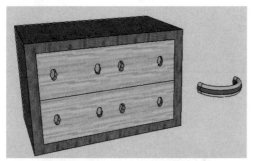

Figure 3-48

4. Trim to get the holes for the handles (Figure 3-48). If this model were to actually be built, the cabinet itself would be complete, including the holes that would need to be drilled in the front faces.

Figure 3-49

5. Now that the holes are made, you can replace the handles (Figure 3-49). This is easy to do now because the handle component has edges where it meets the holes.

Note

This might not be a perfect real-world example because a real cabinet handle would be attached with screws. But you get the idea of how the technique is used.

3.6 Intersecting Only Selected Objects

Problem

You need intersection edges only on selected objects.

Solution

Select what you want to intersect, and choose Intersect→Intersect Selected.

Discussion

While Intersect with Model takes the entire model into consideration when intersecting, Intersect Selected limits which intersection edges are drawn. This has two advantages: you don't get stuck erasing edges you don't need, and you get faster results. Intersect with Model can be a heavy operation, particularly if you have curved objects with many segments. Limiting the intersection edges to get only what you need can save you some CPU time.

To understand how Intersect Selected works, you'll cut windows in a building that has external and internal walls, as shown in Figure 3-50. You want the windows cut only in the external walls. The grouped cylinders are the cutting object. If you right-click on the group, the only Intersect option is Intersect with Model.

If you run Intersect with Model and then hide the group, you would see intersection edges on *all* walls, internal and external (Figure 3-51).

To cut windows only on the outside walls, you can first select what you want to intersect and then use Intersect Selected.

1. Start with a model that has interior and exterior walls with different colors or materials, and add a grouped cutting shape, as shown in Figure 3-52. You can create your model from scratch, or download my Intersect Selected model from the 3D Warehouse.

2. First, you need to select what you're going to intersect. To select all of the external walls, you could click both front and back faces (four total faces), but there's an easier way: Right-click on any external face and choose Select→All with Same Material. All external faces are selected (including some you don't need, but they don't intersect with anything).

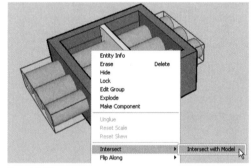
Figure 3-50

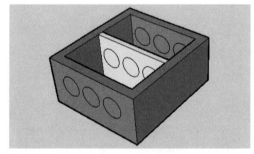
Figure 3-51

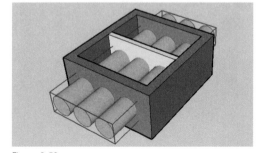
Figure 3-52

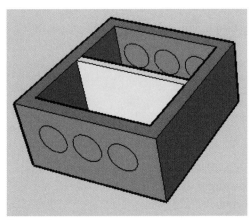

Figure 3-53

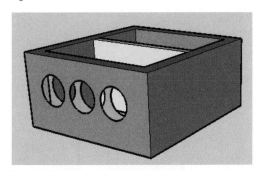

Figure 3-54

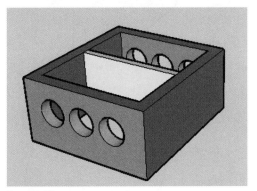

Figure 3-55

3. To add the cutout group to the selection, select it while pressing Shift. Then right-click on any selected object and choose Intersect→Intersect Selected.

4. Hide the group (right-click on it and choose Hide), and you have intersection edges only on the external walls (Figure 3-53).

5. Remove the circular faces from the four walls where they appear. Because the cutout group is gone, there are no window frames, just holes within a shell (Figure 3-54).

6. To complete the window frames, you need to keep portions of the cutout group. Bring the group back by choosing Edit→Unhide→All. Then right-click on the group and choose Explode.

   The edges on the walls automatically cut the exploded cylinders, so you can easily trim the cylinders, as shown in Figure 3-55.

3.7 Intersecting Within a Group or Component

Problem

You need to get intersection edges within a group or component, without intersecting with the rest of the model.

Solution

Edit the group or component, and use Intersect with Context.

Discussion

If a group or component intersects objects outside itself, these objects will be included in the calculation when you use Intersect with Model. If you want to keep intersection edges only within the group or component, use Intersect with Context.

A simple doorknob example demonstrates this. The knob and handle shown in Figure 3-56 is a group.

If you open the group for editing and choose Intersect→Intersect with Model, you will get edges where the knob meets the door (blue arrow in Figure 3-57) and edges where the knob handles meet the cylinder (red arrow). So the cylinder is intersected with objects both inside and outside the group.

If you want only edges within the group, use Intersect with Context.

1. Start with the model shown in Figure 3-56 of a door, with a knob made of a cylinder and two pulled-up hexagons. The cylinders protrude slightly into the hexagons, and the entire knob is a group. You can create your model from scratch, or download my Intersect with Context model from the 3D Warehouse.

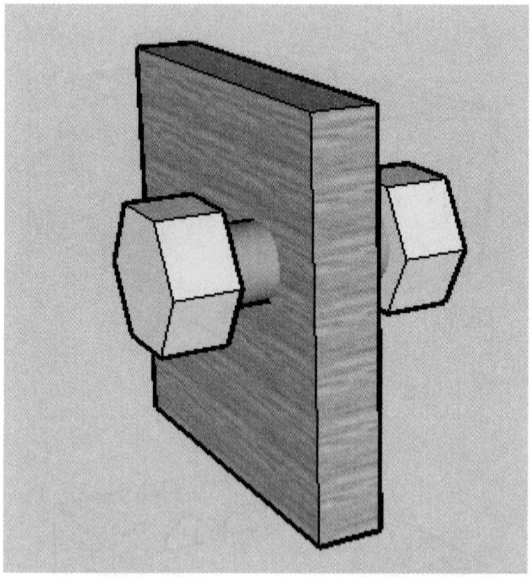

Figure 3-56

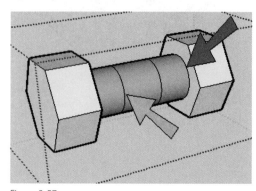

Figure 3-57

Want to Create This Model Yourself?

1. In the flat plane, draw a pulled-up hexagon and a cylinder for the knob and handle, respectively.
2. Move the cylinder into the knob so that it's protruding inside just a bit. To avoid stickiness, first move the cylinder straight up in Front view and then position it exactly over the handle while in Top view. Then back in Front view, move the cylinder straight down.
3. Copy another handle to the other end of the cylinder and make the entire knob into a group.
4. Make a thin box to represent the door, and use Move and Rotate as needed to place the knob in the door.

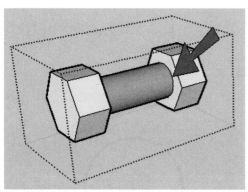

Figure 3-58

2. Open the group for editing and hide the rest of the model. (To hide the model, open the Model Info window to the Components page and select the Hide checkboxes.) Right-click on the cylinder and choose Intersect→Intersect with Context. Edges are created within the group only, where the knobs meet the cylinder (Figure 3-58).

3. Close the group.

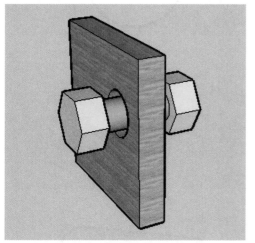

Figure 3-59

The advantage of Intersect with Context in this example is that the cylinder remains whole, without edges along its length. If you create a larger hole in the door to accommodate the knob, you can see that the cylinder itself has no intersection edges (Figure 3-59).

3.8 Using Intersect to Trim Components with Themselves

Problem

You have a series of overlapping components, and you want to trim them relative to one another.

Solution

Open one component for editing and use Intersect with Model to get edges where the component meets neighboring components. Then trim the edited component, which updates all other components.

Discussion

In the chapter's previous recipes, you've seen how groups and components can intersect other objects. Here you'll investigate what happens when components intersect with themselves. This technique is useful when you have overlapping linear copies or rotated copies of a component that need to be trimmed to fit exactly with their neighbors. Components can remain intact (not exploded), which keeps your file size low and allows for easy editing of each component.

In the main example, you'll start with a simple cylinder component, make overlapping linear copies of it, and intersect it a few different ways to result in a log cabin. In "Other Uses," you'll see how the same technique can be used on rotated copies to transform a ring of cube components into a bracelet.

Flatten the Logs

In this example, you'll start with cylinder components and intersect them with each other so that they can be flattened and therefore easy to stack.

1. Start with a circle in Front view. Add a construction point by right-clicking on the circle edge and choosing Point at Center (Figure 3-60). This construction point will make it easier to move log components into place later.

2. Pull the circle into a cylinder and make the whole thing into a component. Then paint it (Figure 3-61).

3. Stack three cylinder components, evenly spaced, so that they overlap, as shown in Figure 3-62.

4. Check the Components page of the Model Info window to ensure that components are hidden while editing. Open the middle component for editing. Right-click on the cylinder face and choose Intersect→Intersect with Model. This creates two edges on the top and two on the bottom, where the middle log meets the top and bottom ones (Figure 3-63).

— **Note** —

You can download my Log Cabin model from the 3D Warehouse, which contains scenes that show the steps for this example.

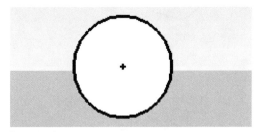
Figure 3-60

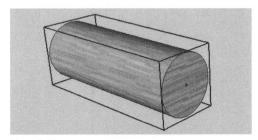
Figure 3-61

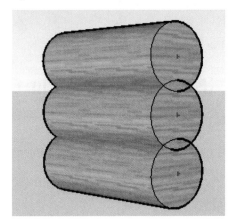
Figure 3-62

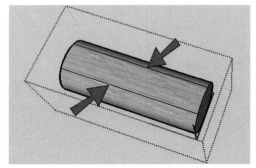
Figure 3-63

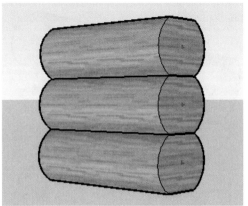

Figure 3-64

5. Draw lines on the front face to connect the intersection edges, and use Push/Pull to shave off the top and bottom. Close the component, and you now have flattened logs (Figure 3-64).

Note

You could also flatten the logs without using Intersect with Model. While editing the middle log, if the other logs are visible, you could use intersection points to add edges manually. But while the other logs are visible, it's harder to see where to shave off the top and bottom. How you do this is just a matter of preference.

Make the Notches

The logs must be notched at each end so they can stack. Here's how to do it.

1. First you need to rotate and move the top log so that is sits between the bottom two, in order to get the necessary intersection edges. Rotate the top log 90 degrees, using the midpoint of the top edge as the center of rotation (Figure 3-65).

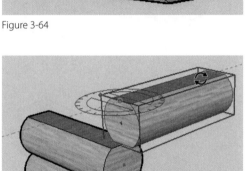

Figure 3-65

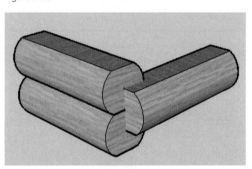

Figure 3-66

2. Move this rotated log down midway between the other two, as shown in Figure 3-66. This is where the construction point comes in handy; you can use it as the first move point.

3. When real logs are stacked to make a cabin, they extend past the notch. So each log needs to protrude past where they all currently meet. Change the Components page of the Model Info window so that other components are now visible while editing. Edit any log and extend its front so that all logs overlap (Figure 3-67).

4. Close the component.

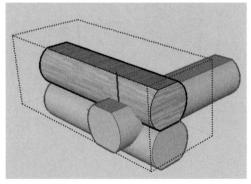

Figure 3-67

5. When creating the notches, you'll need surfaces from the neighboring logs to form the notch faces at the intersections of the log you are working on. So the components must be exploded. Select all three components, right-click on one of them, and choose Explode from the pop-up menu.

6. With all three logs still selected, run Intersect with Model. This gives you some (but not all) of the edges you need to make the notch. You still need the edges in the middle half of the log.

7. Erase the top and bottom logs, leaving only the one in the middle (Figure 3-68).

8. To make the following steps easier, paint this top face (mine is blue, as you can see in Figure 3-69).

   The notch has to be created so that half of the top half, and half of the bottom half, are removed. (In other words, the top and bottom quarters will be removed.) Therefore, the log has to be divided vertically into four sections. An easy way to do this is to copy the painted face from top to bottom and create three faces in between.

9. Select the painted face and copy it straight down to the bottom, as shown in Figure 3-70. (You can press Shift to lock in the blue direction, and click anywhere on the bottom of the log. Or you can tap the up arrow and then click the bottom of the log.)

10. Enter 4/ to create the four spaces between copies. You can check in X-Ray or Wireframe mode to make sure that three copied faces are inside the log.

11. Remove the top painted face. You should see the first copy of it inside the log (Figure 3-71).

12. Move the side edges of this face outward so that the face extends past the sides of the log (Figure 3-72).

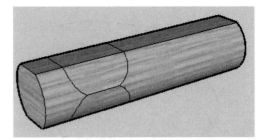

Figure 3-68

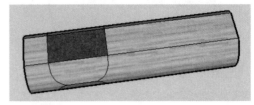

Figure 3-69

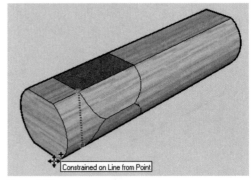

Constrained on Line from Point

Figure 3-70

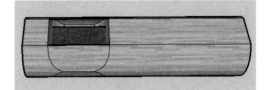

Figure 3-71

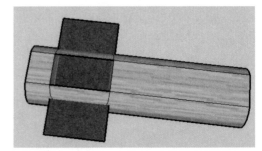

Figure 3-72

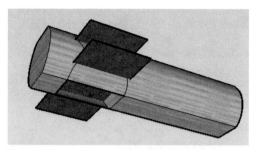

Figure 3-73

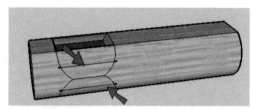

Figure 3-74

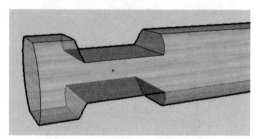

Figure 3-75

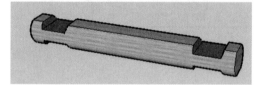

Figure 3-76

13. Do the same on the bottom of the log: remove the lowest face and extend the sides of the next copy. (Yours won't be painted, but I painted mine to make it easier to see, Figure 3-73.)

14. Select both of these extended faces and run Intersect with Model. Trim the faces, and you're left with some new intersection edges, indicated in Figure 3-74.

15. Trim the top and bottom quarters of the notch, until you're left with the faces shown in Figure 3-75. When erasing the edges along the sides of the log, work in X-Ray mode so you easily see the internal edges to erase. (You could also use the Eraser with the Ctrl or Option key, which smoothes the edges but doesn't erase them.)

16. To make the log notched on both of its ends, rotate-copy the half-log you've made and erase the dividing line (Figure 3-76).

17. Erase the construction point; it is no longer needed, because it was placed there only to help move the logs.

18. Make the entire log back into a component.

Put It All Together

Now that you have a log component, it can be copied and stacked to complete the cabin.

1. Make a stack of logs and rotate-copy the stack 90 degrees. Use similar points on the notches to move the logs into place (Figure 3-77).

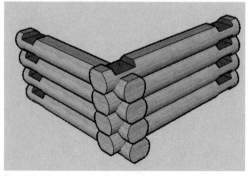

Figure 3-77

2. Copy both stacks to the other notches (Figure 3-78).

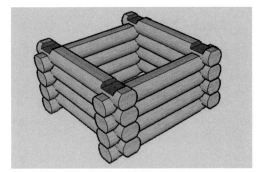

Figure 3-78

3. To cut a door in one wall, make a grouped cutout shape (Figure 3-79).

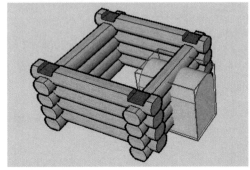

Figure 3-79

4. Explode all of the log components cut by the group and explode the group as well. (Again, this is because the logs will need to "borrow" surfaces from the cutting shape.) Intersect and trim. Done (Figure 3-80)!

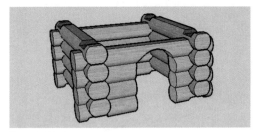

Figure 3-80

Other Uses

The log cabin used cylinder components copied in a linear pattern. Figures 3-81 and 3-82 show two models of bracelets, in which the initial component for each is a cube copied in a rotated pattern. The boxes are trimmed against one another, and rounded for a smoother look.

To see how this was done, download my Beaded Bracelets model from the 3D Warehouse.

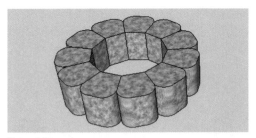

Figure 3-81

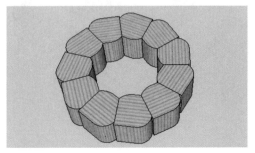

Figure 3-82

CHAPTER 4

Advanced Intersect and Follow Me Techniques

The Follow Me and Intersect tools are used together frequently to create complex 3D objects. Follow Me is used to create individual objects by extruding a face along a path, and the Intersect tool is then used to get edges where the Follow Me objects meet themselves or other objects. After these intersection edges are created, trimming is easy.

This chapter offers some advanced techniques for using them in tandem as well as separately. Specifically, you'll learn to do the following:

- Create temporary faces for a Follow Me face

- Make round corners

- Create lathed shapes

- Quickly create a complex roof with a uniform slope

- Create "dummy" Follow Me paths when the existing path is not easy to select

- Extend Follow Me paths to make intersecting and trimming easy

- Use Intersect to create a 3D Follow Me path

--- **Note** ---

Before using these tools together, it is important that you understand how to use them individually. If you haven't already, read Chapters 2 and 3 before continuing.

4.1 Creating Temporary Faces for Follow Me

Problem

You want to round a sharp corner, but the model contains no face on which you can easily draw a Follow Me face.

Solution

Create a temporary face on which to draw the Follow Me face.

Discussion

Consider the box in Figure 4-1, which has a Follow Me face (shown in dark brown) drawn on one face.

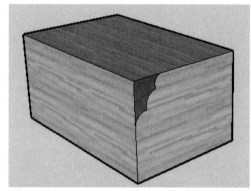

Figure 4-1

If you use the top face as the Follow Me path, the Follow Me face is extruded around the top of the box, removing volume (Figure 4-2). This example is simple because it was clear where to draw the Follow Me face.

But if you are starting with a box with rounded vertical corners like the box in Figure 4-3, you have no face on which to draw the Follow Me face.

The solution is to create a temporary face on which to draw the Follow Me face. After the Follow Me is complete, you can easily remove the temporary face.

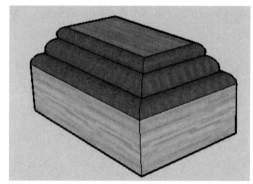

Figure 4-2

In this recipe's first example, you'll start with the model shown in Figure 4-3 and use Follow Me to make a jewelry box with a rounded top. Adding a notch in the box will give you a temporary face for the Follow Me face; you can fill in the notch after the top is rounded. The second example starts with a round object and ends with a round casserole dish with a rounded lid. You'll get there by creating a temporary face from one of the object's straight segments.

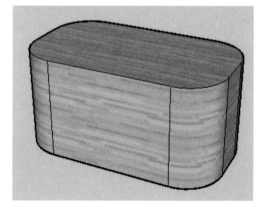

Figure 4-3

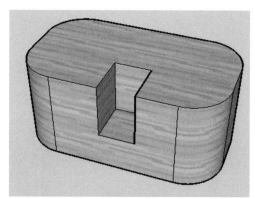

Figure 4-4

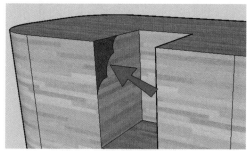

Figure 4-5

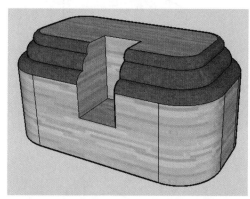

Figure 4-6

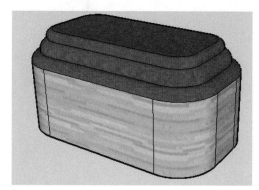

Figure 4-7

Example 1: Jewelry Box

In this example, you will round the top edge of a box that has rounded vertical corners.

1. Start with a box with rounded corners like the box in Figure 4-3. You can create your model from scratch, or download my Jewelry Box model from the 3D Warehouse.

Want to Create This Model Yourself?

There are two ways to create a box like this.

One method is to draw the basic rectangle in Top view, and draw arcs in each corner. When the arc preview is magenta, you know it is equidistant from the corner along both edges. Trim the corners to make a rounded rectangle and then pull it up.

Alternately, you can draw a rectangle and pull it up. Then draw arcs in each corner of the top face, and use Push/Pull to push each arc face down to the bottom of the box.

2. Draw a rectangle on the top or front face and push the rectangle inward, making a small notch (Figure 4-4).

3. Draw the Follow Me face on one of the vertical faces of the notch (Figure 4-5).

4. Select the Follow Me path. To do so, you could click each individual edge, but an easier way is to double-click the top face and then Shift-click to unselect the top face *plus* all four edges that compose the notch. Then use Follow Me to extrude the face around the remaining selected edges (Figure 4-6).

5. To close the notch, pull one of the side faces of the notch to the other side of the notch. Then erase the extra lines (Figure 4-7).

Example 2: Casserole Dish

This example also relies on a temporary face for the Follow Me face. Because the main object is round, however, you need to take advantage of hidden geometry in order to create temporary objects.

1. Start with an oval and pull it up. You can create your model from scratch, or download my Casserole Dish model from the 3D Warehouse.

> ### Want to Create This Model Yourself?
> 1. Draw a circle in the flat (red-green) plane.
> 2. Select the circle and activate Scale.
> 3. Drag one of the side handles to create an oval.
> 4. Pull the oval up.

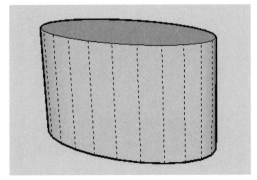

Figure 4-8

2. To be able to draw or edit anything on a round face, you need to see the flat segments that compose the face. Choose View→Hidden Geometry to see the dashed lines that indicate where the hidden edges are (Figure 4-8).

Note

If you work with round objects often or hide objects often, it's helpful to create a keyboard shortcut for the View→Hidden Geometry toggle. I prefer the Function keys (F1, F2, and so forth) for all display commands, which also include Wireframe, X-Ray, and so on. Setting up shortcuts can be done via the Preferences window.

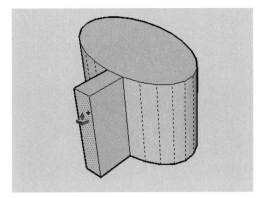

Figure 4-9

3. Use Push/Pull with the Ctrl/Option key to pull out one of the segments (Figure 4-9). One of the vertical faces created by this operation will be used to create one of the Follow Me faces.

4. Erase the top face of the oval cylinder and use Push/Pull with Ctrl/Option again to pull out the inside face of this new box. Extend it almost to the other side (Figure 4-10). One of these vertical faces will be used to create another Follow Me face.

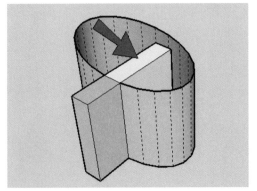

Figure 4-10

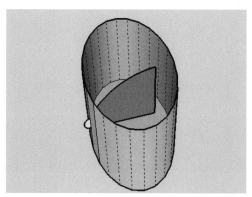

Figure 4-11

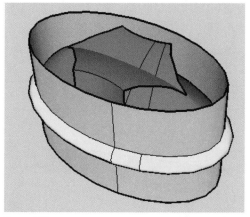

Figure 4-12

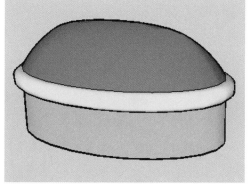

Figure 4-13

5. Erase all new faces except for one vertical face on the inside and one vertical face on the outside. Draw a small half-circle face on the outside vertical face (shown in Figure 4-11 in yellow) and a tall arc (shown in orange) on the inside vertical face. The orange face will be used to create the lid, and the yellow face will be used to create the lip around the bottom of the lid. Trim the rest of the temporary vertical faces. If you paint your new faces, be sure to paint both the front and back face, to ensure that the colors will show even if the Follow Me operation reverses the faces.

6. Hide the hidden edge indicators by toggling the View→Hidden Geometry command.

7. Select the bottom face of the cylinder so that its boundary edges will be used as the Follow Me path, and extrude the half-circle outside the cylinder. Then use the same path to extrude the larger arc face (Figure 4-12).

8. Select everything and use Intersect→Intersect with Model to get edges where the lid intersects itself. Then you can erase all faces above the lid and any extra edges on the lid to get the final dish (Figure 4-13).

4.2 Rounding Corners

Problem

You want to extrude a rounding face around a path with corners, and you want the corners rounded rather than *mitered* (sharp).

Solution

Use Push/Pull instead of Follow Me, and create separate objects to fill in the rounded corners.

Discussion

Consider a model of a box with a Follow Me face (shown in yellow in Figure 4-14) along one edge.

If you use Follow Me to extrude the face around the top of the box, the corners are sharp, or mitered (Figure 4-15).

If you want these corners to be rounded, you need to use Push/Pull instead of Follow Me to create the straight sections. Then for the rounded parts, use Follow Me with a circular path.

The first example demonstrates how to use this technique to create round corners on the rectangular table shown in Figure 4-15. In the second example, you'll create similar rounded corners on a hexagonal table, taking advantage of groups to keep existing objects intact after using Follow Me.

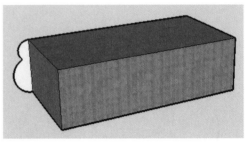

Figure 4-14

Figure 4-15

Example 1: Rectangular Table

In this example, you will create round corners on a rectangular table with sharp corners.

1. Start with a model of a table top. Along one edge, add a rounding face (shown in Figure 4-14 in yellow) that will be pulled around the table top. You can create your model from scratch, or download my Table Top model from the 3D Warehouse.

2. Use Push/Pull to pull the rounding face along one edge (Figure 4-16).

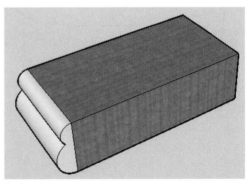

Figure 4-16

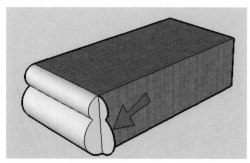

Figure 4-17

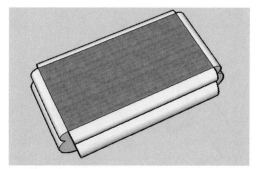

Figure 4-18

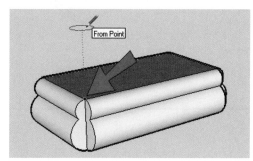

Figure 4-19

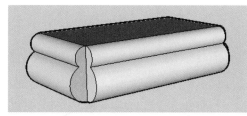

Figure 4-20

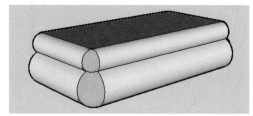

Figure 4-21

3. For the next edge, you need to copy the rounding face so that is perpendicular to the edge. Select the front face of the Push/Pull operation you just completed and activate Rotate. Place the protractor at the corner of the table, keeping it oriented to the table top (the protractor's preview color should be blue). Press Ctrl/Option for copying and make a 90-degree copy (Figure 4-17).

4. Pull this copied face along the next edge.

5. Repeat steps 2 through 4 for the remaining two edges of the table (Figure 4-18).

6. At each corner, you need a rounded version of the rounding face. Therefore, you need to draw a Follow Me circle. This circle must be located away from the table so that it won't break the table's geometry. Activate Circle and orient it to the table top (again, the preview color should be blue). Since the circle will be located above this corner, move the mouse directly up, watching for the blue inference line (Figure 4-19).

7. Make the circle any size you want and be sure to align it to the red or green axis.

8. To make it easier to copy the round object to other corners later, paint the rounding face a different color (shown in Figure 4-20 in cyan). Because it's hard to know which side of the rounding face will appear after Follow Me, you should paint the back face too. The easiest way to do this is to right-click on the painted face and choose Reverse Face. (This switches the back and front faces.) Paint the reversed face the same color you just used for the first side. Now this face is painted on both sides.

9. Use the Follow Me circle as the path for the newly painted Follow Me face, to create the rounded object in the corner (Figure 4-21).

10. You no longer need the Follow Me circle, so erase it.

11. Only a quarter of this round object is showing; the rest of it is within the box. But the whole object needs to be copied to each corner. Right-click on the round corner and choose Select→All with Same Material, which selects the entire object. Then copy the round object to each corner (Figure 4-22).

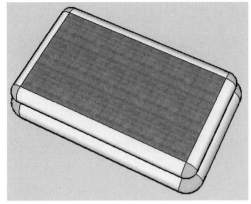

Figure 4-22

12. The table top looks fine from the top, but it's always a good idea to keep your object count low by erasing unnecessary faces and edges. Orbit to see the underside. Because the profile edges at each corner cut the rounding faces, no Intersect operation is needed. Erase faces and edges so that the round borders and corners form an empty shell (Figure 4-23).

13. To replace the bottom face, trace any edge along the bottom.

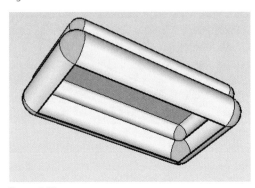

Figure 4-23

Example 2: Hexagonal Table

This example uses the same Follow Me technique to make rounded corners. To prevent the rounded corner objects from breaking the rest of the table, you will use the grouping technique within Follow Me, which is described in Recipe 2.3.

1. Start with a hexagon-shaped box and place a point at the center (right-click on the top hexagon edge and choose Point at Center). This point makes it easier to copy objects later.

2. Draw a rounding face on one vertical face (Figure 4-24).

3. Copy the rounding face 90 degrees from the vertical face, erase the original, and pull the face along one edge.

> **Note**
>
> You can download my Hexagon Table model from the 3D Warehouse, which contains scenes that show the steps for this example.

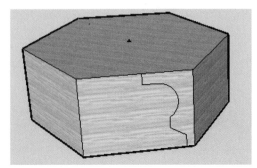

Figure 4-24

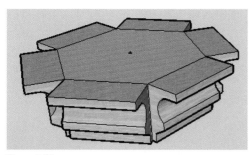

Figure 4-25

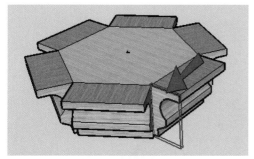

Figure 4-26

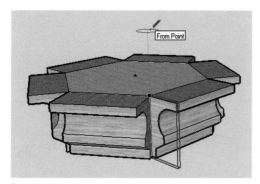

Figure 4-27

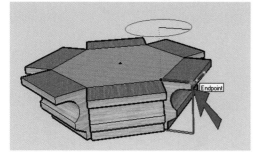

Figure 4-28

4. Rotate-copy the pulled faces along each side of the hexagon (Figure 4-25).

   It you were to make a round object for the corner now, using the technique from "Example 1: Rectangular Table," the top face of the table would be broken by the top face of the Follow Me object. To protect the existing faces of the table, you need to use a group.

5. Activate Select and double-click one of the vertical end faces of the pulled rounding faces. This selects both the face and its surrounding edges. Right-click on the face and choose Make Group. The face will then appear with bold edges and surrounded by a bounding box (Figure 4-26).

6. The next step is to draw the Follow Me circle, and it is important that the circle have the correct number of sides. Because this model is based on a hexagon, the number of circle sides should be divisible by six. This ensures that the segments of the circle, and therefore the segments of the resulting round corner, will align with the edges of the Push/Pull faces. Activate Circle and make sure the number of sides is a multiple of six (24 is a good number). As you did for the rectangular table, place the center directly above the corner of the table (Figure 4-27). Do not click yet to complete the circle.

   ─── **Note** ───────────────────────────

   You can set the number of sides of a circle by entering the number before you place the circle's center point. After you place the center, you can still change the number of sides by typing *24s* either before or right after clicking the point along the radius.

   ──

7. To establish the radius of the circle, click on any point along the top edge of the group. This ensures that a circle segment will start just above the group, so the round Follow Me object will align perfectly with the Push/Pull objects (Figure 4-28).

8. Use the Edit Group method to make the round object: Select the circle as the path, activate Follow Me, edit the group, and click the face (Figure 4-29).

9. While the group is still open for editing, run Intersect with Model on the whole group. This creates edges where the group meets the rest of the table. If there are any edges that aren't created but should be, trace them manually. This is easiest to do with the rest of the model displayed, which can be set in the Components page of the Model Info window. Be sure to check that all edges are drawn, including those on the top and bottom faces of the rounding object.

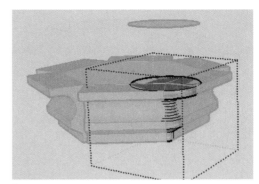
Figure 4-29

10. While the component is still open, open the Components page of the Model Info window to hide the rest of the model, and trim away the extra portions of the group (Figure 4-30).

11. If you have curved faces with small edges along them, use the Eraser with the Ctrl/Option key pressed to smooth the edges.

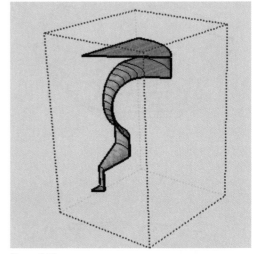
Figure 4-30

12. Close the group and rotate-copy it to the other five corners (Figure 4-31).

13. For the final cleanup, select all six groups, right-click on one of them, and choose Explode. Then you can erase the extra edges on the top and bottom of the table (Figure 4-32).

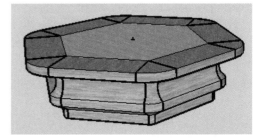
Figure 4-31

14. To hide remaining edges along the rounded border, you can select the entire table, right-click, and choose Soften→Smooth Edges from the pop-up menu. Adjust the sliders to smooth the faces.

— **Note** —
Another way to create the same table involves offsetting the table top, rounding the sharp corners of this new offset face, and using Follow Me to extrude the rounding face along the new edges. You can download my Hexagon Table Alternative model from the 3D Warehouse, which contains scenes that show the steps for this method.

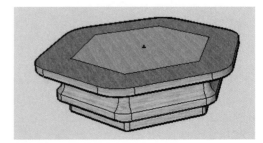
Figure 4-32

4.3 Creating Lathed Shapes

Problem

You want to create a lathed table leg and place it below a rounded box.

Solution

Use Follow Me around a circle to make the lathed shape and Intersect to create the rounded box.

Discussion

Lathed shapes are a common design element in woodworking and furniture design, and a table leg is perhaps the most common lathed shape. Two steps need to be completed for this model:

- Create the rounded box to house the leg, which is modeled by using Intersect.
- Create the lathed shape itself, which is done by extruding a face around a Follow Me circle.

In this recipe, you'll create the box first and then work your way down to complete the leg.

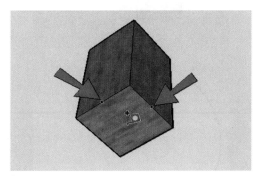

Figure 4-33

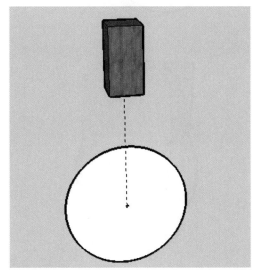

Figure 4-34

1. Start with a square and pull it up.

> **Note**
>
> You can download my Table Legs model from the 3D Ware-house, which contains scenes that show the steps for this recipe.

2. Because the rest of the table leg will be created relative to the center of this box, you need to mark the center with a construction line. Activate Tape Measure and start the construction line on the bottom of the box, where the red and green directions meet from adjacent midpoints (Figure 4-33).

3. Draw the construction line straight down.

4. Draw a vertical circle centered on the construction line endpoint (Figure 4-34).

5. Because the box corners are to be rounded evenly, the rounding must be based on a sphere whose extents meet the box corners. So draw a horizontal circle, perpendicular to and concentric with the large circle. The number of sides should be a multiple of four, because the circle has to align with the four corners of the box. To establish the radius, click on a corner of the box above the circle (Figure 4-35).

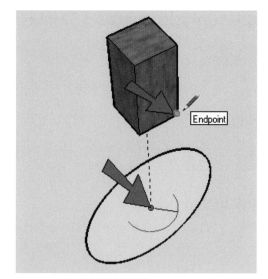

Figure 4-35

6. To create the sphere, select the larger circle as the Follow Me path and use Follow Me on the smaller circle (Figure 4-36).

7. Move the sphere straight up into the middle of the box.

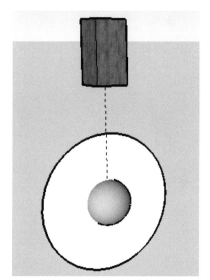

Figure 4-36

8. Leave the sphere selected. The next step is to move the sphere back down so that the rounding of the corners will start from the base of the box. In order to see how to move the sphere, choose View→Hidden Geometry from the main menu, which displays the dashed lines indicating hidden edges (Figure 4-37).

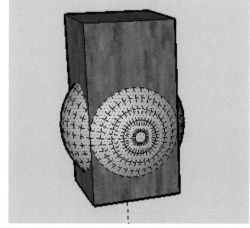

Figure 4-37

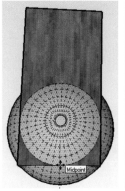
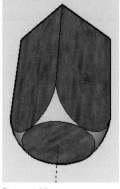

Figure 4-38   Figure 4-39

9. Move the sphere straight down so that the lowest point on any of the protruding sides meets the midpoint of a lower edge (Figure 4-38). This establishes the corners of the box that need to be trimmed.

10. Turn off the display of hidden edge indicators by choosing View→Hidden Geometry again. Run Intersect with Model, and trim both the box and sphere (Figure 4-39). Check the model in X-Ray or Wireframe view to erase all extra edges.

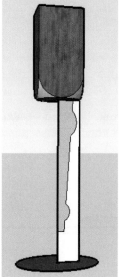
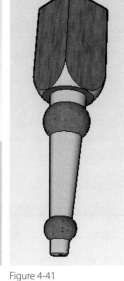

Figure 4-40   Figure 4-41

11. To make the lathed shape, draw a vertical rectangle below the box, sharing an edge with the construction line. On this rectangle, draw a section for the leg, like the one shown in Figure 4-40 in yellow. For the Follow Me circle, draw a horizontal circle at the bottom of the rectangle, centered on the construction line.

12. Use Follow Me to extrude the leg section around the circle. Then erase the circle and trim the rectangle, as shown in Figure 4-41.

13. Make the leg a component and make three more copies to support a table.

Figure 4-42

14. For the table top, draw a rectangle on top of the set of four legs. Offset the rectangle outward and pull it up. To make the table top more interesting, you can also extrude a Follow Me face around the table top (Figure 4-42).

4.4 Roofing with a Uniform Slope

Problem

You want to make a uniformly sloped roof atop a building.

Solution

Draw the roof section, use Follow Me to extrude the section along the building edges, and use Intersect to trim the roof.

Discussion

Roofs can be a difficult part of building design, but by combining Follow Me and Intersect, you can quickly make a complex-looking roof. There are three basic steps:

- Draw a face to represent the roof section with the correct slope.
- Use Follow Me to extrude the face around the building.
- Use Intersect with Model to get edges where the roof faces meet themselves, and trim the extra edges.

Use this technique when you want the same roof slope all around the building. To demonstrate, this recipe uses the technique on a simple roof with a known slope. In the "Other Uses" section, you'll see more complex roofs created using the same technique.

Note

Other roofing solutions are discussed in Chapter 5.

---

1. Start with an L-shaped building.

2. To start the roof section, draw a short horizontal line from the top corner of one of the front faces (Figure 4-43).

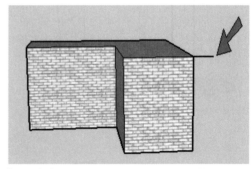

Figure 4-43

3. The Protractor tool (Tools→Protractor) is used to create an angled construction line at a known angle from an existing edge. Activate Protractor and click points 1 and 2 in Figure 4-44 to set the baseline for the construction line along the top of the building. Then move the mouse up and click point 3 to create the construction line at a 45-degree angle. (You can look for this angle in the Angle field, or type *45* and press Enter.)

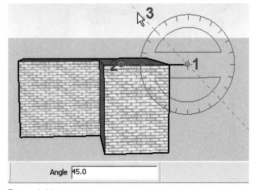

Figure 4-44

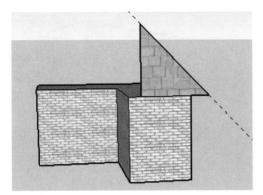

Figure 4-45

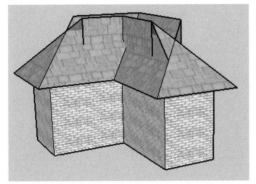

Figure 4-46

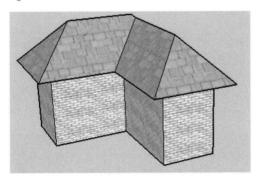

Figure 4-47

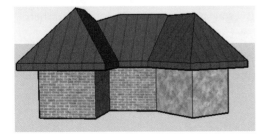

Figure 4-48

> **Note**
>
> Even though the field at the bottom of the window is labeled Angle, you can also enter a roof pitch in the rise-run format. For example, an 8/12 slope is entered as 8:12.

4. Use the construction line to create the triangular roof face as shown in Figure 4-45. The face should extend past the midpoint of the front face, so that the profile will not fall short of the center of the widest part of the building.

5. Select the top face of the building as the Follow Me path. Then use Follow Me to extrude the roof face around the building (Figure 4-46).

6. Select the entire roof and run Intersect with Model to get the edges where the roof intersects itself. Then trim away the extra edges (Figure 4-47).

7. Even when the roof looks "clean," you should check your model in X-Ray or Wireframe mode to erase any extra edges inside the roof.

Other Uses

This section contains two examples of more complex roofs, created using the same Follow Me and Intersect technique. The first example is an overhanging roof, and the second uses curved faces on both the building and roof.

Overhanging roof

Figure 4-48 shows a house with a thick, overhanging roof. The roof is based on a 2D Follow Me face, which is extruded around the top face of the building. The resulting roof faces are intersected and trimmed.

To see how it's done, download my Overhanging Roof model from the 3D Warehouse.

Curved faces on the roof and building

Figure 4-49 shows a building with curved faces, and a roof section that also has curves. The easiest way to create a roof section like this is to first create a vertical face on which to draw the roof section. After running Follow Me and Intersect with Model, the trimming of extra edges can take a while. But the results are worth the effort.

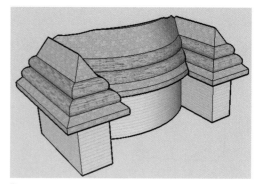

Figure 4-49

To see how it's done, download my Curvy Roof model from the 3D Warehouse.

4.5 Creating "Dummy" Follow Me Paths

Problem

You want to intersect two sets of faces created by Follow Me, but you're having trouble defining and selecting paths.

Solution

Copy the edges needed for the path so that the path can easily be selected away from the rest of the model. Alternatively, move the Follow Me faces away from each other so that their paths can easily be identified and the resulting faces won't interfere with each other.

Discussion

The problem discussed in this section deals with different Follow Me faces that are extruded around edges of the same shape. In these cases, you might have difficulty selecting a path in advance, particularly if edges are broken by other operations. The solution is to copy a set of edges elsewhere so that they can be easily selected. Another problem encountered in the same model is that two sets of Follow Me faces within the same closed shape can interfere with one another. The solution here is to temporarily move one of the faces away, run Follow Me on it, and then move it back into place. After all faces are in place, they can be intersected and trimmed.

The main example that will demonstrate these techniques is a skate park, in which two Follow Me faces create the skate ramp and the spectator seating. In "Other Uses," you will see the same technique applied to a picture frame.

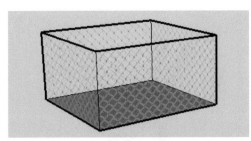

Figure 4-50

Figure 4-51

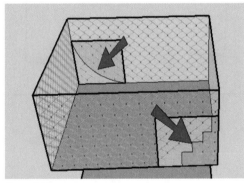

Figure 4-52

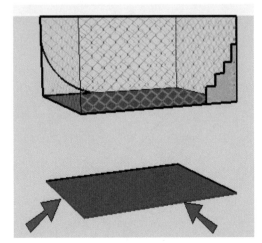

Figure 4-53

1. Start with a box and remove the top. Paint the four sides with a material from the Fencing material category (Figure 4-50). Many of these fencing materials have alpha transparency, which means the white background of each image is interpreted by SketchUp as transparent.

— Note —

You can download my Skate Park model from the 3D Warehouse, which contains scenes that show the steps for this recipe.

2. Make a copy of the bottom of the box, straight up or down. The edges around this face will be the "dummy" paths.

3. Select the original box (not including the copied face) and make it a group (Figure 4-51). This is so that the fence faces won't be broken when objects are added inside the box.

4. Using the faces of the box group to draw on, draw two identical rectangles in opposite corners on which to make the Follow Me faces. On one face, draw an arc section for the skate ramps (shown in Figure 4-52 in beige) and on the other, draw a section for steps (shown in green).

5. Trim the extra edges from these faces.

6. Because the fence box is a group, you can't select edges within it to define a Follow Me path. So you'll use the edges of the face you copied from the bottom of the box. Select the two edges of the face shown in Figure 4-53.

7. With this path defined, run Follow Me on the arc face. Here you can see the second problem: the Follow Me faces interfere with one another. The arc faces were not completed, and the face with the steps has disappeared (Figure 4-54).

8. Undo the Follow Me.

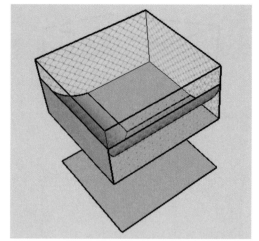

Figure 4-54

9. Move one of the Follow Me faces to a location directly above the box. I chose to move the section for the steps, as shown in Figure 4-55.

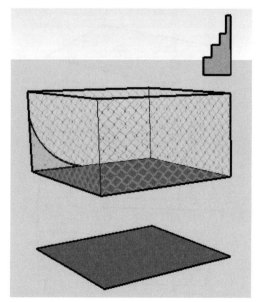

Figure 4-55

10. Use the two edges indicated in Figure 4-56 as the Follow Me path for the arc face.

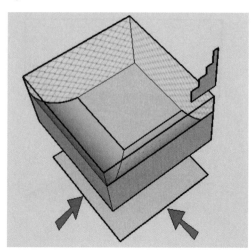

Figure 4-56

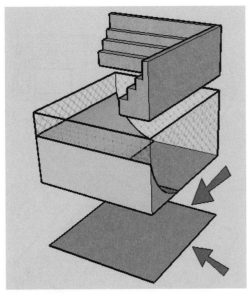

Figure 4-57

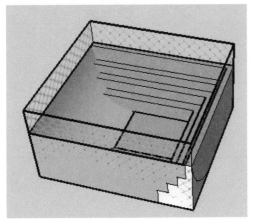

Figure 4-58

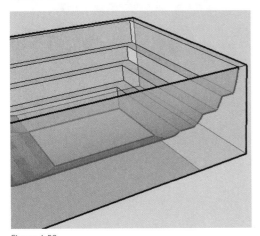

Figure 4-59

11. Use the other two edges as the Follow Me path for the steps (Figure 4-57).

12. Move the steps back down inside the fence (Figure 4-58).

> **Note**
>
> If you don't want to bother moving up and down, you could have made the arc and step sections into groups. Then you could use the Edit Group method within Follow Me, without having to move anything. But you would have to Explode both groups before intersecting.
>
> You could also make just one of the sections a group.

13. Hide the fence group and run Intersect with Model on the arcs and steps. Then trim away all the extras. Check in X-Ray or Wireframe mode to be sure all extra edges are erased (Figure 4-59).

14. Bring the hidden group back.

15. The hard part is finished, but you can make this model a little more usable. There's no way to get in or out of this park, so an entrance is needed. First, move the ramps and steps out of the group and add a cutting shape inside the group (Figure 4-60).

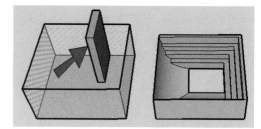

Figure 4-60

16. Move the ramps and steps back inside, intersect them, and trim away the entrance. To cut a hole in the fence, edit the fence group and add a tall rectangle for an opening. Then erase the opening face. Figure 4-61 shows the result.

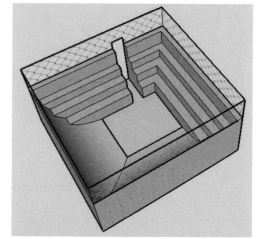

Figure 4-61

Other Uses

You can use the same technique to create an interesting picture frame. In this example, you would copy the inside face of the frame for the dummy paths, and you would move one of the Follow Me faces above or below the model. After Follow Me is complete for both faces, move everything back into place, intersect, and trim (Figure 4-62).

—— **Note** ——————————————————————

Using graphics in your model is covered in Chapter 9.

—————————————————————————————————

Figure 4-62

4.6 Extending Follow Me Paths

Problem

You want to trim two sets of Follow Me objects, but you want to be sure there will be enough of an overlap for trimming purposes.

Solution

Extend the Follow Me paths past where they need to be.

Discussion

Using extended Follow Me paths results in Follow Me objects that extend past the faces they are supposed to intersect. This ensures that all faces and edges of the Follow Me objects are long enough to intersect, and it makes trimming after intersection easy.

The main example uses the extended path technique to create a hot tub with curved walls and steps leading down into the tub. The paths for both the tub steps and the curved walls extend past the final limits of the tub, so that extra faces are easy to trim.

In the "Other Uses" section, the same technique will be applied to window frames.

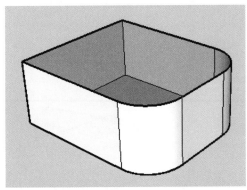

Figure 4-63

1. Start with a box with two rounded corners and no top face (Figure 4-63).

> **Note**
>
> You can download my Hot Tub model from the 3D Warehouse, which contains scenes that show the steps for this recipe.

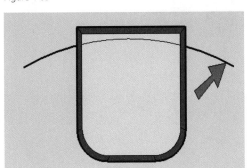

Figure 4-64

2. In Top view, draw an arc on the ground plane, which extends past both sides of the box (Figure 4-64). This path will be used to create the steps that lead down into the tub.

3. Copy one of the side faces of the box to the end of the arc. On this face, draw a cross-section for steps (Figure 4-65).

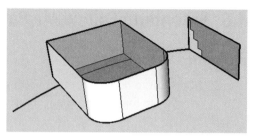

Figure 4-65

4. Using all three segments of the arc as the Follow Me path, and the step section as the Follow Me face, create the steps (Figure 4-66).

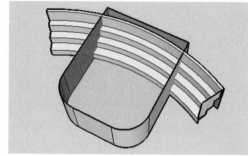

Figure 4-66

5. On the back of the box, make a face like the one indicated in Figure 4-67, using tangent arcs.

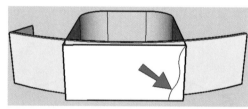

Figure 4-67

6. The Follow Me path for this face is another extended path, going past the back of the tub steps, so the curved walls will be easy to trim behind the steps. Select all of the top edges of the box as the Follow Me path (not including the edge along the back face) and run Follow Me on this face. This creates the curvy walls of the hot tub. If you have extra vertical faces around the tub, erase them (Figure 4-68).

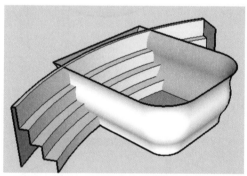

Figure 4-68

7. Run Intersect with Model on the entire model, and trim the walls and steps that extend past each other (Figure 4-69). Because the paths for these objects were extended, trimming is easy.

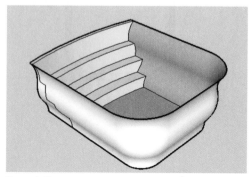

Figure 4-69

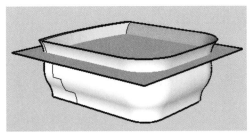

Figure 4-70

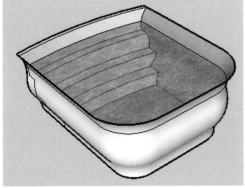

Figure 4-71

Figure 4-72

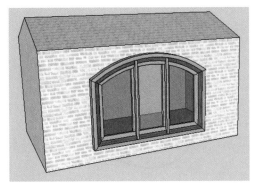

Figure 4-73

8. The last step is to fill the tub with water. The easiest way to make a face to represent the water level is to make a simple box next to the hot tub, at the height you want for the water. Remove all but the top face of this box, and move edges until they intersect the tub (Figure 4-70).

9. Intersect and trim. You can paint this face with a translucent water material from the Water category (Figure 4-71).

Other Uses

The extended path technique can be applied to window frames. This section shows two examples of such windows: a stained-glass window that you might see in an old church and a more modern three-paned window.

Stained-glass window

Figure 4-72 shows windows whose frames have two parts, created using two separate Follow Me faces. The Follow Me paths are extended past one another, and each Follow Me face is a group. After both Follow Me face groups are extruded along their paths, they are exploded, intersected, and trimmed. After the window is made into a component that cuts walls, it can be inserted into walls.

To see how it's done, download my Stained Glass Window model from the 3D Warehouse.

Three-paned window

Figure 4-73 shows a window with three panes. The window frame is created using Follow Me on the frame face. The muntins separating the panes are created with a simple Push/Pull, starting and ending past the window frame. Intersect and trim, make the window a component, and insert.

To see how it's done, download my Three Paned Window model from the 3D Warehouse.

4.7 Using Intersect to Create a 3D Follow Me Path

Problem

You want to use Follow Me along a 3D path, but it is difficult to draw the path.

Solution

Use the Intersect tool to create the path.

Discussion

Recipe 2.7 demonstrated how to use grouped reference geometry to create a 3D Follow Me path. This recipe presents another technique for creating a 3D path, in which intersection edges between two objects create the Follow Me path. This technique is helpful in cases where reference geometry is not easy to draw, but you do know the basic 3D parameters of the path.

In this recipe, you will model a pair of glasses. The frame around each lens proceeds along a 3D path, which is the intersection of a partial sphere and the frame shape. In the "Other Uses" section, the same technique is used to create a window frame around a curved window.

Create the Lens

This section demonstrates how to intersect two objects to produce the 3D Follow Me path. You'll create one lens for the glasses, whose border edges form the 3D path.

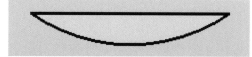

Figure 4-74

1. In Top view, use Arc and Line to make a face (Figure 4-74).

2. Make a vertical circle centered at the line's midpoint (Figure 4-75).

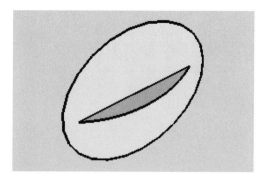

Figure 4-75

3. Use the large circle as the Follow Me path for the lens face. After you run Follow Me on the lens face, you will have a partial sphere. Erase the circle. What remains is the curved glass from which the lens will be cut (Figure 4-76).

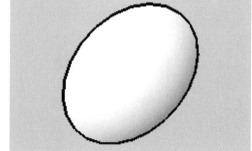

Figure 4-76

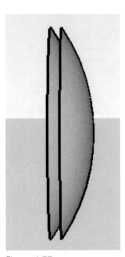

Figure 4-77

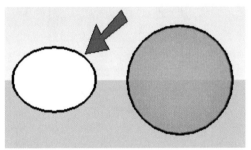

Figure 4-78

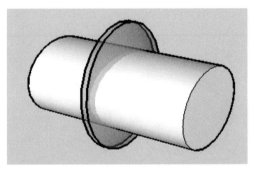

Figure 4-79

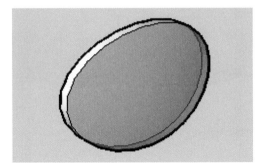

Figure 4-80

4. To give the lens glass some thickness, make a copy of it slightly in front or behind (Figure 4-77).

5. Paint the lens glass with a translucent material.

6. In Front view, in some blank space next to the lens, draw a shape for the lens frame (Figure 4-78). My frame is a simple oval (created by using the Scale tool on a circle), but you could use a rectangle with rounded corners, a star, or whatever shape you want.

7. Pull out the lens shape and move it into the lens glass (Figure 4-79).

8. Intersect and trim (Figure 4-80).

Make the Lens Frame

The border around the front of the lens will be used as the 3D path, and this path will be used to create the frame.

1. On one side of the lens, draw a shape to use as the Follow Me face for the frame (Figure 4-81). My Follow Me face is a rectangle, but you could try a curved shape.

2. To prevent the Follow Me frame from breaking the lens, make the Follow Me face a group.

3. You know that when a face is 2D, you can select it to define its boundary as the Follow Me path. But when the path is 3D, you need to select the Follow Me edges, and not the face. To select the edges bordering this face, double-click the front face of the lens and then Shift-click to unselect the face. This leaves only the edges selected.

4. Run Follow Me on the frame shape group. To remove the little edges throughout the frame, select everything inside the group, right-click, and choose Soften→Smooth Edges. Adjust the sliders until the edges disappear (Figure 4-82).

5. Close the frame group.

6. To make the second lens and frame, copy the framed lens next to the original and leave the copy selected.

7. To ensure that the pair of glasses is symmetric, activate Scale, which will be used to turn the copy inside-out. Click the drag handle in the direction you want to scale (Figure 4-83).

8. For the scale value, enter −1. Then move the copy so that the spacing between the lenses looks correct (Figure 4-84).

Note

Another way to mirror an object is to right-click on it and choose Flip Along with the relevant axis direction.

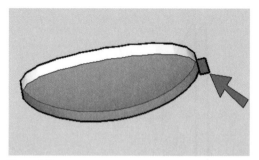

Figure 4-81

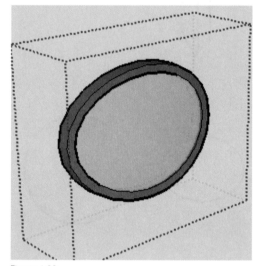

Figure 4-82

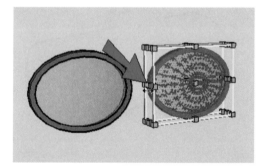

Figure 4-83

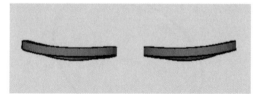

Figure 4-84

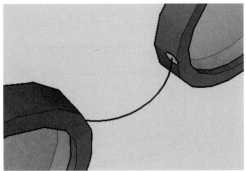

Figure 4-85

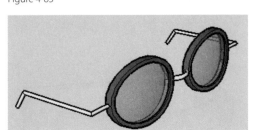

Figure 4-86

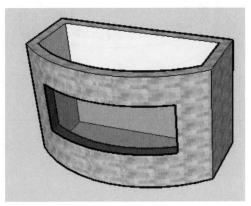

Figure 4-87

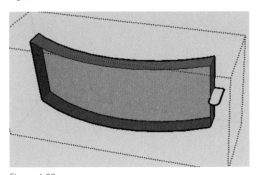

Figure 4-88

9. To make the nosepiece, add an arc between the frames, plus a small Follow Me face (Figure 4-85). Because the frames are grouped, these new objects don't stick to them.

10. Finish the nosepiece and make the ear pieces the same way: Use Follow Me and then make an inside-out copy. The completed pair of glasses is shown in Figure 4-86.

Other Uses

This technique can be used to add a frame to a curved window.

The method to create the window itself is described in Recipe 3.4. In the example in Figure 4-87, the window glass is along the front of the window, not the back or middle. This makes it easier to define the path for the frame. The window itself is a component.

Edit the window component and add a shape for the frame (shown in Figure 4-88 in yellow). Make the frame shape a group.

Extrude the frame around the border of the glass and smooth the edges. Run Intersect with Model on the frame, to get the edges where the frame meets the walls of the building (Figure 4-89).

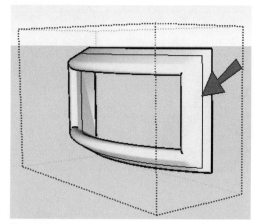

Figure 4-89

Trim the frame, close the frame group, close the window component, and you have a window with a curved frame (Figure 4-90).

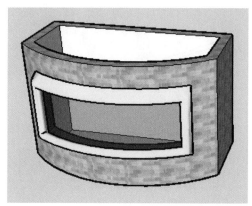

Figure 4-90

CHAPTER 5

Roofs: Constraints and Inferences

Inferences in SketchUp are those colored dots and dashed lines, and helpful text boxes, that appear while drawing, such as *On Red Axis*, *On Face*, *Midpoint*, and so forth. You can use inferences to ensure that you are drawing lines in the correct direction (red, green, or blue), starting a line at the right place (on an edge, endpoint, or midpoint), or drawing an object on a face. In addition to those basic uses, inferences also can be used to constrain objects, either to another object or to a direction. *Constraining* means you are forcing an object to have a certain geometric characteristic, such as a direction or start point.

To master SketchUp, understanding constraints is a must. You know the basics: a red preview line means a line will be drawn parallel to the red axis, and so on. You may even be an old hand at Shift-locking, aware that pressing and holding Shift while a preview line is red keeps the line in the red direction. But have you used double constraints or tried using the arrow keys? In this chapter, you'll learn about these and many more powerful ways constraints can help you work more accurately and effectively.

Most of the recipes involve roofs, which can pose vexing problems in building design but benefit from well-applied constraints. Even if you're not an architect, keep reading. The techniques presented are great for a wide variety of projects, because learning how to use SketchUp's constraints is simply essential to efficient design.

5.1 Creating an Overhanging Roof

Problem

You want to create an overhanging roof on a simple, rectangular house.

Solution

Use Push/Pull to create the overhanging parts of the roof, and use inferences and Shift-locking to fill the resulting gap.

Discussion

One quick and easy solution for adding an overhanging roof to a simple, rectangular building is to create both the roof thickness and overhang by using Push/Pull. Unfortunately, the method also results in an unwanted gap at the ridgeline. This recipe demonstrates two ways to fix that gap. The first approach is to fill in the gap with constrained lines, forming a new face that can be pulled along the entire ridge. The second option is to move the top edges of the roof while locking constraints.

--- **Note** ---

For more suggestions on working with overhanging roofs, see Recipe 4.4, which presents a solution for creating a uniform overhanging roof on a building with several sections, or Recipe 5.4, which demonstrates using Autofold and a planar constraint for creating overhangs.

1. Start with a house like the one in Figure 5-1. (Make a simple box with a line between midpoints along the top face. Then use Move to move this line straight up.)

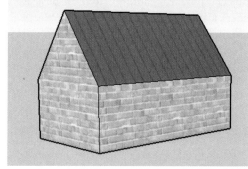

Figure 5-1

2. To give the roof some thickness, use Push/Pull with Ctrl/Option to pull out one roof face. Press Ctrl/Option again and double-click the other roof face to pull it out the same amount (Figure 5-2).

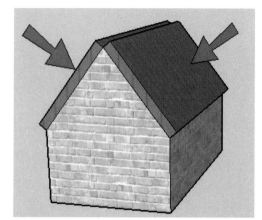

Figure 5-2

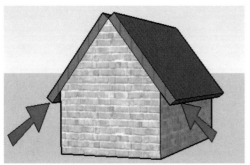

Figure 5-3

Figure 5-4

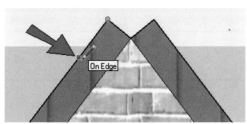
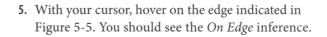

Figure 5-5

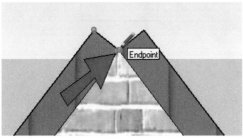

Figure 5-6

3. Use Push/Pull again to pull down both bottom faces (Figure 5-3).

   Notice the gap at the top of the roof. You can fix it in a couple of ways.

4. The first method of closing the gap is to add lines. Start a line at the point indicated in Figure 5-4.

5. With your cursor, hover on the edge indicated in Figure 5-5. You should see the *On Edge* inference.

6. Hover the cursor over the valley point indicated in Figure 5-6; look for the *Endpoint* inference.

7. You have just "reminded" SketchUp of the geometry of that edge and point, so SketchUp can produce inferences from them. Move the cursor straight up from the valley point, keeping the dotted blue inference line. Stop when you also see a magenta preview line starting from the endpoint of the angled edge you hovered over (Figure 5-7). This means that the point you are about to click is the endpoint of the extension of that edge, and is also directly above the valley point. This is a *double constraint*.

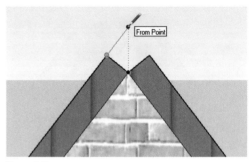
Figure 5-7

8. Click this point. Then complete the small diamond-shaped face by connecting another line to the opposite corner of the gap. Pull this small face to the other side of the house (Figure 5-8).

9. If you were to continue with this method, you would erase the extra lines. Instead, choose Undo until the gap is back, and move on to the second method.

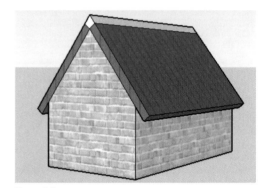
Figure 5-8

10. Select the edge indicated in Figure 5-9. This edge will be moved into place by using another double constraint.

Figure 5-9

11. Activate Move. For the first move point, click the corner point indicated in Figure 5-10.

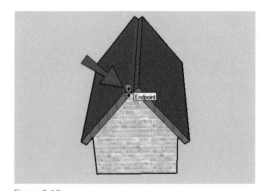
Figure 5-10

Figure 5-11

12. Hover over the lower edge of the same side of the roof, indicated in Figure 5-11.

Figure 5-12

13. Move the cursor slightly out from the edge, until you see the *Parallel to Edge* inference (Figure 5-12).

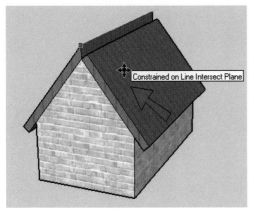

Figure 5-13

14. Press Shift to lock the magenta inference, and click anywhere on the opposite sloped roof face. This moves the edge so that both constraints are satisfied—the new edge is still parallel to the edge below, and it lies on the extension of the opposite roof face (Figure 5-13).

15. Repeat steps 10 through 14 to move the other gap edge the same way, and erase extra lines.

You'll use this model again in Recipe 5.2's "Example 2: Coplanar Dormer." You can either save your model now or download a fresh model later, if you prefer.

5.2 Creating Dormers

Problem

You want to place a dormer in a roof.

Solution

Use inferences and locking constraints to create dormers.

Discussion

Dormers, which are vertical windows cut into a roof, present interesting design challenges. How do you project the side edges of a dormer to reach the slope of the roof, or how do you keep the dormer face coplanar with the rest of the house? Inferences and constraints make this easy. You can constrain points to edges, faces, or axis directions, and the Shift key enables you to use double constraints (for example, constraining a point to both the red direction and to a specific face). Arrow keys can also be used to lock the red, green, and blue directions.

This recipe demonstrates the advantages of inference locking and constraints by using three types of dormers, which get progressively more complex. The first dormer is a simple box cut into a straight roof. The second is created on an overhanging roof, constrained to the side of the house below the roof. The third has a peaked shape, and points on its front face are constrained to existing objects (windows) on the house.

Example 1: Simple Dormer

The first example is a simple review of the basics of locking a direction. You will create a dormer from a rectangle drawn in a roof. With the help of direction locking, you'll position the dormer and place a copy in relation to other model elements (existing windows).

1. Start with a model like the one in Figure 5-14. You can create your model from scratch, or download my Simple Dormer model from the 3D Warehouse.

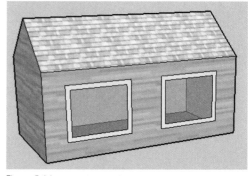

Figure 5-14

2. Draw a rectangle in the roof. For the side of the dormer, start a line at the lower corner (where indicated in Figure 5-15). Move your cursor (don't click yet) straight up or down, in the blue direction. Press and hold Shift to lock this direction. The blue preview line turns bold to indicate that its direction is locked.

Figure 5-15

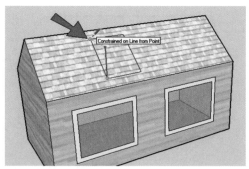

Figure 5-16

3. With Shift still pressed, hover over any point along the back edge of the dormer rectangle. This sets the height of the dormer wall to match the height of the back edge of the rectangle. The inference should read *Constrained on Line from Point* (Figure 5-16).

Figure 5-17

4. Click to finish the line and then add the horizontal edge to complete the triangle (Figure 5-17). This is the side of the dormer.

5. Use Push/Pull to complete the dormer.

Figure 5-18

6. To change the flat roof into a sloped one, use Move to slightly push down the front edge (Figure 5-18).

Figure 5-19

7. Hide the top face of the dormer and cut a hole in the roof below the dormer (Figure 5-19).

8. Unhide the top of the dormer and add a glass window to the dormer front.

9. The next step is to move the dormer directly above one of the windows already on the house, which will require direction locking. Select the whole dormer and activate Move. Click the dormer's lower-left front corner and start to move the dormer in the green direction (or red, depending on how you made your house). Press and hold Shift to lock the direction. Then click any point along the left edge of the window below. This aligns the left side of the dormer with the left side of the window below it (Figure 5-20).

Figure 5-20

10. To make the dormer the correct width, select all of the vertical edges on the right side (use a left-to-right selection window and check your selection in Wireframe mode). Move the selected edges by any point on the right edge, Shift-lock the green (or red) direction, and click any point on the right edge of the window below the dormer (Figure 5-21).

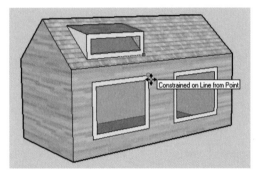

Figure 5-21

11. Copy the entire dormer to the right, so that it sits above the other window (Figure 5-22). For the move points, use similar reference points on the windows below.

Figure 5-22

Example 2: Coplanar Dormer

The dormer in this example is cut into an overhanging roof. The front face of the dormer will lie in the same plane as the side wall of the house. For this design, you need a constraint that locks two faces.

1. Start with a model like the one shown in Figure 5-23. You can reuse your model from Recipe 5.1, or you can download my Coplanar Dormer model from the 3D Warehouse.

Figure 5-23

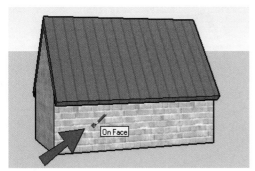

Figure 5-24

2. The front face of the dormer will lie in the same plane as the side of the house. Activate Line (don't click yet) and hover over the side face (Figure 5-24). Press and hold Shift.

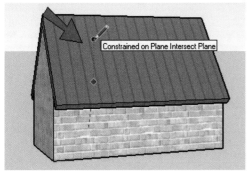

Figure 5-25

3. Move the cursor up to the roof face. The black point at the end of the dashed black inference line follows the cursor, and the dark blue point lets you know where the line will meet the roof face. This is a double constraint: *Constrained on Plane Intersect Plane*. Click where you want to start the dormer (Figure 5-25).

Figure 5-26

4. Draw the four lines for the dormer face (Figure 5-26). Make sure to draw the vertical lines in the blue direction.

Figure 5-27

5. For the side face, start a line at the lower-left dormer corner and hover over the side edge of the roof to inference the slope of that edge. Draw a line parallel to that edge (Figure 5-27).

6. For the next line, Shift-lock the green (or red) direction and click the lower-right corner (Figure 5-28).

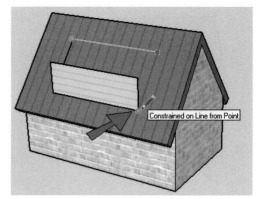

Figure 5-28

7. Add two more lines to complete the two sides (Figure 5-29).

Figure 5-29

8. The roof of the dormer should have some thickness. Use Push/Pull with Ctrl/Option to pull the roof up. Then pull out the three exposed sides of the roof (Figure 5-30).

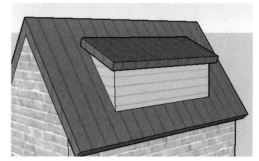

Figure 5-30

9. One way to fill the gap between the dormer roof and the main roof is to add lines. Start a line at the back corner (shown by the yellow arrow in Figure 5-31) and hover over the top side edge (blue arrow).

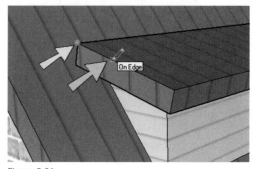

Figure 5-31

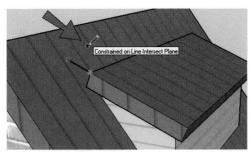

Figure 5-32

10. Press and hold Shift to lock the line to the direction of the side edge, and click the main roof face (Figure 5-32).

11. Complete the triangle to fill the gap on the side. Then pull the triangle to the other side of the dormer.

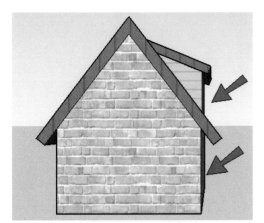

Figure 5-33

12. If you want to make sure your dormer is coplanar with the house side, orbit to the view shown in Figure 5-33. The two faces should line up.

Figure 5-34

Example 3: Peaked Dormer

The last dormer is a bit more complicated, because its main shape is peaked rather than a straight rectangle. This dormer will start directly above one of the existing windows. This example also uses the arrow keys, which provide another way to both find and lock the red, green, and blue directions.

Draw the peaked dormer face

In this phase, you'll use constraints to draw the front face of the peaked dormer.

1. Start with a house like the one in Figure 5-34. The windows have frames that protrude slightly from the side wall of the house. You can create this model from scratch, or download my Peaked Dormer model from the 3D Warehouse.

2. The front of the dormer will be coplanar with the front of the blue window frame. Activate Line and hover over the corner point indicated in Figure 5-35. Then start to move up or down in the blue direction.

Figure 5-35

3. Press and hold Shift, and hover on the roof face. The red point indicates where the line would start (Figure 5-36), but don't click. There is another way to obtain the same point by using arrow keys instead of Shift.

4. You should still be using the Line tool. Hover again over the same point on the window frame shown previously in Figure 5-35.

5. Tap the up arrow or down arrow on your keyboard (you don't have to keep it pressed). This is similar to using Shift to lock the blue direction, with the added bonus that the arrow will also "find" the blue direction for you. Then click anywhere on the roof face to start the first dormer line.

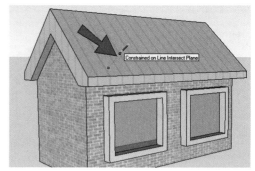

Figure 5-36

Note

Tapping the arrow key again will toggle off the direction constraint.

---

6. To complete the line, tap the left arrow to lock the green direction, and click anywhere on the right edge of the blue window frame (Figure 5-37).

Note

The left arrow key locks the green direction, and right arrow locks the red direction (think *R locks R*). Although the up or down arrow key locking blue is obvious enough, I don't use the other arrows very often because it's hard to tell which one I need when the axes are not displayed. I tend to Shift-lock red and green instead, but of course, it's a matter of preference. The arrow keys do have the added benefit of finding the direction for you, which is especially useful when using Autofold (described in Recipe 5.4).

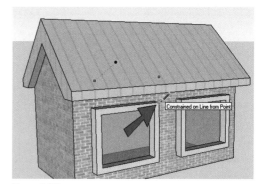

Figure 5-37

7. Complete the peaked dormer face. Make sure the peak is centered and that it is lower than the top of the main roof (Figure 5-38).

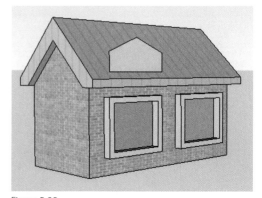

Figure 5-38

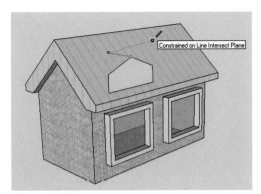

Figure 5-39

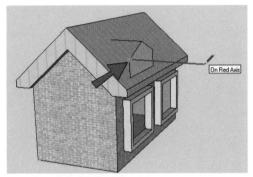

Figure 5-40

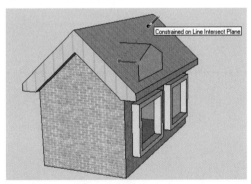

Figure 5-41

Figure 5-42

Complete the dormer

There are two ways to complete the dormer: by using Intersect with Model or by using constraints. To use Intersect with Model, you would pull the dormer face straight back through the roof, run Intersect with Model on it, and use intersection edges to trim the back faces away. You would then have to hide one of the house or roof faces to see where to cut the dormer into the roof, make the cut, and then unhide the face. For an example of using one object to trim another object, see Recipe 3.1.

This example details a different method: using constraints. There are a few more steps involved than when using Intersect, but you will save the steps of hiding and cutting the roof face. When you understand both methods, you can decide for yourself which you prefer.

1. While still using the Line tool, click the peak point, tap the right arrow key to lock the red direction, and click the roof face (Figure 5-39).

2. You can Shift-lock a constraint even when a line starts out in the opposite direction. Start the next line where indicated in Figure 5-40, and move the cursor away from the house in the red direction. Press and hold Shift.

3. Click the roof face, and the line snaps back in the correct direction (Figure 5-41).

4. Add two more lines to complete the two faces on one side of the dormer (Figure 5-42).

5. You could use the same method to complete the other side of the dormer, but if the dormer has all its sides, you'd need to hide a face in order to cut the hole in the roof. The bottom face of the dormer should be completed so that the roof hole can be cut first; then the remaining sides of the dormer can be created. Start the line at the back of the peak and hover over the corner indicated in Figure 5-43.

Figure 5-43

6. Move in the red direction then hold Shift while clicking the roof face (Figure 5-44). This is another way to use a double constraint.

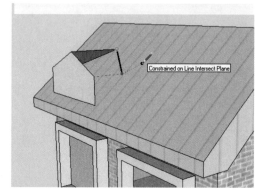

Figure 5-44

7. Complete the edges for the hole in the roof and erase the hole face (Figure 5-45).

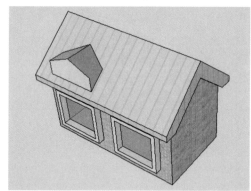

Figure 5-45

8. Then complete the dormer sides (Figure 5-46).

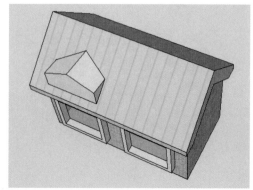

Figure 5-46

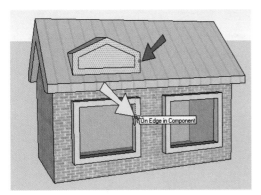
Figure 5-47

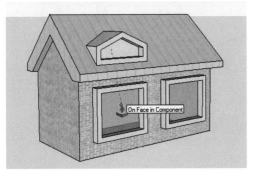
Figure 5-48

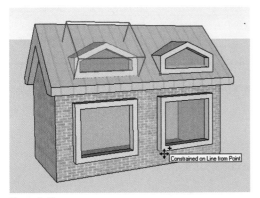
Figure 5-49

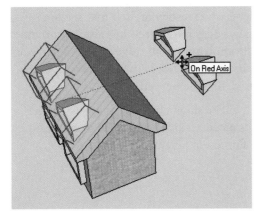
Figure 5-50

Create finishing touches

Now you can add a window in the dormer and make copies of it.

1. The first step is to add a frame to the dormer face, to match the frames of the windows below it. Activate Offset and click the dormer face on its right edge (indicated by the red arrow in Figure 5-47). Then complete the offset by clicking on the inner-right edge of the window below (yellow arrow). This makes the dormer frame the same thickness as the window frame.

2. For the glass, start the Push/Pull on the inner dormer face and end it by clicking the glass below (Figure 5-48).

3. As you should always do when something in your model will repeat, make the entire dormer a component.

4. Copy the dormer, constraining it to the green direction by using either the left arrow key or the Shift-locking method (Figure 5-49).

5. To copy both dormers to the other side, copy them in the red direction into some blank space (Figure 5-50).

6. There are a few ways to flip objects, but I prefer using the Scale tool. A scale value of −1 makes an "inside-out" copy.

Note

Using Scale to flip components is a great way to create symmetric objects. This will be shown in Recipe 7.11.

---

7. To move the copied dormers back to the roof, move them by a peak point, lock the red direction, and click the roof face (Figure 5-51).

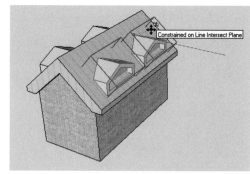

Figure 5-51

8. Use Intersect with Model to cut roof holes, and your four dormers are complete (Figure 5-52).

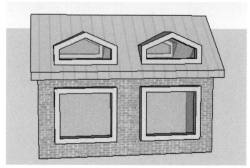

Figure 5-52

5.3   Working with Roof Intersections

Problem

You have roofs of different heights or slopes on various parts of a building, and you want to resolve the ridge and valley lines where the roofs meet.

Solution

Create new edges at the intersections by using double constraints.

Discussion

When you have roof faces of different slopes and heights, start resolving their intersections by thinking about the existing edges and faces that the new edges must meet. It is also important to understand which face will meet new ridge lines. By knowing which ridge line is higher, you can figure out where roof volume needs to be added and where it needs to be removed. After you establish this, you can apply double constraints to define the new edges.

Using double constraints to resolve intersecting roofs will be shown by two examples. In the first example, one roof meets roofs of different heights on either side, in the middle of the other roofs (not at corners). In the second example, roofs of different heights meet at corners.

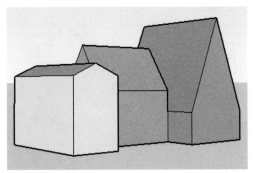

Figure 5-53

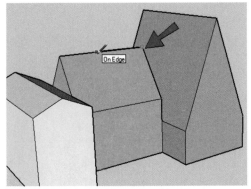

Figure 5-54

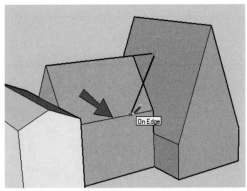

Figure 5-55

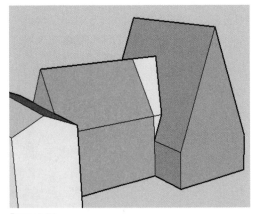

Figure 5-56

Example 1: End-Middle Intersections

In this example, you must contend with three roofs of alternating directions, each with a different height and slope. The middle roof meets the outer roofs in the middle, not at their corners. Edges are needed at each end of the middle roof, to resolve the roof to its neighboring faces.

1. Download my Roof End Middle model (shown in Figure 5-53) from the 3D Warehouse. The green roof in the middle is perpendicular to the roofs on either side and meets the other roofs in the middle (not at corners).

Want to Create This Model Yourself?

1. In Top view, draw three rectangles for the footprint. The outer rectangles should have longer vertical edges, and the middle one should have longer horizontal edges.
2. Rotate all three rectangles slightly. This removes the ability to use red and green directions (just to make this a little harder).
3. Pull up the yellow rectangle higher than the green, and the green higher than the purple.
4. Add ridge lines across each top, and move them up so that the purple peak is the highest, followed by green, followed by yellow.

---

2. Resolve the green-purple intersection first. Start a line at the closest ridge point of the green roof, indicated in Figure 5-54. Then hover over the green ridge line.

3. Press and hold Shift to lock the direction of this edge. Then click the closest purple roof face. This extends the green ridge line until it meets the purple roof.

4. The next line will continue from the previous line you created. Hover over the edge indicated in Figure 5-55.

5. Hold Shift and click the same purple face. This extends the edge you hovered over, to meet the purple roof.

6. Add two more lines to complete the extension of the roof face and the wall face (Figure 5-56).

7. Add the same edges on the other side of the green roof and erase extra lines. The intersection of the green and purple roofs is shown in Figure 5-57.

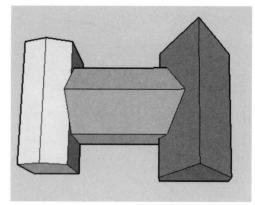

Figure 5-57

8. Now the green-yellow intersection will be resolved. Because the green ridge is higher than the yellow ridge, the far yellow face will need to have material added to it. Start a line as before, from the green ridge endpoint indicated in Figure 5-58, and then hover over the green ridge.

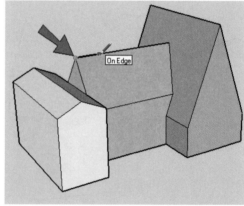

Figure 5-58

9. Shift-lock this line to the far yellow face. Depending on your roof slopes, the line might end somewhere past the current ridge line or instead end somewhere within the line (as in this example, shown in Figure 5-59).

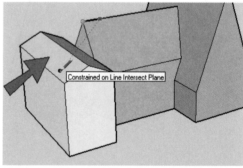

Figure 5-59

10. Start a new line at this new endpoint. Then hover over either green roof face and hold Shift. Constrain this line to end on the yellow ridge line by clicking the yellow ridge line (Figure 5-60).

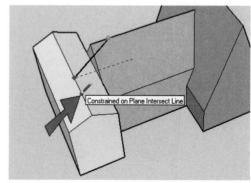

Figure 5-60

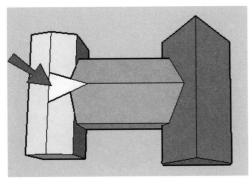

Figure 5-61

11. Draw the same line for the other side of the green roof. This creates the triangle that needs to be added to the far yellow face (Figure 5-61). If your triangle cuts into the green faces, trim the extra faces.

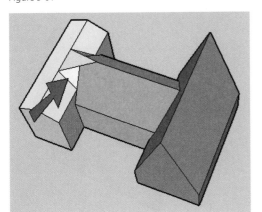

Figure 5-62

12. Complete the intersection by adding the line indicated in Figure 5-62, on both sides.

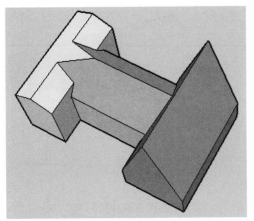

Figure 5-63

13. Erase extra lines. The completed resolved roofs are shown in Figure 5-63.

Example 2: Corner Intersections

This example shows the slightly more complex scenario of fixing roofs when they meet at corners.

1. Download my Roof Corners model shown in Figure 5-64 from the 3D Warehouse. This building has three sections that meet at the corners. None of the edges is along the red or green axis, and each section has its own peak face to use for the roof. The green peak is the highest, followed by the red, and the yellow peak is the lowest.

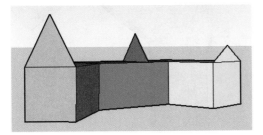

Figure 5-64

2. Pull the green and yellow roof faces back, along their side walls (Figure 5-65).

3. Use Push/Pull with the Ctrl/Option key to extend the red roof in both directions, beyond the outer sides of the green and yellow roofs.

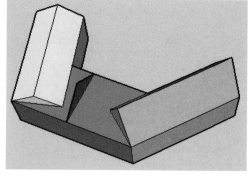

Figure 5-65

4. Select everything, right-click on a selected face, and choose Intersect→Intersect with Model. This creates intersection edges on all roof faces (Figure 5-66).

5. The first corner to resolve is the red-green corner.

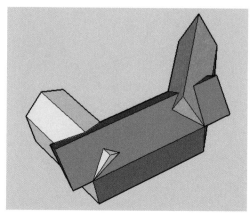

Figure 5-66

Because the red roof is lower than the green one, you need to add material to the back red face. Start a line at point 1 in Figure 5-67, hover over edge 2 and hold Shift, and constrain the endpoint of the line to face 3.

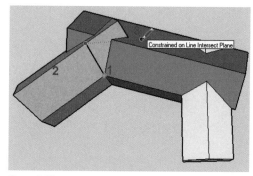

Figure 5-67

6. From this new endpoint, draw two lines that meet the red ridge line, as indicated in Figure 5-68.

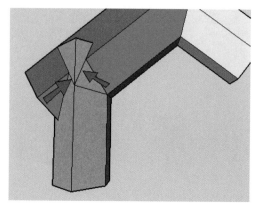

Figure 5-68

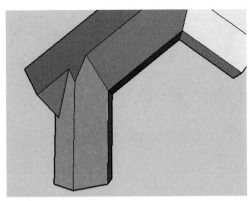

Figure 5-69

7. Trim edges to clean up the green roof (Figure 5-69).

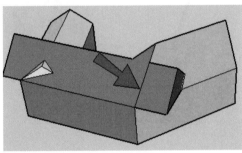

Figure 5-70

8. To finish resolving this corner, orbit around to the back and add the line indicated in Figure 5-70.

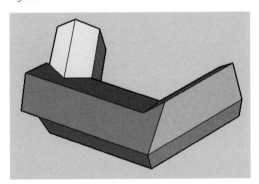

Figure 5-71

9. Now you can trim the rest of the red faces. While you're here, also trim the portions of the yellow faces that stick out from the back red face (Figure 5-71).

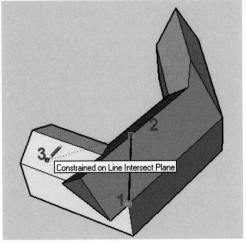

Figure 5-72

10. Now for the other corner. Start a line at point 1 in Figure 5-72, hover over edge 2 and hold Shift, and constrain the endpoint of the line to face 3.

11. Add the line indicated in Figure 5-73.

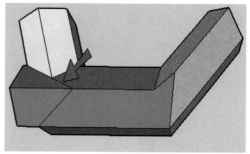

Figure 5-73

12. Trim to resolve the corner (Figure 5-74), and you're finished.

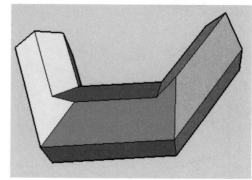

Figure 5-74

5.4 Creating Overhangs with Autofold

Problem

You want to create overhanging faces by using an existing face as a plane constraint.

Solution

Use Push/Pull to make horizontal overhangs and then use Autofold with a planar constraint to move the overhang faces into place.

Discussion

Sometimes when you try to move objects in certain ways—such as when you try to move objects within a face out of the plane of that face—SketchUp doesn't allow it. At these times, turn to the Move tool's Autofold feature. With it you can "force" edges and faces to move in a way that SketchUp wouldn't otherwise permit.

This recipe examines two cases in which Autofold is useful: to create a peaked point, and to move overhanging faces to be constrained to an existing plane.

In this recipe, you'll veer away from roofs to design a beach umbrella. You'll create the umbrella flaps horizontally and then move them down using Autofold. In the "Other Uses" section, you'll see how the same technique can be applied to an overhanging roof (you can't stray too far from roofs in this chapter).

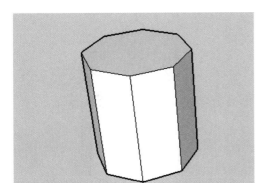

Figure 5-75

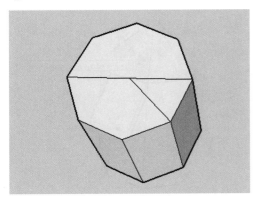

Figure 5-76

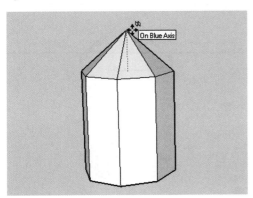

Figure 5-77

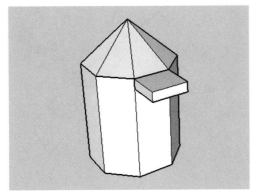

Figure 5-78

— Note —

For a stepped, detailed model of this example, download my Umbrella model from the 3D Warehouse.

1. Start with an octagon and pull it up (Figure 5-75).

2. The next step is to establish the center point of the top octagon and pull it up, to create the top umbrella point and define the slope off the umbrella flaps. You could draw separate lines from the center to each of the eight corners, but Autofold provides an easier way. Create just the two lines shown in Figure 5-76.

3. Activate Move, click the midpoint of the longer line, and try to move the point up. Without Autofold, you can move this point only within the red-green plane.

4. There are two ways to implement Autofold. Either press the Alt/Cmd key while moving or just tap the up arrow key. Now you can move the center point straight up. SketchUp breaks faces and adds edges where necessary, to accommodate the moved point (Figure 5-77).

5. On one of the vertical faces, draw a thin rectangle at the top and pull it out (Figure 5-78).

6. Select the front face of this rectangle, indicated in Figure 5-79. Activate Move and click any point along the top edge of this face.

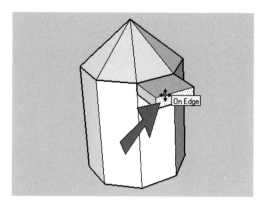
Figure 5-79

7. Use the Move tool, with the up arrow or the Alt/Cmd key to activate Autofold, and move the face straight down. Click the triangular face above it, constraining the move point to that face (Figure 5-80).

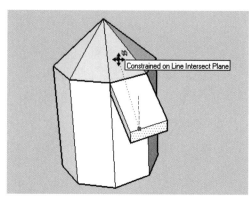
Figure 5-80

8. Erase the vertical walls (Figure 5-81).

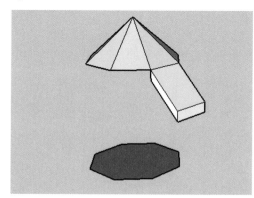
Figure 5-81

9. To cut a round shape into the flap, draw the horizontal arc face indicated in Figure 5-82.

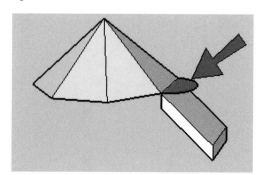
Figure 5-82

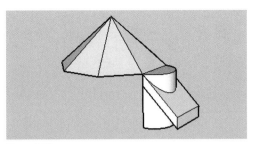

Figure 5-83

10. Pull the arc down to create a vertical half-cylinder. Then select everything, right-click on a selected face, and choose Intersect→Intersect with Model. This produces intersection edges where the flap meets the half-cylinder (Figure 5-83).

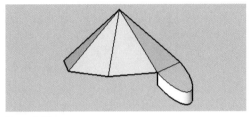

Figure 5-84

11. Trim the faces to get a new, round flap (Figure 5-84).

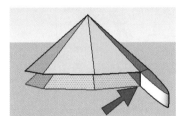

Figure 5-85

12. To give the triangular parts of the umbrella roof the same thickness as the round flap, copy the eight triangular faces straight down to meet the bottom of the round flap (Figure 5-85).

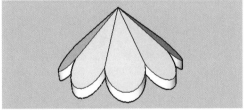

Figure 5-86

13. Rotate-copy the round flap around seven times and erase extra edges (Figure 5-86).

14. Also erase the edges on the underside of the umbrella roof.

Figure 5-87

15. Finally, to make the pole, create a circle at the center point of the original octagon and pull it up (Figure 5-87).

Other Uses

You can use the same Autofold-constraint technique to make a uniformly sloped, overhanging roof.

Start with a basic house form and draw a face at the top for the roof cross-section (Figure 5-88).

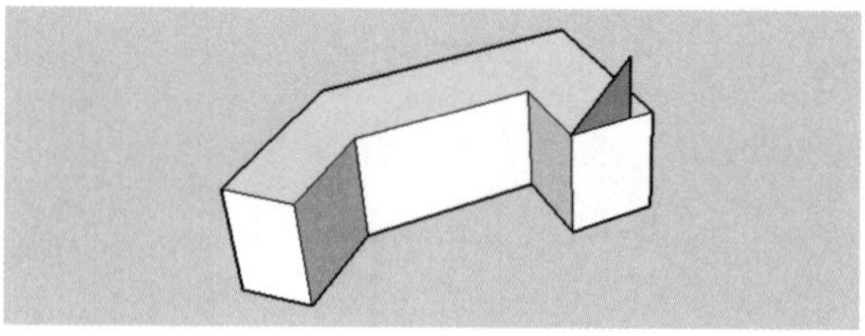

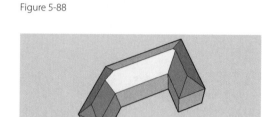

Figure 5-88

Use the Follow Me and Intersect technique to create the roof (Figure 5-89). This technique is detailed in Recipe 4.4.

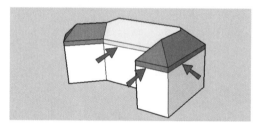

Figure 5-89

Start the new overhang faces by copying all of the lower roof edges straight down (Figure 5-90).

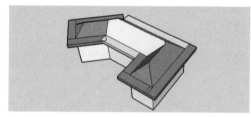

Figure 5-90

Pull out each of these new faces by the same distance (Figure 5-91).

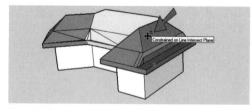

Figure 5-91

To make the overhangs, select all of the new vertical faces, and move them down with Autofold, constraining them to one of the existing sloped roof faces (Figure 5-92).

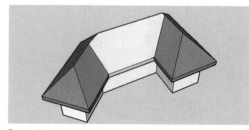

Figure 5-92

You will have to do some cleanup on the roof and house faces, possibly adding some edges or running Intersect with Model to break faces that need to be erased. You will also have to fix the roof corners, both on top and on the underside. In the end, you're rewarded with a nice overhanging roof (Figure 5-93).

Figure 5-93

CHAPTER 6

Groups: Protect and Defend

Groups are SketchUp's way of "sealing off" geometry, protecting one or more objects from affecting other objects and from being affected by other objects. A grouped set of objects also has the advantage of being selected as one object with one click, eliminating the need for dragging selection windows.

Many users are not clear on when to create a group and when to create a component. Geometrically, the two types of objects behave the same way: they are selectable as a single object, they are "sealed" from other objects, and they can be changed only when open for editing. As a general rule, these objects should be made into a group rather than a component:

- Objects that need to be kept separate from other objects

- Objects that will be used only once (will not be copied)

- Objects that will eventually be exploded (such as objects used only for cutting or trimming)

Note

Components are covered at length in Chapter 7, in which their advantages and many uses are discussed.

Creating a Group

To create a group, you first select the objects to include in the group. You can then either choose Edit→Make Group from the main menu, or right-click on one of the selected objects and choose Make Group from the pop-up menu.

A group usually consists of more than one object. But you can still make a group from a single object. If only one face or edge is selected, Make Group will not appear in the pop-up menu, but you can still choose Edit→Make Group from the main menu. If you want to make a single face into a group, you can activate Select and double-click the face. This selects both the face and its edges, which means more than one object is selected, and Make Group appears in the pop-up menu.

After a set of objects is grouped, the objects are "sealed" inside and protected from other objects. This means that nothing will stick to or change the group, and the group will not stick to or change any of the surrounding geometry.

Note

Unlike a component, a group is created without a name. If you are working on a complex model with numerous groups, however, naming the groups can be helpful and make the groups easier to locate later. To assign a name to a group after it is created, right-click on the group and choose Entity Info. The Entity Info window has a field in which you can assign a name. You can also assign group names in the Outliner, which is described in Recipe 7.15. The Outliner can then be used to locate a specific group in your model.

Editing a Group

To make any changes to the group, the group must be open for editing. There are three ways to open a group:

- Right-click on a group and choose Edit Group.

- Activate Select and double-click on the group.

- Select the group and choose Edit→Group→Edit Group from the main menu.

During editing, the contents of the group appear within a dotted-line bounding box. Only the group contents are available for editing; the rest of the model cannot be touched and appears faded in the background. If you prefer to hide the rest of the model during group editing, open the Model Info window to the Components page and select the second Hide checkbox (Figure 6-1).

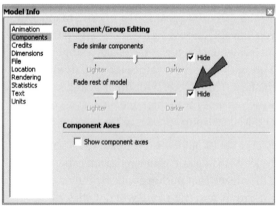

Figure 6-1

When the editing is complete, there are three ways to close the group:

- Right-click outside the group and choose Close Group.

- Activate Select and click anywhere outside the group.

- Choose Edit→Close Group→Component from the main menu.

Exploding a Group

When you no longer need a group to remain a group, you can *ungroup* it. This is also called *exploding*. To explode a group, right-click on it and choose Explode. If multiple groups are selected and you choose Explode from the pop-up menu, all selected groups will be exploded.

If you have *nested groups*, which are groups within other groups, exploding works on only one level at a time. For instance, consider a car group in which each tire is its own group. If you explode the car, the tire groups remain intact. You would then have to explode the tire groups separately.

--- **Note** --------------------------------

If you work frequently with groups and components, you should get to know the Outliner. The Outliner is a great way to organize complex models, enabling you to easily find components and groups, as well as edit, lock, and rename them. The Outliner is the focus of Recipe 7.15.

6.1 Ungluing Faces

Problem

You create a new object that shares a face with an existing object. When you try to move the new object, the object cannot move away from the plane of the shared face.

Solution

Make the new object a group and unglue the group from the wall.

Discussion

When you place an object along the face of another object, the two objects are "glued" together at their shared face and cannot be separated. Making either object into a group will protect the object from this stickiness.

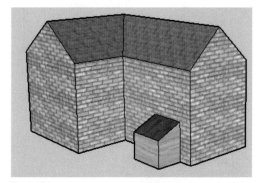

Figure 6-2

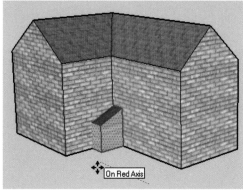

Figure 6-3

Consider the house model in Figure 6-2, which has a small shed connected to one wall. The goal is to move the shed from its current wall to the red brick wall, which is in a different plane.

If you select the whole shed and try to move it, you'll see that it is glued to the current wall. You can move the shed off the wall itself, but it still remains glued to the wall's plane, as shown in Figure 6-3.

The main example demonstrates how to use a group to unglue this shed from the house. In the "Other Uses" section, you'll see how to use groups to separate connected plates.

1. Start with a house and shed model like the one in Figure 6-2. You can create your model from scratch, or download my House with Shed model from the 3D Warehouse.

Want to Create This Model Yourself?

1. Start with an L-shaped footprint and pull it up.
2. Draw the two ridge lines on the top, starting from the midpoint of each building section.
3. Select both ridge lines and move them up.
4. For the shed, draw a rectangle on the ground next to one wall and pull it up.
5. To slope the shed roof, use the Move tool to push down one edge.

2. Use a left-to-right selection window to select the entire shed and make it a group.

3. Select the shed (which you can now do with one click) and move it. Because the shed originally shared a wall with the house, it is still "glued" to that wall even after being made into a group. So when you move the shed, it cannot leave the plane of the wall (Figure 6-4).

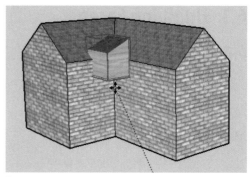

Figure 6-4

4. To break the link between the group and the wall, right-click on the group and choose Unglue.

   The Unglue option is available only for groups and components, so the only way to unglue the shed from the wall is to make it a group or component.

5. Now you can move the shed to the red wall, which sits on a different plane (Figure 6-5).

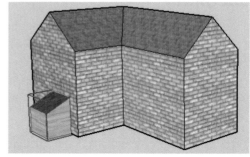

Figure 6-5

--- **Note** --------------------------------

An alternate way to place the shed on the red wall, without having to group it, is to simply copy it. Then you would only need to erase the original.

_____

Other Uses

Another case in which you would use a group is shown in Figure 6-6: two plates that need to be separated by a set distance. The two plates are initially side by side.

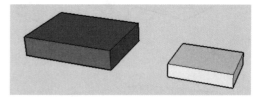

Figure 6-6

If neither plate is a group and you place one atop the other (Figure 6-7), you will be able to move the plates only against one another (Figure 6-8). Because the faces are glued together, you cannot raise one plate above the other.

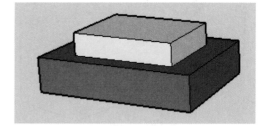

Figure 6-7

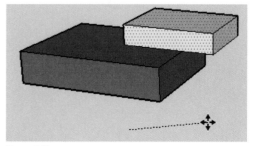

Figure 6-8

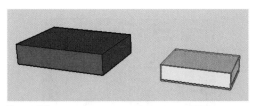

Figure 6-9

The solution in this case is to start with side-by-side plates in which one plate is a group. In Figure 6-9, the yellow plate is a group.

Now when you place one plate atop the other (Figure 6-10), you can move the top plate above the bottom one (Figure 6-11).

Figure 6-10

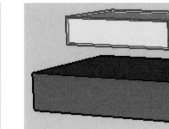

Figure 6-11

6.2 Unsticking Edges

Problem

You create an object that shares edges with an existing object. When you try to move the new object, the shared edges move also.

Solution

Make the new object a group.

Discussion

In Recipe 6.1, you saw that objects that share a face become glued together at the shared face. In this recipe, the objects share edges. The situation is similar: The objects are stuck together at the common edges. When one object is moved, the edges remain stuck, which distorts the object not being moved.

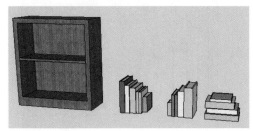

Figure 6-12

This example demonstrates how to prevent stacks of books from sticking to a bookcase. Consider the model shown in Figure 6-12; no objects are grouped. The goal is to place the books on the shelves and to move the books within the shelves without affecting the bookcase itself.

In Figure 6-13, each stack is placed so that the lower-left corner meets the front-left corner of the shelf. So each stack shares two edges with the bookcase itself.

Figure 6-13

If you try to move the vertical stack on the bottom shelf, the corner of the shelf moves with the books (Figure 6-14).

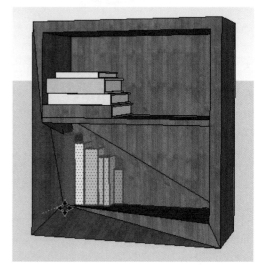

Figure 6-14

Similarly, if you move the stack on the top shelf, the corner of that shelf moves (Figure 6-15).

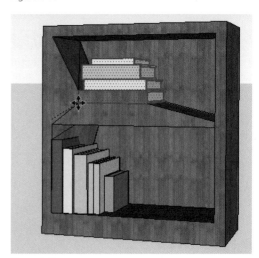

Figure 6-15

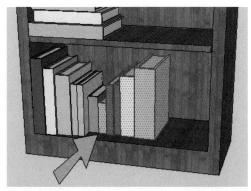

Figure 6-16

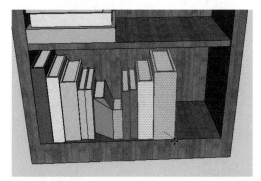

Figure 6-17

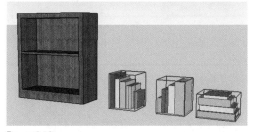

Figure 6-18

Because the books themselves are not grouped, other books will stick to them. In Figure 6-16, the second vertical stack is moved next to the stack currently on the bottom shelf, so that the adjacent orange and pink books share a face.

If you try to move the new stack so that the large cyan book aligns with the front of the shelf, the face and common edges shared with the orange book move, too (Figure 6-17).

The solution to this problem is to make each stack of books into a group. In addition to preventing stickiness, each book stack will be easy to select, using one click instead of selection windows that can select more or less than you need. (You could make the bookcase itself into a group, too, but that won't solve the problem of books sticking to each other.)

1. Download my Bookcase model (shown previously in Figure 6-12) from the 3D Warehouse.

2. Make each stack of books into its own group (Figure 6-18).

3. Move one of the vertical stacks to the front-left corner of the bottom shelf (Figure 6-19).

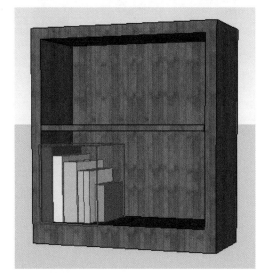

Figure 6-19

4. Move the stack a bit to the right (Figure 6-20), and the bookcase remains unchanged.

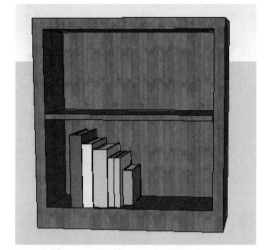

Figure 6-20

5. Place the other vertical stack so that the adjacent orange and pink books share a face (Figure 6-21).

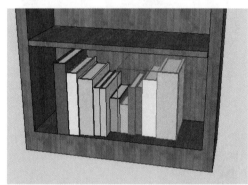

Figure 6-21

6. This new stack protrudes into the back of the bookcase, so it needs to be moved a bit forward. Move it so that the cyan book aligns with the front of the bookcase. As shown in Figure 6-22, the two stacks remain separate; the pink book does not remain stuck to the orange book.

You could also move the stacks apart; they are not glued at their common plane.

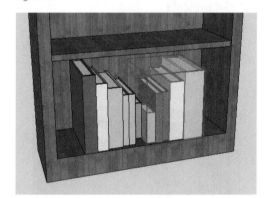

Figure 6-22

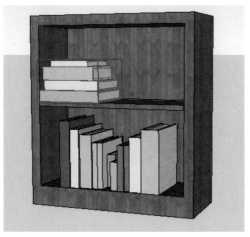

Figure 6-23

7. Place the horizontal stack on the top shelf; align it at the front corner of the shelf (Figure 6-23).

8. Move the stack up (perhaps to make room for more books). The bookcase remains unchanged (Figure 6-24).

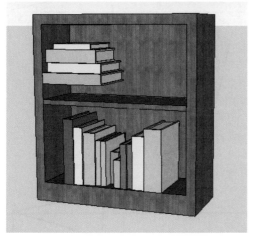

Figure 6-24

6.3 Protecting from Edits

Problem

You have a floor and walls for a room, but when you create new objects in the room, the walls and floor are changed.

Solution

Protect the room by making it a group. You can still use the faces and edges in the room group as a basis for new objects.

Discussion

Objects inside a group cannot be changed (unless the group is open for editing). You can still inference faces, edges, and points of grouped geometry when creating new objects, so you can draw objects outside or around grouped walls and floors. But any objects created outside the group will not affect anything inside the group.

Consider the room shown in Figure 6-25, which has two walls and the floor displayed. The goal is to add a bureau in the corner where the rectangle is drawn on the floor, and to add a clock to the wall where the circle is drawn.

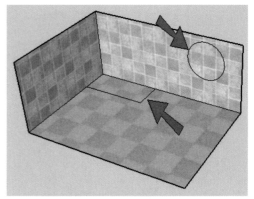

Figure 6-25

If the room is not grouped, there are three problems you could encounter:

- When you pull out these shapes, the objects that are created have the same material as the face from which they were pulled (Figure 6-26). Obviously, you could change the materials, but that takes some extra steps.

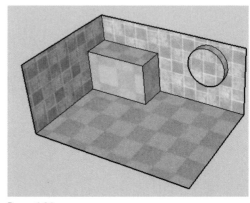

Figure 6-26

- The Push/Pull operations affect the back faces of the walls and floor (Figure 6-27). You could keep the walls and floor whole by using the Ctrl/Option key with Push/Pull, but the wall and floor faces would still be divided by the original clock and bureau edges.

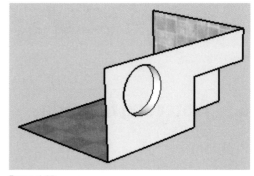

Figure 6-27

- If you select and move the bureau, the walls and floor become distorted (Figure 6-28), because two edges of the bureau are shared with the walls and floor, and they remain stuck together while moving. (You should recognize this problem from Recipes 6.1 and 6.2.)

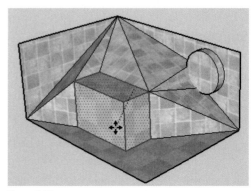

Figure 6-28

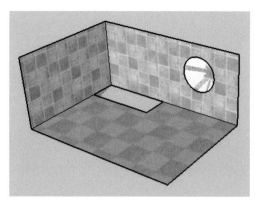

Figure 6-29

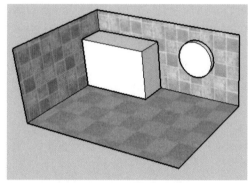

Figure 6-30

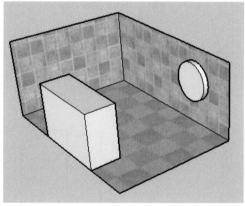

Figure 6-31

You can solve all three problems by grouping the room.

1. Start with a box and remove two sides and the top.

2. Paint the walls and floor.

3. Make the room into a group.

4. Draw a circle on the wall for a clock, and draw a rectangle on the corner of the floor for the bureau (Figure 6-29). Even though the referenced faces and edges are inside a group, you can use them as a basis for the new objects. The edges of these new shapes are bold, which means they are not integrated into the walls and floor, and the new faces are created in the default face color.

Note

The circle and rectangle faces can appear to have distorted, or shimmering, materials when you orbit around the model. This is due to SketchUp's *face confusion* or *Z-fighting*. These faces occupy the same exact planes as other faces, so SketchUp doesn't know which material to assign. This is why it looks like both materials are visible when you orbit around. After you give either new face some thickness, the material distortion disappears.

---

5. Pull the faces out. As shown in Figure 6-30, the new objects have the default color, and if you orbit to the back, you'll see that the backs of the walls and floor are not affected.

6. Move the bureau to another part of the room, and the walls and floor remain intact (Figure 6-31).

6.4 Cutting and Slicing

Problem

You want to make slices of a model in order to create floor plans, stripes, or other types of patterns.

Solution

Make grouped faces to use as the slicing objects, and use the Intersect tool to create the slices.

Discussion

If you read Chapter 3, you're familiar with the Intersect tool and with various ways that groups and components can be used as cutting tools. This recipe focuses on using copied groups to slice objects at set intervals.

The main example demonstrates using slicing groups to create floor plans for a tower. In the "Other Uses" section, you'll see how slicing groups can produce linear and rotational stripes.

1. Start with a tower model like the one in Figure 6-32. You can create your model from scratch, or download my Tower Floor Plans model from the 3D Warehouse.

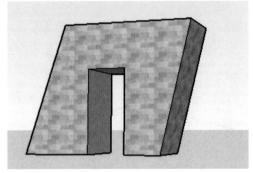

Figure 6-32

Want to Create This Model Yourself?

1. Create two identical, rectangular towers that have the same height.
2. To make the top, horizontal portion, draw a rectangle at the top of one of the towers and pull it to meet the other tower.
3. Erase extra edges.
4. To slope the sides, move the top-right and bottom-left edges.

2. To make the first slicing group, switch to Top view and draw a rectangle in blank space, large enough to contain the entire tower.

The reason for drawing it in blank space is so that the rectangle won't affect the bottom of the tower. If the rectangle touches any part of the tower, it will create edges on the tower.

3. Make the rectangle into a group (Figure 6-33).

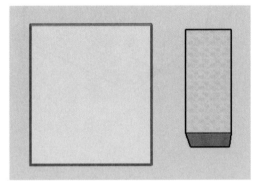

Figure 6-33

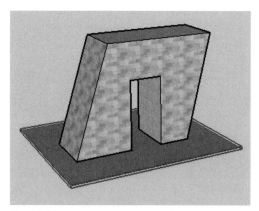

Figure 6-34

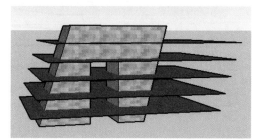

Figure 6-35

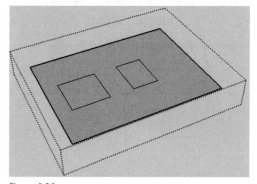

Figure 6-36

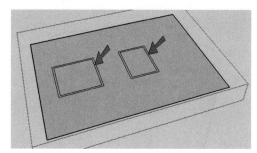

Figure 6-37

4. Move the grouped rectangle so that it encompasses the bottom of the tower (Figure 6-34).

5. Make several vertical copies of the group, from bottom to top (Figure 6-35). Erase the groups at the very bottom and the very top.

   To create edges where the groups meet the tower, you could use the Intersect tool on the tower itself, which would give you edges for each floor. But these edges would be visible from the outside of the tower and would break up the tower walls. To keep the building exterior clean, with no edges along the walls, you need to edit the groups instead.

6. To create one of the floors, open any of the slicing groups for editing.

7. Editing these groups is easier when the rest of model is hidden while editing. So open the Model Info window (Window→Model Info) to the Components page, and select the Hide checkbox for Rest of Model.

8. Right-click on the rectangle and choose Intersect→Intersect with Model.

   As you can see in Figure 6-36, the result is edges on the face where the group meets the walls of the tower.

9. Because these edges are along the tower walls, they would be visible from outside the tower. To create the floor so that its edges cannot be seen from the outside, use the Offset tool to offset the new faces slightly inward (Figure 6-37). After you complete one offset, you can double-click subsequent offset faces to offset them by the same distance.

10. Erase everything in the group except for the offset faces (Figure 6-38).

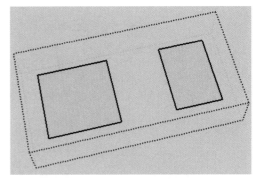

Figure 6-38

11. Close the group. As shown in Figure 6-39, you can see the floor inside the tower by switching to X-Ray view.

12. For each remaining group, edit and intersect it, and then offset the edges to create the floors. Figure 6-40 shows the results in X-Ray view.

The advantage to using groups in the tower is that they enable you to easily create one offset floor at a time, without having the rest of the model in view. You could get the same results without using grouped rectangles, but it would be much harder to create the offsets and erase the edges along the walls. If the building were uniform, with each floor identical, you could have used components for the slicing planes instead of groups.

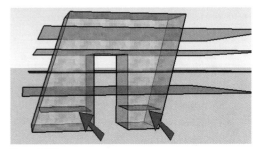

Figure 6-39

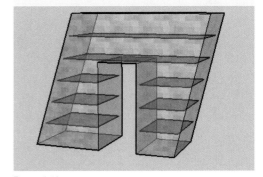

Figure 6-40

Other Uses

You can use slicing groups to create stripes as well. The advantage to using groups in these cases is that they are easy to erase when they are no longer needed.

Striped bowl

The bowl shown in Figure 6-41 was created by using the Follow Me tool to extrude a tall, oval shape around a wavy path.

--- **Note** ---

For details on using Follow Me to create round objects, see Recipe 2.5.

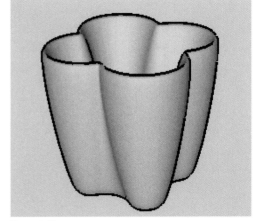

Figure 6-41

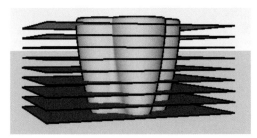

Figure 6-42

Create the slicing groups (again, be sure to create the initial rectangle away from the bowl, group it, and then move it into place). Make several copies along the height of the bowl (Figure 6-42).

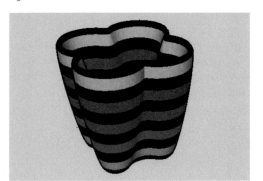

Figure 6-43

In this example, you do not need to intersect each individual group. Instead, right-click on the bowl itself and choose Intersect→Intersect with Model. This produces the edges along the bowl, at which point the groups are no longer needed. You can erase each group with a simple click; erasing would be much more difficult if groups were not used. Figure 6-43 shows the results after painting the stripes.

Beach ball

In Recipe 2.6, you can see how to use two circles and the Follow Me tool to make a sphere. In this example, after the sphere is created, the larger of the two circles is then made into a group and rotate-copied all around the sphere (Figure 6-44). To make copying easier, it is helpful to add a center point to one of the circles and switch to Wireframe view when copying.

Figure 6-44

Run Intersect on the sphere and erase each group to produce the beach ball shown in Figure 6-45.

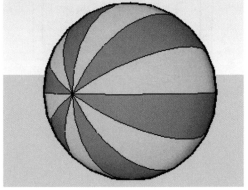

Figure 6-45

6.5 Two-Sided Coloring

Problem

You want to paint both sides of a set of faces.

Solution

Make the faces into a group. When you paint a group, that material or color is applied to all sides of all faces that are not already assigned a material.

Discussion

When you paint a face, only the side you click gets the material. (The exception to this is when you paint with a translucent material, which is applied to both sides of a face.) Even when you use the Shift or Ctrl/Option key to paint multiple faces, either all front faces or all back faces are painted, but not both sides. This is by design; "real-world" faces indeed have two sides. But in some cases, you might want to paint both sides of a face, and you can use groups for this.

> **Note**
>
> Using the Shift and Ctrl/Option keys to paint multiple faces is discussed in Recipe 8.4.

The main example shows how to paint both faces of walls of a house. In "Other Uses," you'll see how two-sided painting helps while making cut-throughs.

Consider the model of a house with a painted roof shown in Figure 6-46. All faces other than the tops of the roof have the default front and back colors.

Figure 6-46

If a wood material is activated, and is applied to any front face while the Shift key is pressed, all front faces are painted with wood (Figure 6-47). The back faces still have the default back color.

> **Note**
>
> If you want to paint both sides of a set of faces without using groups, you can use the Reverse Faces option. Select the faces to paint, and paint all of the sides that are showing. Leave the faces selected, right-click on one of them, and choose Reverse Faces. This switches the front and back sides of the face, so you can apply the same material to the sides that are now showing.

Figure 6-47

Figure 6-48

To paint the back faces to look like Figure 6-48, you must Shift-click one of the inner walls.

If you want to paint both sides of faces at once, the solution is to make a group that includes the faces you want to paint.

1. Create a house like the one in Figure 6-46, whose walls have the default colors and a painted roof. Cut holes for windows so you can see the inside walls.

2. Make the entire house a group.

3. Activate a material and click the group. (Do not open the group for editing; simply click the group while it is closed.) As shown in Figure 6-48, both sides of the default-painted walls get the new material. The only faces not painted are those at the top of the roof, because they already had an assigned material. (The underside of the roof faces do get the new material, assuming you didn't paint those faces before you made the group.)

Other Uses

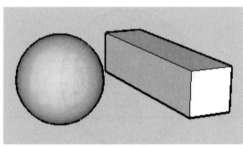

Figure 6-49

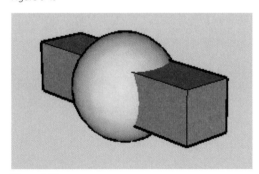

Figure 6-50

Recipe 3.3 demonstrated how to use groups or components to cut through objects. The basic steps are as follows:

- Group the cutting object.
- Move the cutting group into place.
- Use the Intersect tool to get intersection edges.
- Explode the group.
- Trim extra edges.

If you want the cut faces of the trimmed object to have the same color as the cutting object itself, both sides of the cutting object's faces should be painted. (You could just paint the back faces, but that's rather difficult when an object is closed.)

Consider a sphere like the one in Figure 6-49 that needs a rectangular hole cut through it. The cutting object is a long box that will pass through the sphere when moved into place. The box is not a group (yet).

To paint the entire box, pick a color (green, in this case), press and hold Shift, and click any face of the box. As you can see in Figure 6-50, the outside faces become green. But the inside faces of the box are not painted. After painting, move the cutting object into place.

The result after Intersect and trimming is shown in Figure 6-51. The cutout walls have the default color, because the inside faces of the cutting box had the default color.

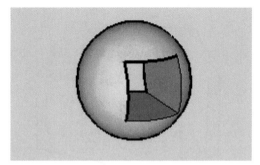

Figure 6-51

Go back to the beginning. If the cutout face color is to match the color of the cutting object, the cutting object should be a group. Then paint the group (Figure 6-52).

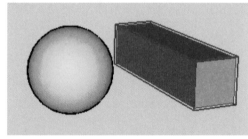

Figure 6-52

Figure 6-53 shows the result after you move the group into place, intersect, explode, and trim: the cutout walls have the cutout color. This is because both front and back faces of the cutting object were painted as a group.

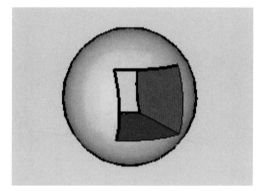

Figure 6-53

6.6 Locking a Group

Problem

You want to prevent a group from being moved, erased, or edited.

Solution

Lock the group.

Discussion

If there is a portion of your model that you know will not change, or you want to prevent objects from accidental changes or deletion, the solution is to make these objects into a group (or a component) and lock it. Lock (and Unlock) are available on a group's pop-up menu, as well as on the pop-up menu of a group in the Outliner.

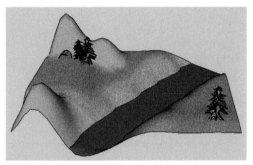

Figure 6-54

Figure 6-54 shows a piece of terrain upon which a model is to be built. For this example, you know that no parts of the terrain, including the stream, hills, and trees, will change, and you want to make sure these objects will not inadvertently be moved or edited by you or anyone else who works on the file.

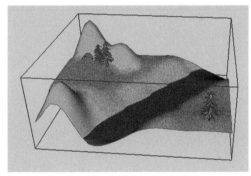

Figure 6-55

The solution is to make all of these objects into a locked group. Create the group and then right-click on the group and choose Lock. The bounding box and edges of a locked group are displayed in red (Figure 6-55).

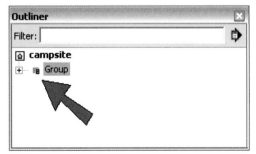

Figure 6-56

If you open the Outliner (Window→Outliner), the group's symbol has a lock symbol, as indicated in Figure 6-56.

> **Note**
>
> When you use the Get Current View tool to import terrain from Google Earth into SketchUp, the terrain is imported into SketchUp as a locked group. This is to prevent the terrain from being moved or edited. For more information, see Recipe 13.9.

CHAPTER 7

Components: Efficiency in Repetition

An essential feature of SketchUp, components can greatly increase your modeling efficiency as well as keep your file size as trim as possible. Components are geometrically similar to groups in that they are "sealed" and protected from other geometry and are selectable as a single object. Because components offer additional features, however, you can do much more with components than with groups.

If you're unsure about when to use a component versus a group, the general rule is that groups are mainly used for keeping objects separate from other objects, and they generally do not repeat. Components are the better choice for the following objects:

- Objects that will be repeated at least once in the model

- Objects that will be saved into their own file

- Objects that have specific alignment or insertion properties

- Objects that will cut faces, such as windows and doors

- 2D objects that are to always face the camera

The best-known feature of components is that they can be used for repeated objects; if you edit one, all copies of that component change as well. Components can also cut faces, align to specific faces, and always face the camera. Using repeated components, rather than copying faces and edges, can greatly decrease your file size, because SketchUp has to recognize only one set of geometric objects, and needs only location and size information for each component instance.

This chapter delves into the many uses and features of components, which no serious SketchUp modeler can live without.

7.1 Creating a Component

Problem

You want to combine several objects into a component.

Solution

Use the Create Component window.

Discussion

To create a component from objects in the model, first select the objects to include in the component. You can then do one of the following:

- Choose Edit→Make Component from the main menu.
- Right-click on one of the selected objects and choose Make Component from the pop-up menu.
- Click the Make Component icon.

This opens the Create Component window.

In the Create Component window (Figure 7-1), you can assign a name for the component or accept the default name. The description is optional.

Here is a quick description of the other options in the Create Component window:

- Alignment options are used for objects that are meant to align to all or specific faces (Recipe 7.10).
- The "Cut opening" checkbox is selected for objects such as windows, which cut the faces within which they are inserted (Recipe 7.12).
- Use "Always face camera" for 2D "cutout" components such as people, animals, trees, and shrubs, which always face the camera no matter the model orientation, giving the illusion of 3D volume (see Recipe 9.4). The "Shadows face sun" option is relevant for these types of components as well, to correct "skinny" shadows when the component's edges are along the sun's orientation.
- Set Component Axes is used to define the component's insertion point and orientation.
- If the "Replace selection with component" checkbox is selected, the selected objects will be replaced with the new component. Always look at this option when creating a component, because this option is not always selected by default.

> **Note**
>
> Although a component usually consists of more than one object, you can make a component from a single object. If only one face or edge is selected, Make Component does not appear in the pop-up menu, but you can choose Edit→Make Component from the main menu, or use the Make Component icon. If you want to make a single face into a component, you can activate Select and double-click the face. Because this selects both the face and its edges (more than one object is selected), Make Component appears in the pop-up menu.

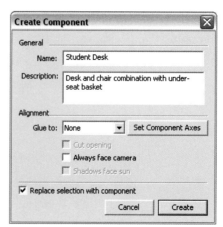

Figure 7-1

7.2 Using the Components Window

Problem

You want to find, view, and insert components.

Solution

Use the Components window.

Discussion

From the Components window (choose Window→Components), you can view and manipulate the components in your model, as well as find external models to use as components.

Figure 7-2

Figure 7-3

SketchUp comes with a few components installed, which you can access through the Components window (Figure 7-2). Users of the free version see only a Components Sampler folder in the window, and Pro users also have a folder with training examples for dynamic components (Chapter 14). The models in these folders are stored on your hard drive, where SketchUp is installed. (If you don't see these folders in the Components window, click the Select tab, click the arrow next to the house icon, and choose Components from the resulting drop-down menu.)

Note

The Components Sampler folder contains many dynamic components, which are identifiable by the green and white icon in the thumbnail. Free users can insert and interact with dynamic components, just not create their own. This folder also contains some "regular" (nondynamic) components. This chapter focuses only on "regular" components; dynamic components are described in Chapter 14.

Additional sampler components by Google are stored in the 3D Warehouse. To access them, make sure the Select tab is active and then click the arrow next to the house icon to open the drop-down menu (Figure 7-3). Choosing one of the links—Architecture, Landscape, Construction, or People—takes you directly to the selected collections on the 3D Warehouse website. To insert a 3D Warehouse model directly into your model, click its thumbnail and click again in the model. Clicking on a model's name or a collection's name will open that component's page in the 3D Warehouse, where there are options to open or save the model.

─── **Note** ───────────

For more details on finding models in the 3D Warehouse, see Recipe 13.1.

When you insert a component into your model, Sketch-Up automatically includes it in your In Model folder. To open this folder, click the Select tab's house icon (Figure 7-4).

To view or edit component properties, highlight the component in the In Model folder and click the Edit tab. (You can also right-click on a component thumbnail in the Components window and choose Properties from the pop-up menu to open the Edit tab.) From the Edit tab, you can change any of the properties (alignment, openings, and so on) that were set when the component was originally created.

The Statistics tab shows how many edges, faces, images, and the like are included in the component. This is a great way to see how complex, and therefore resource-heavy, a component is. The Statistics tab also lists Component Instances, which refers to the number of nested components within the selected component, not the number of components found in the model. The number of component instances in the model is listed at the bottom of the Statistics list (in Windows), or can be found in a component's Entity Info window.

Figure 7-4

─── **Note** ───────────

If you delete all instances of a component from your model, the component will still appear in the In Model folder. This is intentional, with the thought that you might change your mind and want to use the component after all. There is a Purge Unused option that will clean out your Components window of unused components. Purging components can greatly speed up a heavy model.

7.3 Inserting a Component

Problem

You want to insert a SketchUp model into your model as a component.

Solution

Use the Components window, or drag and drop from your file browser, or choose File→Import from the main menu.

Discussion

Components that you do not create yourself from scratch within your current model come from external SketchUp files. There are a few ways to insert models from outside your file:

- As discussed in Recipe 7.2, you can find models in the Components Sampler folder and in sampler collections in the 3D Warehouse. To insert one of these models, click the model thumbnail in the Components window, and click again to place the component in your model.

- If the SketchUp model you want to use as a component is on your hard drive, you can import it. From the main SketchUp menu, choose File→Import. In the Import window, make sure you are searching for SketchUp files (as opposed to graphic files), and browse to the file you want to insert as a component.

- If the model file is on your hard drive, you can also use your computer's file browser to insert the model. Simply click and drag the filename and drop it directly into the SketchUp window.

7.4 Editing or Exploding a Component

Problem

You need to make changes to a component, or explode it so that it is no longer a component.

Solution

To change a component, you open it for editing, make changes, and close the component. To explode a component, right-click on it and choose Explode.

Discussion

Editing and exploding a component is done the same way as for groups, which is covered in Chapter 6. The difference with components is that when you edit one, all identical components automatically get the same changes.

Exploding a single component, however, does not affect other components. If you want to explode more than one component, select them in advance. When you choose Explode from the pop-up menu, all selected components will be exploded.

Note

If you work with layers, keep in mind this strange behavior of exploded components: If the original objects composing the component are on Layer0 (SketchUp's default layer), and the component is on a different layer, the original objects will take on the new layer after the component is exploded. This does not happen if the original objects are on layers other than Layer0.

7.5 Renaming a Component

Problem

You want to rename a component.

Solution

Use the Definition Name field of the Components window or the Entity Info window.

Discussion

When you insert a component from the 3D Warehouse or import a SketchUp model as a component, SketchUp inserts the component by using a name identical to the filename of the inserted model. You might want to change this name. You might also want to change the name of a component you created yourself, even though you assigned it a name upon creation. There are two ways to change a component's name: directly in the Components window or in the Entity Info window.

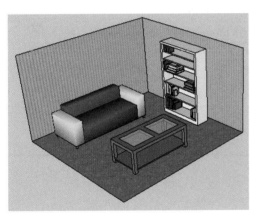

Figure 7-5

Figure 7-5 shows a room with three components: a sofa, coffee table, and bookcase. When you examine these in the Components window's In Model folder (opened by clicking the house icon as indicated in Figure 7-6), you see that their names (listed in bold next to each component thumbnail) were taken from the original model files and are a bit awkward.

— **Note** —————————————

Component names appear in Detail view but not in Thumbnails view. The view can be set by clicking the View Options icon, located to the left of the house icon in the Components window.

Figure 7-6

One way to rename a component is directly in the Components window. Select a component, such as the bookcase, and enter a new name in the top field (Figure 7-7). Keep in mind that if you select a component to rename this way, SketchUp thinks you want to insert the component, and attaches an instance of the component to your cursor when you move back to the model. You can end this insertion mode by pressing the Esc key.

Figure 7-7

The second way to rename a component is to use the Entity Info window. If this window is not already open, right-click on the component to rename, and choose Entity Info from the pop-up menu. If the Entity Info window is already open, just select the component you want to rename. Rename the component by entering the new name in the Definition Name field (Figure 7-8).

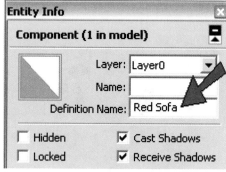

Figure 7-8

7.6 Saving a Component in Its Own File

Problem

You have objects in your model that you want to use in another model.

Solution

Make the objects into a component, and use the Save As option in the pop-up menu.

Discussion

If you want your entire model (which has not been made into one component) to be used later as a component, the solution is simply to save the file. When you are ready to import the model into a new file, you then choose File→Import, and find the saved model. It will be inserted as a component, surrounded by a bounding box.

But what if you want to save only selected objects of the model for later use as a component?

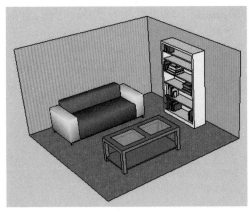

Figure 7-9

Figure 7-9 shows a model of a room containing a sofa, bookcase, and coffee table. For this example, assume that all of these objects were built from scratch within SketchUp, not imported as components from external files. The goal is to save the coffee table into its own file, so that it can be imported into other models. Make the coffee table into a component (Recipe 7.1); right-click on the component, either in the model itself or in the Components window; and choose Save As from the pop-up menu. The default filename is the name you assigned to the component when it was created; you can change it if you want. After the file is saved, it can be imported as a component in future files.

What you are saving into their own file are the objects inside the component and not an instance of the component. The component's axes become the model axes for the saved objects.

Keep in mind that many models in the 3D Warehouse were not saved this way; they were first made into components within their original file and then uploaded to the 3D Warehouse. A component like this will have a double bounding box when you insert it into your model. Some 3D Warehouse models also have issues with axes and insertion properties, which are explained in Recipe 7.10.

7.7 Accessing Local Components

Problem

You have folders of SketchUp model files on your hard drive and want to be able to access these folders from the Components window.

Solution

Add the folders to your Components window's Favorites.

Discussion

Google makes storing your models and collections easy in the 3D Warehouse, by providing unlimited space and access, as well as providing security and privacy options. But some users prefer to keep their component models local, stored either on their hard drive or on an internal company network.

— Note —

For details on storing your own models and collections in the 3D Warehouse, see Recipes 13.3 through 13.7.

Figure 7-10

The first step is to organize your models on your hard drive. Figure 7-10 shows the folder My SketchUp Components with three subfolders for Appliances, Cabinetry, and Furniture. The Furniture folder itself has three subfolders. These folders contain SketchUp models.

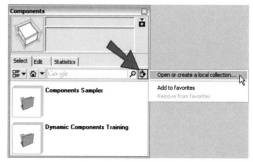

Figure 7-11

To open My SketchUp Components from the Components window, click the Details arrow indicated in Figure 7-11. From the pop-up menu that opens, choose "Open or create a local collection." Browse to My SketchUp Components and click OK. This folder is now displayed in the Components window, and you can see its subfolders (Figure 7-12).

To be able to access this folder without having to browse for the folder each time, click the Details arrow again and choose "Add to favorites." My SketchUp Components will now appear in the drop-down menu of component folders.

To remove a folder from Favorites, open the folder and use the "Remove from favorites" option from the Details arrow pop-up menu.

Figure 7-12

7.8 Painting Components

Problem

You want to paint components different materials or colors.

Solution

Use the default material for faces you want to paint. When you apply paint to a closed component (a component not open for editing), all faces that have the default color will get the new material.

Discussion

If repeating objects are identical except for their colors, there is no need to model each object separately. The efficient solution is to make one component in which you leave the default material for those faces you plan to paint later. Faces that already have a material assigned will keep that material when the component is painted; only faces with the default material will be painted when this technique is used. Because the face is painted from "without," not during component editing, the paint applies only to the individual component you are painting.

In the main example, you will create several identical houses that have different materials for the walls, but the same materials for the roofs, doors, and windows. In the "Other Uses" section, you'll see how this technique can be applied to make colored racecars, and different gemstones in identical settings.

Figure 7-13

1. Create a simple house with one window and one door (Figure 7-13). Paint the roof, door, and window, but leave the walls in the default color.

2. Make the entire house into a component (Recipe 7.1).

3. Make several copies of the house component.

4. To paint each house, simply activate a material and click the house component. All inside and outside walls are painted, but the front faces of the roof, door, and window keep the materials they were originally assigned (Figure 7-14).

   To change the colors on the door, roof, or window, you would need to edit the component (Recipe 7.4).

> **Note**
>
> Painting a component or group this way is a great way to quickly paint both sides of a set of faces. For details, see Recipe 6.5.

Figure 7-14

Other Uses

Here are some other examples in which you can paint components different materials.

The race car component shown in Figure 7-15 has a painted windshield and tires, and the car body has the default material. If you paint the cars different colors, the car bodies will have the new colors, but the tires and windshield colors will not change.

Figure 7-15

Figure 7-16 shows a chain of gemstone-setting components in which the setting is painted gold, but the stone is left in the default color. Painting each component a different color makes for an interesting bracelet.

Figure 7-16

7.9 Repeating Objects with Different Sizes

Problem

You want to use repeating objects that differ only in scale.

Solution

Use one component to represent all of the similar objects, and use different scale values so that they appear at different sizes.

Discussion

If repeating objects are identical except in scale, it is inefficient to model each object separately. Besides the additional work, the high number of repeated objects will cause your file size to balloon. The solution is to use one component for all of the similar objects, and use the Scale tool to resize them from "without." With this technique, SketchUp needs to store the geometric data only for the original component. For each instance of the component, SketchUp needs to know only location and scale data, which are much less resource-heavy than geometric data.

The main example uses one book component to make stacks of different-sized books in a bookcase. In "Other Uses," you'll see how this technique can be applied to tree components to make a random-looking landscape.

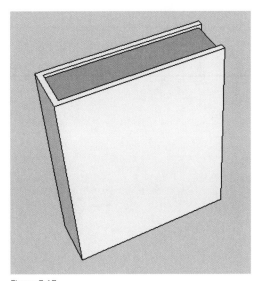

Figure 7-17

1. Start with a model of a book (Figure 7-17). You can create your model from scratch or download my Books model from the 3D Warehouse. In this model, the faces representing the pages are painted gray, and the faces for the covers and spine are left with the default color. This will make it easier to color the books later.

2. Make the book into a component (Recipe 7.1).

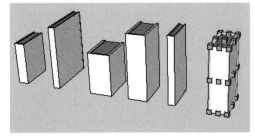

Figure 7-18

3. Make several copies of the book component. To change the size of a book, select it (do not open the component for editing) and activate the Scale tool. Use the drag handles to make the book taller, shorter, thicker, and so on (Figure 7-18).

You can use these books to fill a bookcase, as shown in Figure 7-19. Not only can you use the Scale tool to make the books various sizes, but you can also use the Rotate tool to place books at various angles, like the ones on top of the bookcase. Because the book covers were left the default color, you can paint each book separately, using the technique shown in Recipe 7.8. The pages of all books remain gray because they were already painted and do not have the default material.

Figure 7-19

Other Uses

This scaling technique is particularly useful in landscaping. Figure 7-20 shows a model in which three tree components are used at different scales, producing a random-looking landscape.

Figure 7-20

2D Trees Versus 3D Trees

Tree and other landscaping components generally come in two flavors: 2D Face Me components and "normal" 3D components. The trees pictured in Figure 7-20 are 2D, which are much smaller in file size and always face the camera. (Face Me components trick the eye into thinking they are 3D, but they are actually like cardboard cutouts.) However, 2D components have issues with shadows, and these components can look a bit less realistic than the resource-heavy 3D trees (though you can use digital images to make realistic-looking 2D trees, as described in Recipe 9.4).

In addition to trees and other landscaping components, 2D Face Me components can be used to represent people, street lamps, trash bins, and basically anything that does not need to change shape when it spins around.

If you prefer using 3D tree or other landscaping components, you can edit the component and hide its edges. This will make display regeneration faster, despite the potentially heavy model size.

7.10 Aligning and Gluing

Problem

You want to use Model A as a component in Model B, but when you import Model A into Model B, the component does not align properly or has an incorrect insertion point.

Solution

Determine where you want Model A's insertion point to be, and align this point with Model A's origin. Also, save Model A with the proper alignment properties, set in the Model Info window.

Discussion

Alignment issues are common when you use models downloaded from the 3D Warehouse, because many of the uploaded models there were saved without alignment properties or a proper insertion point.

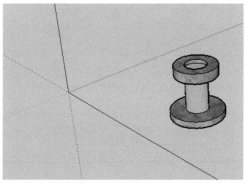

Figure 7-21

Figure 7-22

For example, consider the dresser handle model shown in Figure 7-21, created away from the model origin and oriented vertically. When this handle is placed in the dresser model shown in Figure 7-22, it remains vertical and the insertion point is rather far from where you actually want to place the handle.

A model that is to be used as a component should be placed so that the origin is located at the model's insertion point: the point you will use to drag the component into the next model and snap to a specific placement point. In addition, before saving, set the proper alignment properties in the File page of the Model Info window.

The main example demonstrates how to create a dresser handle so that it can be imported correctly into a dresser model. In the "Other Uses" section, you'll see how the same technique can be applied to a framed picture and to a window.

1. Create a model of a dresser handle, similar to the one shown in Figure 7-23. Orient it so that it is vertical (start the model in the red-green plane), and place the handle so that the origin coincides with the center of the lowest face. This is the point by which the handle will be dragged and placed into the dresser model. Pay attention to the dimensions while creating the handle, so that it is approximately the right size. (The diameter of the handle base should be about 4 inches.)

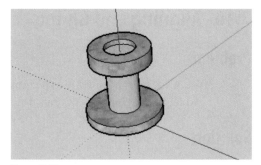

Figure 7-23

   You do not have to make the handle into a component. When imported or inserted from the Components window, the entire handle model will automatically be inserted into the dresser as a component.

2. Open the Model Info window (Window→Model Info) to the File page. At the bottom of this window, set the "Glue to" option to Any. This means that the current contents of the red-green plane will align to any face of the dresser model. (You could also set the alignment to only vertical faces, if you know that your dresser front will be vertical.)

Figure 7-24

3. Save this model.

4. In a new file, create a model of a dresser (Figure 7-24) or download my Dresser model from the 3D Warehouse. If you create your own dresser, pay attention to its dimensions so that the size will be correct relative to the size of the handle.

5. Use the Tape Measure tool to place construction lines marking the centers of the handles for the top drawer, as shown in Figure 7-25. This is where you would drill holes on an actual dresser.

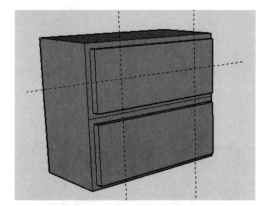

Figure 7-25

6. From the main menu, choose File→Import, and make sure the file type is set to look for SketchUp models. Import the handle model. Place its insertion point at the intersection of the construction lines, as shown in Figure 7-26. Because the handle is set to align to any face, it aligns correctly with the front of the dresser.

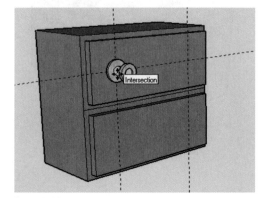

Figure 7-26

Figure 7-27

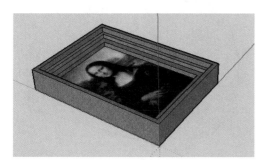
Figure 7-28

Figure 7-29

7. To complete the dresser, find the handle in the In Model folder and place a handle at the other side of the top drawer. Place two more on the bottom drawer, as shown in Figure 7-27. Then erase or hide the construction lines.

Other Uses

In this section, you'll see how to apply the insertion and alignment technique to a framed picture placed on a wall, and to a window placed in a roof.

Framed Picture

The model shown in Figure 7-28 is a framed picture that will be imported into another model, as a picture on a wall. The origin coincides with the lower-left back corner of the frame. Before saving, set the "Glue to" property to Any or Vertical faces.

Figure 7-29 shows the model with the walls. Note that the insertion point is at the lower-left back corner of the frame, and the picture aligns to the vertical face of the wall.

Window

The model shown in Figure 7-30 is an octagonal window. The origin coincides with the lower-back midpoint of the window frame. For windows, you generally want the component to cut the face onto which it is imported, which will be set in the Model Info window. The red-green plane defines where this cutting will occur: the boundary of the frame that lies in the red-green plane is the cutting boundary.

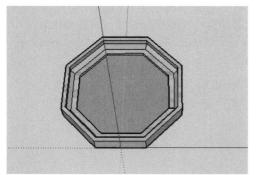
Figure 7-30

The alignment is set to Any face, so that the window can be imported into a sloped face. Also, "Cut opening" is checked in the Model Info window (Figure 7-31), so that the window will cut the face on which it is positioned. The model with the imported windows is shown in Figure 7-32. The windows align to the sloped face and cut the face of the roof.

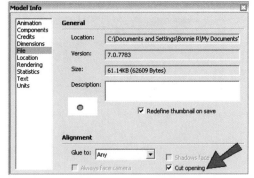

Figure 7-31

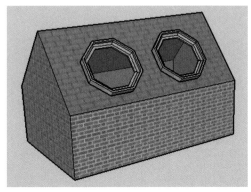

Figure 7-32

7.11 Using Components for Symmetric Models

Problem

You are creating a symmetric model and want to save time and keep the file size low.

Solution

Decrease your file size and make editing easier by using two mirrored components.

Discussion

With this efficient technique, you create half of the model and make it a component. The second half of the model is a mirrored copy of the component, joined to the original. If needed, you can hide edges where the two components meet. Editing a symmetric model is easy, because you have to edit only half of the model, and file size is reduced because you are creating only half of the geometry.

The main example demonstrates modeling half of a house. In "Other Uses," you will see how this technique can be applied to symmetric furniture such as a sofa or table.

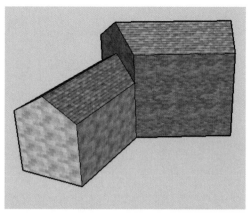

Figure 7-33

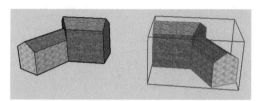

Figure 7-34

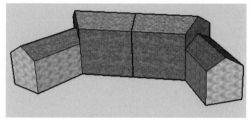

Figure 7-35

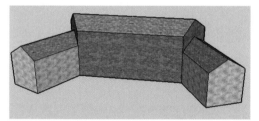

Figure 7-36

Figure 7-37

1. Start with a model of half of a house (Figure 7-33). You can create your model from scratch or download my Symmetry House model from the 3D Warehouse.

2. Make the half-building a component (Recipe 7.1), and make one copy of the component.

3. Keep the copied component selected and activate the Scale tool. Turn the copy inside out by dragging a center-side handle through the component, stopping when the Scale value is –1 (Figure 7-34).

4. Attach the mirrored half to the original half. The two halves appear to be separate objects because of the edges between the components (Figure 7-35).

5. These edges can be hidden. Open either component for editing, select the edges that meet the other half, and hide them. (Hide is available from the pop-up menu or the Edit menu.) After closing the component, you can no longer tell that the model is comprised of two components (Figure 7-36).

6. Edit either component, and add some windows and an arch-shaped door along the common edge. The result is a perfectly symmetric house (Figure 7-37), with a file size much smaller than if you had modeled the entire house. And if you need to make changes, you need to edit only one of the halves.

Other Uses

The symmetric component technique is great for furniture design, because most furniture is symmetric. This section shows a symmetric sofa and a table.

Sofa

The sofa in Figure 7-38 comprises two halves that are mirrored and joined together. Edges between halves are hidden.

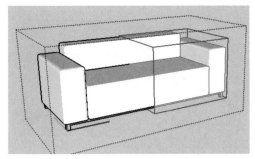

Figure 7-38

Table

Figure 7-39 shows a model of an antique table with double symmetry, composed of four quarter-components. Edges are hidden where the component is joined to other components.

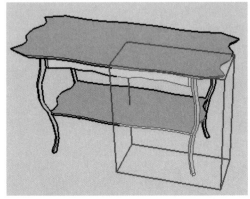

Figure 7-39

7.12 Placing Windows in 3D Walls

Problem

You want to place window components in thick (3D) walls, but a component can cut only one face.

Solution

Use nested components, which can be inserted and exploded, enabling you to cut through the wall.

Discussion

SketchUp components can cut only one face. This is fine for the model shown in Figure 7-40, which consists of 2D, flat walls. When you import a window into a flat wall, the wall is automatically cut. The trouble starts when the walls have thickness, as in Figure 7-41. When you insert a window into the front face of a wall, it cuts only that face. The back face of the wall remains uncut. So all you can see through this window is the back face of the wall; you cannot see inside the building.

Figure 7-40

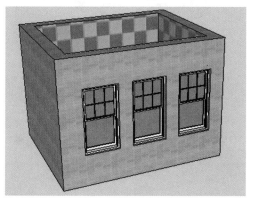

Figure 7-41

There are two ways you can solve this problem, depending on whether you know the thickness of the wall. Example 1 shows how to build a nested window component to cut walls of unknown thickness. Example 2 demonstrates a similar technique for cutting walls of known thickness.

Figure 7-42

Example 1: Window in Walls of Unknown Thickness

This example consists of four main tasks: creating a face to represent the cutting boundary, building a nested window component, placing the component in the wall, and exploding the component so that the hole in the wall can be made.

1. Download my Irregular Window model from the 3D Warehouse (Figure 7-42). If the window is not already a component (if you downloaded it from the 3D Warehouse in your Internet browser and not via the Components window), make it a component now. The alignment and cutting do not have to be set yet, because this component will become part of a nested component.

2. Orbit to a view like the one shown in Figure 7-43, in which you can see the two parts of the frame. The green part will sit in front of the wall, and the brown part will be set into the wall. The thickness of the brown frame is about 5.5 inches, so the wall thickness should be more than 5.5 inches.

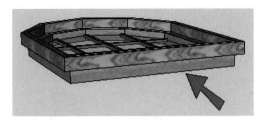

Figure 7-43

3. Orbit to view the back of the window. The cutting face will cover the exterior boundary of the brown frame, along the face shared by the brown and green frames. This is the plane where the window will meet the front face of the wall. Start a rectangle at the corner where the green and brown frames meet (Figure 7-44).

Figure 7-44

4. Complete the rectangle along the cutting plane, extending past the edges of the window (Figure 7-45).

5. Right-click on the rectangle and choose Intersect→Intersect with Model. This creates edges where the cutting face meets the edges of the window component.

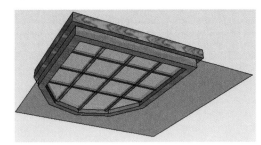

Figure 7-45

6. To make it easier to complete the cutting face, hide the window component (right-click on the window and choose Hide). Your cutting face should look like Figure 7-46, with several extra edges. The innermost face, indicated by the arrows, is where the cutting face meets the interior edges of the brown frame. This face is not needed, so erase its edges.

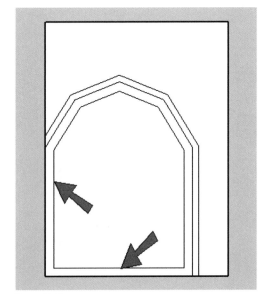

Figure 7-46

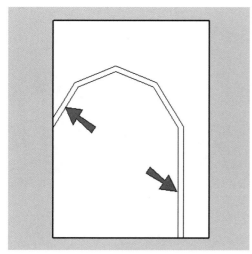

Figure 7-47

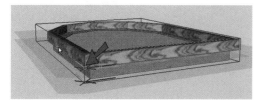

Figure 7-48

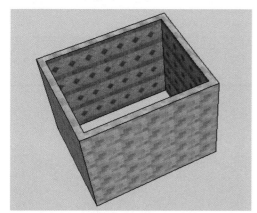

Figure 7-49

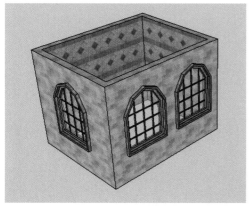

Figure 7-50

7. The innermost face you have now, indicated by the arrows in Figure 7-47, is the boundary you want for the cutting face, because this is where the cutting face meets the exterior edges of the brown frame. Erase everything *except* for the edges of this face.

Note ───────────────────────────

You could have created the same cutting face by simply tracing the outside edges of the brown frame. For this example, there are only seven edges around the cutting face, but if the window had round edges, tracing each edge would require a good bit of work.

---

8. Unhide the window component by choosing Edit→Unhide→All from the main menu.

9. Select both the window and the cutting face and make a new component. Set it to glue to any face. To define the correct insertion point, click Set Component Axes.

10. Define the component origin at the bottom corner of the green frame, because this is where the window will meet the wall. Keep the component's red and green axes in their current directions (Figure 7-48).

11. In blank space, create a box and offset the top face so that the walls are thicker than 5.5 inches. Push down the center of the box to create the 3D walls (Figure 7-49). (You could also create a rectangle and offset it, and then pull up the resulting border face.)

12. From the In Model folder of the Components window, insert a few windows into the walls. The cutting faces align with the front faces of the walls.

13. Explode each window and push the cutting face from the front face of the wall to the back face of the wall. You can use Push/Pull on the cutting face even though it appears behind the window face. You can now see through the walls, into the room (Figure 7-50).

14. Orbit to view the back of the windows. Because the walls are thicker than the 5.5-inch brown window frame, the frame ends in the middle of the wall (Figure 7-51).

If you had made walls thinner than the 5.5-inch window frame, the frame would protrude slightly into the room.

Figure 7-51

After you understand this technique, you can apply it to any window. Most of the windows in the 3D Warehouse are based on rectangles (Figure 7-52), so all you need to do is add a simple rectangle for the cutting face (Figure 7-53), no intersection required.

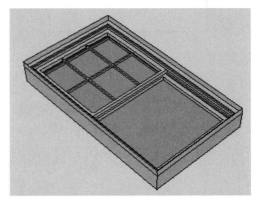

Figure 7-52

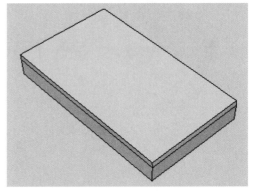

Figure 7-53

Combine the window and the cutting face into one nested component, set the component axes along the cutting face (in this case, along the top of the window), and insert some into a wall. Explode each window and push in each cutting face, and you can see into the house (Figure 7-54).

Figure 7-54

Figure 7-55

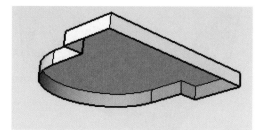

Figure 7-56

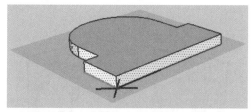

Figure 7-57

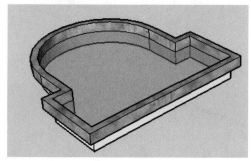

Figure 7-58

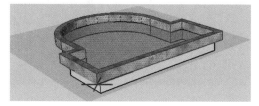

Figure 7-59

Example 2: Window in Walls of Known Thickness

If the thickness of the walls is known, you can employ a neat trick. You can create a component that consists of two cutting components, one for each of the front and back walls. When you explode this component, the nested components inside it are no longer nested, and are "free" to cut the faces. No face pushing is required.

1. Start in Top view and create the basic window shape. The window shape shown in Figure 7-55 is a complex arch shape, but you can use any shape you like.

2. Pull up this face the same distance as the thickness of the wall, such as 6 inches.

3. The window glass will align with the front face of the wall, not the back face. So orbit to the bottom of the window and erase the back face (Figure 7-56).

4. The component that will cut the back face of the wall consists of the side faces of the current model. Select all faces created so far, press Shift, and click the top face to deselect it. This leaves only the side faces selected.

5. Make a component from these selected faces; set to align to any face and to cut openings. The origin for this component should be at the bottom of the faces, because this is where the component will meet the back face of the wall (Figure 7-57).

6. Now you can create the component that will cut the front face of the wall. Use Offset to make the frame and pull it up so that the frame will extend in front of the wall. Paint the window face with a translucent material (Figure 7-58).

7. Select all faces and leave the back component unselected. Make a new component from these faces, with the axes oriented as shown in Figure 7-59. This component should also be set to cut openings.

8. Select both cutting components and make a new component. Set the origin for this component at the bottom of the frame, where the window will meet the front face of the wall. Keep the red and green axes in their current directions (Figure 7-60).

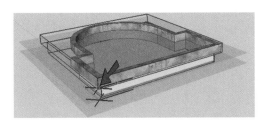

Figure 7-60

9. In blank space, make a box to represent the building. Use the Offset tool to offset the top face inward by the same distance as the thickness of the window, such as 6 inches.

10. From the In Model folder of the Components window, insert some windows in the walls. The cutting face aligns exactly with the front faces of the walls (Figure 7-61).

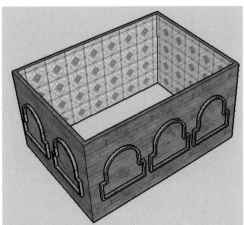

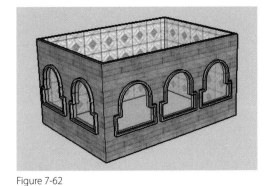

Figure 7-61

11. Explode all of the window components. This reduces each window to its two nested components, which are both set to cut faces. Therefore, the front and back faces are simultaneously cut (Figure 7-62).

Figure 7-62

12. Orbit to view the back of the windows. The window frames fit exactly within the thickness of the walls (Figure 7-63).

Figure 7-63

7.13 Reloading Components

Problem

You want to replace a component with another component, which is a model from another file.

Solution

Use the Reload option, which switches out existing components for components external to the current model; all of the components are swapped at once.

Discussion

Say you have designed a building with 50 identical window components, and your client decides that another window would work better. The Reload option enables you to replace all of the original windows with new ones. Reloading is particularly useful for landscaping components, for example, when you want to switch one type of shrub for another.

This technique is also helpful for solving a common problem in SketchUp: Models with numerous, heavy components may run slowly when you orbit, pan, and so on, because SketchUp has to regenerate each edge of each component with every new view. You can use temporary *placeholder* components in place of the real ones, and use the Reload option to swap them out when your entire design is complete and ready to show.

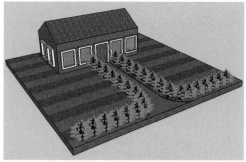

Figure 7-64

Figure 7-65

Consider Figure 7-64's model: the 3D plant used to line the walkway is an imported component that is copied repeatedly. Because of the high number of edges and faces of the components, the model may move quite slowly when you change the view. (Of course, this also depends on your processor speed.)

One sure way to keep your model moving quickly is to use "light" component placeholders, made of simple geometry. When you finalize your design, you can replace these placeholders with the more complex, realistic 3D models. The main example demonstrates how to reload landscape components, and the "Other Uses" section uses the same technique to place desks in a classroom.

1. Download my Hosta model (Figure 7-65) from the 3D Warehouse and save it to your hard drive. Each hosta leaf is the same component at different scales, so the size of this model file is not too large. The edges of the leaves themselves are hidden, which means SketchUp has fewer edges to regenerate when the view is changed. However, there are still edges visible along the stems.

Large Components and Model Speed

Aside from using placeholder components, there are a few other things you can try to make your heavy, component-laden model run a bit faster:

- Switch the view from Shaded with Textures to Shaded (View→Face Style→Shaded). In this mode, all textures are displayed in their base color instead of using graphic images. Faces displayed this way are quicker to regenerate when the view is changed.
- Display the model without edges, either using Shaded mode or Shaded with Textures mode. (Removing edges from the display is done in the Styles window, on the Edge page of the Edit tab.) This prevents SketchUp from having to regenerate edges, but regenerating faces might still cause the model to move slowly. (Not to mention that not everyone likes the edge-free look.)

- Hide edges within the component. To do this, open the component for editing and switch to Wireframe view. This leaves only edges displayed. Select all of the edges and hide them by using the pop-up menu or by choosing Edit→Hide. Switch back to Shaded or Shaded with Textures, and only the component faces will be visible.

---

2. Download my Landscaped Walkway model from the 3D Warehouse. As you can see in Figure 7-66, the landscaped walkway currently includes stick-figure components as placeholders for each hosta plant.

3. To replace the placeholders with the "real thing," right-click on any placeholder component and choose Reload from the pop-up menu. (The Reload option is also available when you right-click on the placeholder component in the In Model folder of the Components window.)

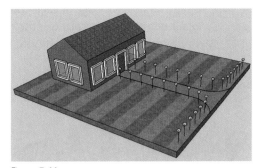

Figure 7-66

4. Browse to where you saved the hosta model and reload it. Each placeholder is replaced with a 3D hosta model (Figure 7-67). Because your model may run slowly now, this technique is best employed at the last moment when all placeholders for all components are in place, and you have settled on the final viewing angle.

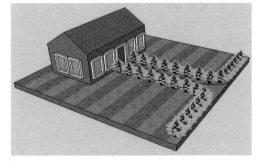

Figure 7-67

Replacing All Versus Replacing Some

The Reload option replaces all components with the new one. But what if you want to replace only some of the components, leaving the rest as they are? The solution for this is to select the components you want to reload and make them unique (right-click on any selected component and choose Make Unique from the pop-up menu). Now you can use Reload on one of the unique components. Note that dynamic components cannot be made unique.

Figure 7-68

Figure 7-69

Figure 7-70

Other Uses

The desk model shown in Figure 7-68 has a high number of edges and faces, particularly in the basket below the chair. Importing many of these into a classroom model might cause the classroom to move slowly. Instead, when you create the classroom, use simple box components as placeholders for the desks (Figure 7-69).

When you use Reload, the orientation of the new components might not be correct (Figure 7-70). You could solve this problem by rotating the model in the original desk file, saving the file, and using Reload again in the classroom. Or you could edit one of the reloaded components in the classroom and rotate it.

7.14 Replacing Components

Problem

You want to replace one or more components in your model with another component in your model.

Solution

Use the Replace Selected option in the Components window.

Discussion

Recipe 7.13 discussed the technique for swapping components with models *external* to the file. This recipe demonstrates how to replace components with other components that are *already in* your model.

1. Download my Flower House model from the 3D Warehouse (Figure 7-71). This model, displayed without edges, contains 10 of the same window components, each with a flower box.

2. The flower boxes are to be removed from all of the first-floor windows. Right-click on any of the first-floor windows and choose Make Unique from the pop-up menu.

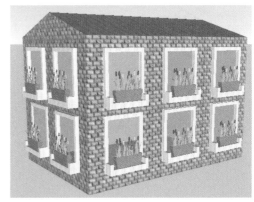

Figure 7-71

3. This component is now different from the other nine windows. Open it for editing and erase the flower box. (The flower box is itself a component, so it can be erased with one click.) Also, push in the windowsill so that the frame is a simple offset (Figure 7-72).

4. Close the edited component.

5. Select the four remaining original windows on the first floor.

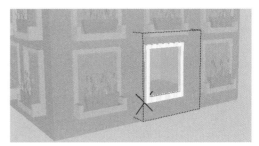

Figure 7-72

Figure 7-73

6. Open the In Model folder of the Components window, where you should see three components: the flower box, the original window with the flower box, and Window#1 (the edited unique component). Right-click on this new component and choose Replace Selected (Figure 7-73).

Figure 7-74

The four selected components are now replaced with the new component (Figure 7-74).

—— **Note** ——————————————————————

Another way to get the same result is to select all of the first-floor windows and make them unique. Then you could edit any one of them, and the changes would be applied to all of them.

Figure 7-75

7. If you want to switch the new windows back to the original ones, you could select each new window and use the same Replace Selected technique. To select all of the new windows at once, right-click on the new component in the Components window and choose Select Instances from the pop-up menu. All of the new windows are selected (Figure 7-75).

Figure 7-76

8. To replace all of these with the original component, right-click on the original window component in the Components window and choose Replace Selected. Now all of the windows are the original components with the flower boxes, as shown in Figure 7-76.

Other Uses

You can use the Replace Selected technique to make a random-looking garden. Start with an orderly garden with rows of each plant component and randomly select some plants to change (Figure 7-77).

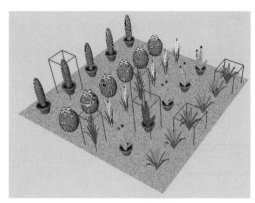

Figure 7-77

In the Components window, right-click on a random plant and choose Replace Selected. This replaces the randomly selected plants with the new plant (Figure 7-78).

Figure 7-78

Continue replacing plants with other plants until the garden looks random. For an even more random look, use the Scale tool to make identical components different sizes, using the technique described in Recipe 7.9 (Figure 7-79).

When using different scale values, keep in mind that the scale values will still be in effect if you replace the components.

Figure 7-79

7.15 Working with the Outliner

Problem

You have a complex model with many components or groups, or nested components or groups, and you want a way to keep track of them.

Solution

Use the Outliner.

Discussion

The Outliner lists all your model's components and groups in a hierarchical form that shows nesting levels. It indicates whether components are selected, open for editing, hidden, or locked. It also provides a search field to locate groups or components by name, which is helpful when your model is too large to see everything, or when you are trying to locate a hidden component or group.

There are two examples in this recipe: The first provides an overview of how the Outliner works and how you can use it to organize groups and components. The second demonstrates using the Outliner to create a staircase with nested components.

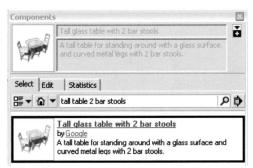

Figure 7-80

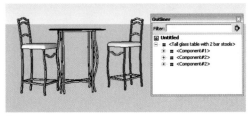

Figure 7-81

Example 1: Organizing with the Outliner

This example uses a nested component composed of a table component with two barstool components to show how the Outliner works, and how you can rename components to better organize your model. In the "Other Uses" section, you'll see how the Outliner helps organize a townhouse development consisting of both components and groups.

1. In the search field of the Components window, enter *tall table 2 bar stools*. Click the thumbnail shown in Figure 7-80 and bring the component into your model. (If you see more than one model in the search results, click the model made by Google.)

2. Open the Outliner (Window→Outliner). When all of the items are expanded, the Outliner lists one main component (Tall glass table with 2 bar stools) and three nested components, one for the table and two for the chairs. The item at the top of the list, Untitled, is the name of the model file (Figure 7-81).

3. In the Outliner, click Component#1, which is the table component. The table is selected in the model, which means that the "parent" component in which it is nested must be opened for editing (Figure 7-82).

4. The names Component#1 and Component#2 are not very informative, so they should be changed. As detailed in Recipe 7.5, you can rename a component in the Components window or in the Entity Info window. You can open the Entity Info window directly from the Outliner: ight-click on Component#1 and choose Entity Info from the pop-up menu.

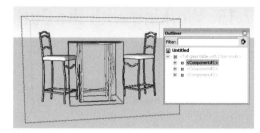

Figure 7-82

— **Note** —————————————————————

The same pop-up menu appears whether you right-click on the component itself in the model or on the component name in the Outliner.

————————————————————————————

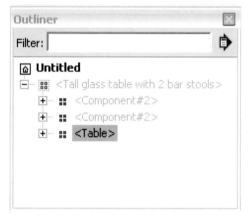

Figure 7-83

5. In the Definition Name field of the Entity Info window, enter something more informative, such as *Table*. The new name appears in the Outliner (Figure 7-83). The Outliner items are listed alphabetically, so the listed order has changed.

6. Rename the other components *Chair*. (You have to rename only one of them; the others will update automatically.)

7. Each chair component consists of two identical nested components. Rename these *Half Chair* (Figure 7-84).

— **Note** —————————————————————

The technique of using half of a component to model a symmetric object is described in Recipe 7.11.

————————————————————————————

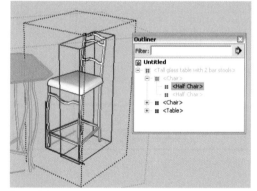

Figure 7-84

8. The two halves of the chair have the same component name, but you can use the Outliner to differentiate between them. Right-click on one of the half-chair components and choose Rename. Enter a new name, such as *Right Half*. The new name appears without angle brackets, while the original component name is listed afterward, inside angle brackets (Figure 7-85). This is a great way to differentiate between identical components.

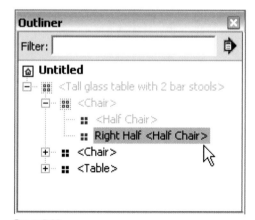

Figure 7-85

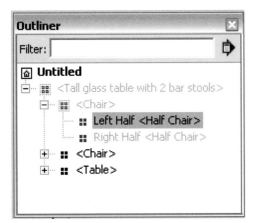

Figure 7-86

Figure 7-87

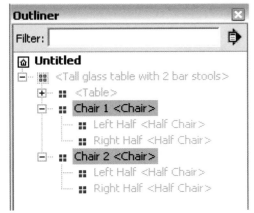

Figure 7-88

9. Rename the other half-chair component (Figure 7-86).

10. Expand the other chair component, and you'll see that it has the same new names for the half-chair components nested in it (Figure 7-87). Because you renamed components nested within a "parent" component, each instance of the parent component has the same renamed nested components.

11. To differentiate between the two chair components, change their descriptive names, such as *Chair 1* and *Chair 2* (Figure 7-88).

This is a simple example, but imagine a much more complex model with multiple rooms each loaded with furniture components. If each furniture component has a unique descriptive name and you need to locate a specific sofa in a specific living room, you could enter the unique name in the Filter field at the top of the Outliner. The Outliner will then display only items that have the specified name.

The Outliner can also inform you of components and groups that are hidden (they are grayed out) and locked objects (the item symbol has a lock added to it).

Other Uses

Another example in which the Outliner can help organize a complex model is the townhouse development shown in Figure 7-89. Each set of three houses is a group, as shown in Figure 7-90. The symbol for a group is a solid square, whereas the component symbol is a group of four small squares. Each group is given the default descriptive name Group.

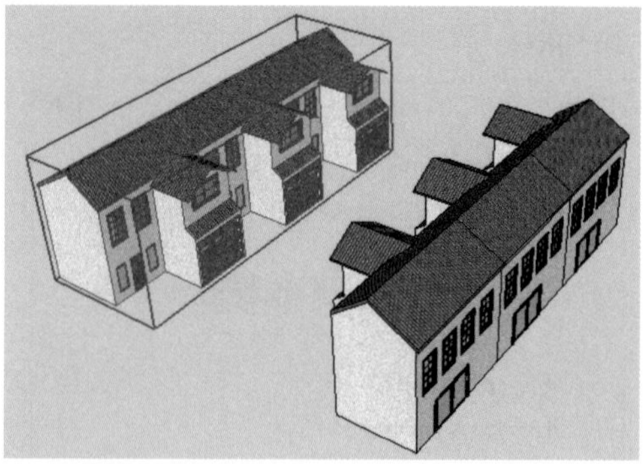

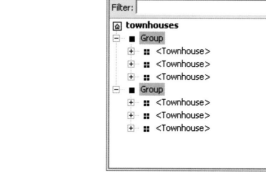

Figure 7-89

Figure 7-90

Groups are given the generic descriptive name Group because, unlike components, they are not assigned a name when created. However, you can assign a descriptive name to a group: use either the Definition Name field in the group's Entity Info window, or the Rename option in the Outliner. Figure 7-91 shows the renamed groups.

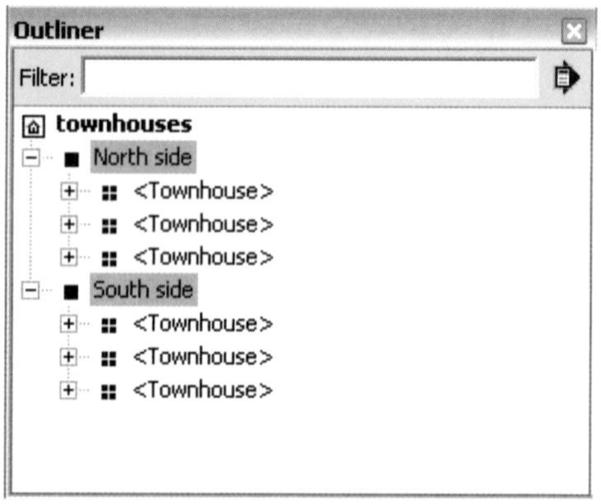

Figure 7-91

To differentiate between each townhouse, use the Rename option. Figure 7-92 shows each component with a street address.

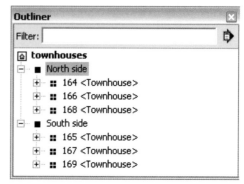

Figure 7-92

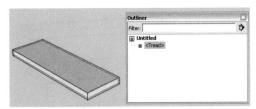

Figure 7-93

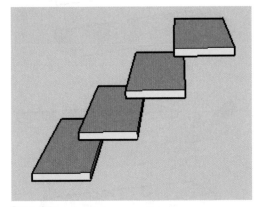

Figure 7-94

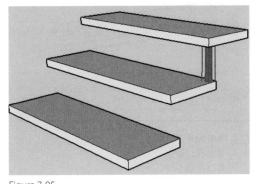

Figure 7-95

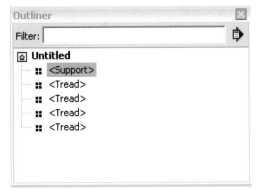

Figure 7-96

Example 2: Using the Outliner to Create Nested Components

In this example, you will create a staircase with the help of the Outliner. This staircase will consist of nested components. In the "Other Uses" section, you will see how to apply this technique to beam connectors in a construction model.

1. Create a simple box to represent one of the stair treads and make the box into a component named Tread. The tread component is listed in the Outliner (Figure 7-93).

2. Make a few copies of the tread, positioned so that the front of each tread extends forward, over the back of the tread below (Figure 7-94). This is easiest to do in Side view.

3. Create a vertical support between any two treads. The support shown in Figure 7-95 is a simple cylinder. Make the support a component named Support.

The Outliner now lists several tread components and one support component (Figure 7-96).

4. Copy the support component to the other side of the tread (Figure 7-97).

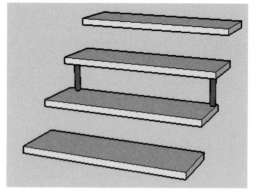

Figure 7-97

5. The next step is to nest the support components into the tread component above them. First you must be able to identify in the Outliner which tread is above the supports. Select the tread above the supports (Figure 7-98).

The selected tread is highlighted in the Outliner.

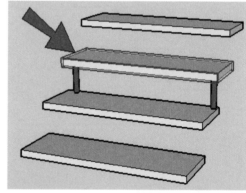

Figure 7-98

6. Remember which tread was highlighted in the Outliner. Then, within the Outliner, select both support components (press the Ctrl/Option key when you want to select multiple items) and drag them just below the tread that was highlighted (Figure 7-99).

 Note

If you have many treads, making it difficult to remember which one was highlighted, you could use the Rename option to give the tread a unique name.

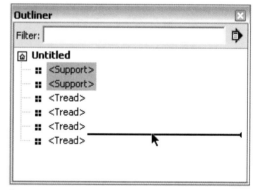

Figure 7-99

Figure 7-100

Figure 7-101

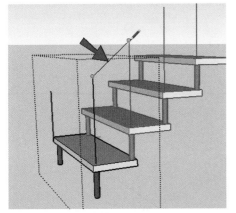

Figure 7-102

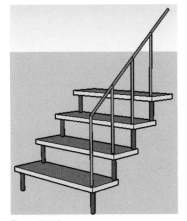

Figure 7-103

This nests the supports within the tread; the change is applied to each tread component (Figure 7-100).

The Outliner lists two supports inside each tread (Figure 7-101).

Note

You could nest the support components without using the Outliner: select the supports and cut them (Edit→Cut). Then open for editing the tread component into which the supports will be nested, and choose Edit→Paste in Place. This technique is shown in Recipe 3.4.

---

7. To add a rail to the staircase, open the bottom tread component for editing, and use the Line tool to create a Follow Me path. Figure 7-102 shows a vertical path starting just above the support, connected to a diagonal path that meets the vertical path from the tread above.

8. The Follow Me face for the rail is a small circle, extruded along the two Follow Me lines. When the rail is completed, make it a component, and close the tread component (Figure 7-103).

   The Outliner shows one rail component inside each tread component.

9. What if you want the rail to appear only at the top of the staircase, and not on each tread? In Figure 7-104, the top tread is the last one listed in the Outliner list. Within the Outliner, drag the rail from this tread and move it just under the filename.

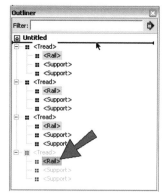

Figure 7-104

This makes the rail a first-level component (no longer nested), and it appears only above the top tread (Figure 7-105). To replace the rail inside each tread, you would move it from its first-level position back into the tread from which you moved it.

Figure 7-105

Other Uses

The Outliner can also be used to nest connector components into each beam of a construction model. Figure 7-106 shows three joist components, which are attached to a single beam component. There are two connector components connecting each side of the leftmost joist to the beam.

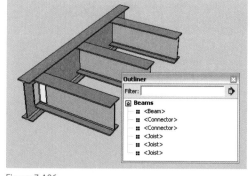

Figure 7-106

Use the Outliner to move the two connectors from their first-level position to a position underneath the joist to which they are attached. The connectors are now nested below all of the joists, and each joist has two connectors (Figure 7-107).

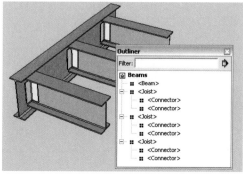

Figure 7-107

CHAPTER 8

Painting, Materials, and Textures

At first glance, materials seem a simple feature of SketchUp: Click the Paint Bucket icon, choose a material from the resulting window, and click a face to apply your choice—even a second-grader can do it. But SketchUp materials have capabilities far beyond simply applying paint to faces. For instance, there are shortcuts to painting multiple faces at a time, you can edit a material's size and color, and you can make changes to a material on just one specific face. In this chapter, you will learn about the more complex aspects of materials, such as editing, positioning, translucency, and alpha transparency.

8.1 Finding Materials and Images

Problem

You want to find materials or images to use in your models.

Solution

Look in the Materials (or Colors) window for local materials, and then search on the SketchUp website or in the 3D Warehouse for additional materials.

Discussion

The Materials window (called Colors on the Mac) houses the folders of materials currently on your system. To access it, choose Tools→Paint Bucket, or click the Paint Bucket icon, or choose Window→Materials. Within the Materials window, you can find all colors and materials used in a particular model in the In Model folder (the Colors In Model folder on the Mac). To open this folder, you can use the drop-down menu or click the house icon (Figure 8-1). Windows permits you to edit materials found in the In Model folder only; no matter what your system, it is the best practice to edit only materials in In Model and not the "source" materials found in the other folders.

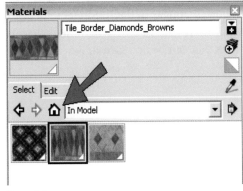

Figure 8-1

As you can see in the Materials window, SketchUp comes with a few folders of sample materials, such as Bricks and Cladding, Roofing, and so on. For an expanded version of the folders you already have (more bricks, more roofing materials, and so on), the free Materials Bonus Pack is available from the SketchUp website. Click the Download link and then the link for Bonus Packs. When you download and install this pack, the materials are placed automatically into the correct folders.

Note ─────────────────────────

You can also try searching the Web for materials. Specific images of items such as bathroom tile, cabinet faces, or custom doors may be found on manufacturer websites.

The 3D Warehouse offers numerous models that contain collections of materials, but be aware that although some are high quality, others are not. Here are some keywords you can try when searching the 3D Warehouse:

- Texture pack, material pack

- Texture collection, material collection

- Fabric textures, fabric materials (or metal, or concrete, or wood, and so on)

- Seamless

- Names of manufacturers of paint, lumber, countertops, cabinets, and so on, to find their collection palettes

A 3D Warehouse model with a collection of materials usually looks something like Figure 8-2. After you download the file and open it in SketchUp, all of the materials appear in the In Model folder of the Materials window. If you want to save these materials as collections that can be accessed in other files, see Recipe 8.3.

Note ─────────────────────────

Be warned: Materials remain in the In Model folder even if they are no longer used in your model, and carrying extra materials in your model will increase your file size and can affect performance, resulting in slow refresh of materials, faces, and edges. Windows users can remove extra materials by clicking the Details arrow on the Materials window (next to the drop-down field) and choosing Purge Unused. On the Mac, Purge Unused is available in the List drop-down menu. Components behave the same way, in that unused ones must be purged manually. If you purge your materials but still have some materials in your In Model list that you are not using, they are probably used by components that have not yet been purged. So purge components first and then materials.

Figure 8-2

8.2 Getting Images into Your Model

Problem

You want to use an image file as a material in your model.

Solution

Create a new material by using the Materials window, or import the image file as either a texture or an image.

Discussion

If you want to use a material or image that isn't available in the Materials window, all you need is the image file you want to use. The method you use to get it into your model depends on what you plan to do.

Figure 8-3

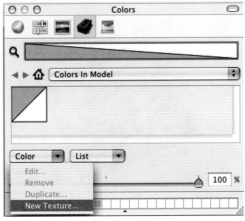

Figure 8-4

Method 1: Create a New Material

When you create a new texture, you bring a material into the Materials window without automatically using it in your model. This is a good method if you are loading a group of materials you plan to paint with later or plan to save as a collection.

In Windows, click the Create Material icon shown in Figure 8-3 to create a new material. If a material is already active in the Materials window, the new material will be based on the active one, which is helpful for making a copy of a material (Recipe 8.6). If the default material is currently selected, the new material will be a blank slate. In either case, the Create Material window opens, in which you can assign the material a name and either pick a color or choose an image. To use an image, select Use Texture Image and browse to the image file. If you want your image to have a specific scale, you can enter a length and height. Click OK, and the new material appears in the In Model folder.

On the Mac, click the Color drop-down menu and choose New Texture (Figure 8-4). Browse to find the image file and then import it. Assign a name and dimensions, or accept the defaults. Once imported, the new material appears in Colors In Model.

Method 2: Import a Material As a Texture

If you want to use the material immediately to paint a face, import the image as a texture: From the main menu, choose File→Import, and make sure you are searching for image file types (as opposed to 3D models). Find the file you want to import, and select "Use as texture" (Figure 8-5).

The image is attached to your cursor, and you can apply it to a face. Click two corner points of the image to bring it in at the size you want (Figure 8-6). The Height or Width field at the bottom of the SketchUp window will tell you the dimension of the image. The image automatically tiles to fill the face (Figure 8-7). Once in use, the material appears in the In Model folder. In Windows, the thumbnail has a small white arrow in the corner to show that the material is being used.

--- Note ---

If you want to bring the image in at its defined size, double-click on the face to place the image. To place it by its center point, hold the Ctrl/Option key. To size it with a different aspect ratio, hold the Shift key.

Sometimes the tiling needs adjusting. Consider a picture frame with an empty face where the painting will go. When you import an image that is smaller than the face on which it is painted, it tiles (Figure 8-8). To fix the painting, move the sides of the frame (Figure 8-9).

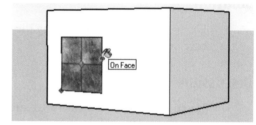

Figure 8-5

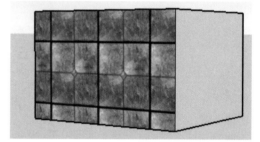

Figure 8-6

Figure 8-7

Figure 8-8

Figure 8-9

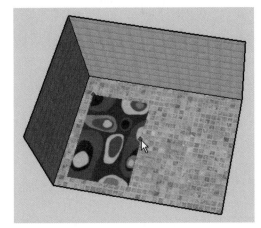

Figure 8-10

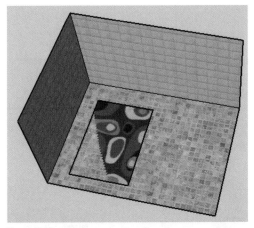

Figure 8-11

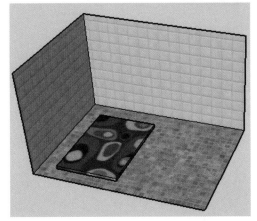

Figure 8-12

Figure 8-13

Method 3: Import a Material As an Image

If you want to import the material on its own face (rather than for painting an existing face), import it as an image. The material will not actually be a usable SketchUp material until you explode the image.

Note

Importing as an image is used mainly for digital photos, rather than for tiling materials. Using digital photos in your model is covered in Chapter 9.

From the main menu, choose File→Import, and make sure you are searching for image file types. Find the image you want to import and select "Use as image" (Figure 8-10).

One example of where you might want to import an image is for painting a rug onto a floor. (Make the floor and walls a group, so that the rug will not stick to the floor.) Click two corner points to define the image size, as shown in Figure 8-11. The Height or Width at the bottom of the SketchUp window will tell you the dimension of the image.

Note

If you want to bring the image in at its defined size, double-click on the face to place the image. To place it by its center point, hold the Ctrl/Option key. To size it with a different aspect ratio, hold the Shift key.

The image is not exactly a face; it is more like a group. It cannot be edited, positioned, or used on any other face. (You can, however, use the Scale, Rotate, and Move tools on an image.) To convert the image into a face, right-click on it and choose Explode. Now the face acts like a normal SketchUp face, and the material appears in the In Model folder.

Because the rug face is now on the same plane as the floor, SketchUp will have some confusion about which material should be displayed (Figure 8-12). This is sometimes called *Z-fighting*, which results in a shimmering effect that shows both materials when you orbit around.

To fix this, pull up the rug face very slightly so Sketch-Up will have no doubt about which face is on top (Figure 8-13).

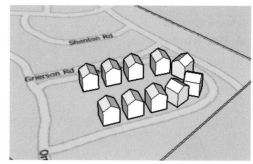

Figure 8-14

In some cases, you don't need to explode an image. If you don't plan on changing the face or using the material elsewhere, you can leave the image as is, such as a map on which you will show houses of a planned development project (Figure 8-14).

8.3 Creating Material Collections

Problem

You have materials in your model that you want to easily access in future models.

Solution

Save the materials as a new collection (Windows) or folder (Mac).

Discussion

Creating a collection or folder of materials in your model is the best way to be able to provide future access to the materials you have compiled. This is useful if you have created your own set of custom materials, or want to save collections of downloaded materials found in the 3D Warehouse or via a web search.

Create a Material Collection in Windows

In Windows, a *collection* is a group of materials. A collection is basically a folder; you can open it as you would any of the folders in the Materials window. First, gather in your model the materials you want to save as a collection. Then click the arrow icon indicated in Figure 8-15 and choose "Save collection as" from the pop-up menu.

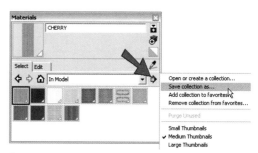

Figure 8-15

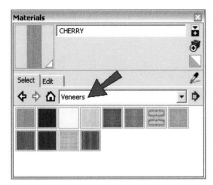

Figure 8-16

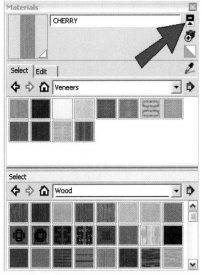

Figure 8-17

Browse to and select an existing folder or create a new one. In Figure 8-16, Veneers is the name of the collection and is listed as the current folder.

If you want this collection accessible in future files, click on the arrow icon again and choose "Add collection to favorites." After the collection is part of your favorites, it will always be listed in the folder drop-down menu, at least until you remove the collection from your favorites.

There is also a very nice drag-and-drop feature that enables you to easily place materials into folders. To add the second folder pane, click the icon indicated in Figure 8-17. In the second pane, open the folder you want, and you can drag materials from one folder to the other.

Create a Material Folder on the Mac

On the Mac, you can save the materials in your model to their own folder. This folder will be available in future files and can be opened as you would open any of the folders in the Colors window. First gather in your model the materials you want to save as a folder. Then click the List drop-down, and choose New (Figure 8-18). Assign a new name for the folder. This name then appears as the current folder.

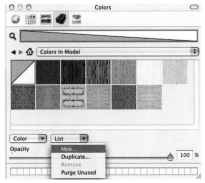

Figure 8-18

If you have a few materials you want to access often, you can save them so that they are always displayed in the Colors window. Simply drag a material's thumbnail into one of the empty spots in the color well, indicated in Figure 8-19.

Figure 8-19

8.4 Painting Multiple Faces

Problem

You want to paint more than one face at a time.

Solution

You can preselect faces, or use the Shift and Ctrl/Option keys while painting.

Discussion

If you want to paint several faces with the same material, clicking each face one at a time can be tedious. To avoid this, you can either select faces in advance or take advantage of the Shift and Ctrl/Option keys.

1. Download my Painting Multiple Faces model from the 3D Warehouse (Figure 8-20).

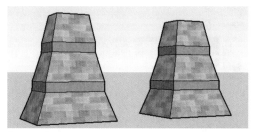

Figure 8-20

2. To change the material of the six front stone faces, select them in advance. Pick a new material and click any selected face. They are all painted at once (Figure 8-21).

3. Choose Undo to restore the stone faces.

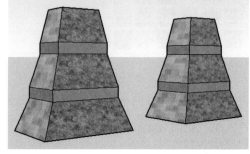

Figure 8-21

4. If you want to replace all of the stone faces with another material, first pick the new material. Then press and hold the Shift key and click any stone face. All of the stone faces in the model are replaced with the new material (Figure 8-22).

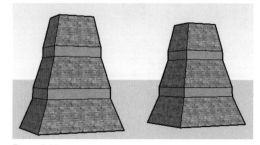

Figure 8-22

--- Note ---

You can also replace one material for another by preselecting all faces of a specific material. There are two ways to do this: right-click on the face in the model and choose Select→All with same material, or right-click on the material in the In Model folder of the Materials window and choose Select (Windows only). After all of the faces are selected, you can pick a new material and click any selected face.

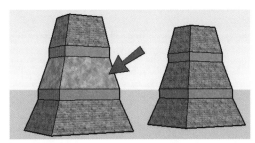

Figure 8-23

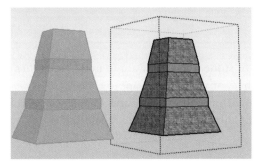

Figure 8-24

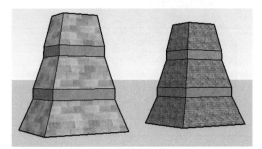

Figure 8-25

5. The Ctrl key (Option key on the Mac) can also be used to paint multiple faces. The difference is that Shift replaces *all* faces of a specific material, and Ctrl/Option replaces all *contiguous* faces of a specific material. To see what this means, pick a new material, press Ctrl/Option, and click the face indicated in Figure 8-23. This paints all faces within the same "stripe." The faces separated by the green stripes, and the faces on the other building, remain unchanged.

6. Choose Undo to return to the original stone faces.

7. If you want to replace all stone faces in one building but not the other, you can use a group. Groups isolate objects from material changes produced by using the Shift or Ctrl/Option keys. Make a group of one building (select the entire building, right-click on it, and choose Make Group from the pop-up menu).

8. Open the group for editing (activate Select and double-click the group). Pick a new material and use the Shift key to replace all of the stone faces (Figure 8-24).

9. Close the group (activate Select and click outside the group). The other building remains unchanged (Figure 8-25).

Note ──────────────────────────────

You could also paint the ungrouped building, which will not affect any faces within the group.

8.5   Changing Material Size and Color

Problem

You want to change the size and scale of a material.

Solution

Find the material in the In Model folder of the Materials window, and edit the material size and color parameters.

Discussion

If you paint faces with a tiling material such as brick or stone, you may want to make the stones or bricks appear larger or smaller, stretched or squashed, or you might want to change the material's base color. To make these changes, find the material in the In Model folder, select the material, and edit it to have a new size or color. You can also save your edited material by right-clicking and choosing Save As.

Note

This recipe demonstrates how to make simple adjustments to a material's size and color. If you want to change size, angle, skew, and placement, you need to position the texture. This is explained in Recipe 8.9.

---

1. Download my Edit Textures model from the 3D Warehouse (Figure 8-26).

2. Open the In Model folder of the Materials window, to see the two included materials.

Note

This example has only two materials, but if your model has many materials, it might be difficult to find the thumbnail for the material you want to edit. To find this material, hold the Alt key while the Paint tool is active (Cmd key on the Mac), and click a face in the model that has the material you want to edit. The thumbnail will then be highlighted in the In Model folder.

---

3. Double-click the brick material, which opens the editing parameters. The name of the image file is listed here (Figure 8-27).

4. To make the bricks appear larger, type a greater size in either the Width or the Height field and press Enter.

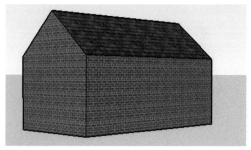

Figure 8-26

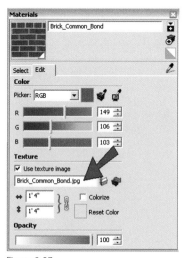

Figure 8-27

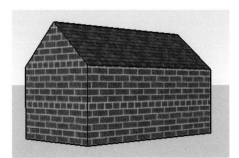

Figure 8-28

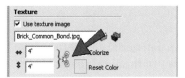

Figure 8-29

Figure 8-30

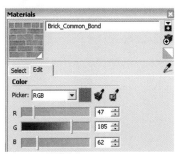

Figure 8-31

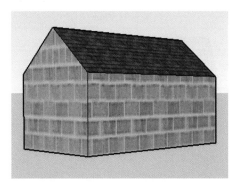

Figure 8-32

The bricks are now larger and easier to see (Figure 8-28).

5. When you change the material size, the default is to maintain the aspect ratio (the width changes by the same ratio as the height). If you want a new aspect ratio, click the lock icon (Figure 8-29) to "break" the connection between the two fields.

6. Now you can enter different values. Enter a higher value for Height, and the bricks become taller, almost square (Figure 8-30).

7. You can also change the base color of the material. Choose one of the color picker methods (Figure 8-31 shows RGB, or red, green, and blue) and set a new color. On the Mac, the color pickers (color wheel, color sliders, etc.) are available via icons at the top of the Edit Material window.

The bricks shown in Figure 8-32 are now green.

8. In Windows, when you are finished editing a material, click the Select tab. On the Mac, click Close at the bottom of the Edit Material window.

It is important to note that the edits you make this way affect only the In Model material. The original material, whether from the SketchUp library or imported from an image, remains unchanged.

You can save your new material if you'll want to use it in other models. Here's how:

- In Windows, right-click the new material's thumbnail in the Select tab, and choose either Save As to add it to a material library, or choose "Export texture image" to save it as an image file.

- On the Mac, edit the material you want to save and click the Edit Texture Image icon. This opens the image file in an external graphics editor, from which you can save the image file to your hard drive.

8.6 Copying a Material

Problem

You want to make a copy of an existing material, which will have a different color or size.

Solution

In Windows, create a new material based on the one you want to copy. On the Mac, use the Duplicate option.

Discussion

This technique is helpful if you want to create a different version of a material already in use, such as a different-color wood or larger bricks. You can make a copy of the existing material, edit the copy's size or colors, and use the new material in your model.

1. Download my Painting Multiple Faces model from the 3D Warehouse (Figure 8-33). The goal is to create a copy of the stone material and then apply this new material to some of the faces in the model.

2. Open the In Model folder of the Materials window, which has two materials. Select the material you want to change—the stone, in this case.

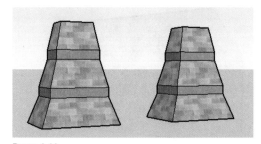

Figure 8-33

3. In Windows, click the Create Material icon indicated in Figure 8-34.

   On the Mac, right-click on the stone thumbnail and choose Duplicate. Enter a new name for the copy.

4. In Windows, you will see the Create Material window. Enter a new name (Figure 8-35), and edit the size or color (or both). When finished, click OK.

   On the Mac, double-click the thumbnail of the new material, and make the changes in the Edit Material window. Click Close when finished.

Figure 8-34

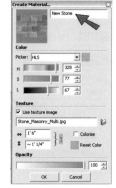

Figure 8-35

5. Find the new material in the In Model folder and use that material to paint some of the faces (Figure 8-36).

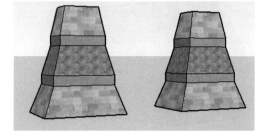

Figure 8-36

8.7 Using Translucent Materials

Problem

You want to make a material translucent.

Solution

Edit the material and adjust the Opacity slider.

Discussion

Translucent materials are generally based on solid colors and used to represent glass. But you can make any material translucent, even when based on a tiled image. (An example of this is a glass-block wall for a shower; you can see the blocks and also see inside the shower.)

When you paint a default-colored face with a translucent material, *both* sides of the faces are automatically painted, unlike with opaque materials. However, you can override this by painting one side either before or after the translucent material has been applied.

The main example demonstrates how to make any solid color or image-based material transparent. In the "Other Uses" section, you'll see how transparent materials can be used to model a glass sculpture and a stained-glass window, and how you can use the double-sidedness of faces to make a one-way window.

Figure 8-37

1. Download my Translucent Materials model from the 3D warehouse (Figure 8-37). The two windows are painted solid yellow, and the skylight is painted with a stone material.

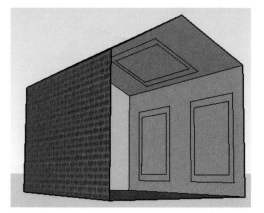

Figure 8-38

2. Orbit to see the inside view of the windows and skylight (Figure 8-38). All faces are painted with the default material.

3. Open the In Model folder of the Materials window and double-click the solid yellow thumbnail to edit it.

4. Drag the Opacity slider to the left (Figure 8-39). The material thumbnail at the top of the window splits diagonally, with the original color at the top and the translucent version at the bottom. While you're moving the slider, watch the yellow windows of the house to see their translucency vary (Figure 8-40).

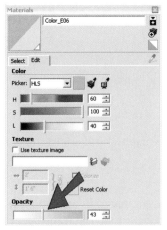

Figure 8-39

5. The next step is to make the skylight translucent. In Windows, stay in the Edit tab, make sure the Paint tool is still active, press the Alt key (the cursor should be an eyedropper), and click the stone material in the skylight. On the Mac, click Close to finish editing the yellow color, then double-click the stone material to edit it.

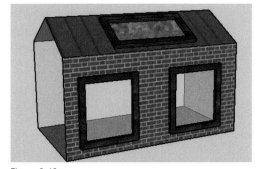

Figure 8-40

6. Adjust the Opacity slider for the stone material. Now you can see through the skylight, while still seeing a faint version of the stone pattern (Figure 8-41).

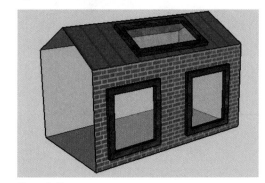

Figure 8-41

7. Orbit again to see the back faces of the windows. They are translucent on this side as well (Figure 8-42). This is because these faces originally had the default color. If you had already painted the back faces with a material or if you paint these faces now, the back faces will get that new material, whether translucent or not. The front faces will still be translucent.

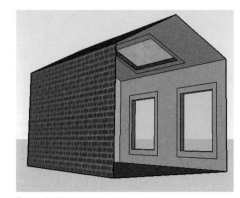

Figure 8-42

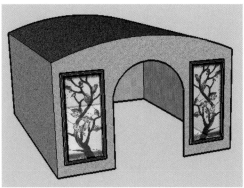
Figure 8-43

Other Uses

Here are some other examples of translucent materials.

Figure 8-43 shows two stained-glass windows. Each is painted with an image whose material was made translucent.

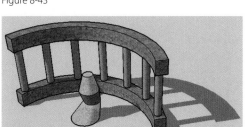
Figure 8-44

Figure 8-44 shows a glass-and-metal sculpture, in which the green bits of the sculpture are translucent. Shadows are turned on to demonstrate a point: with a high Opacity value, the translucent faces will cast shadows.

Figure 8-45

When the Opacity dips below 70 percent, translucent faces will not cast shadows (Figure 8-45).

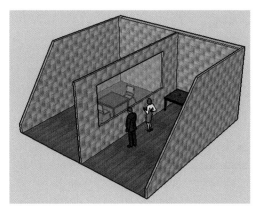
Figure 8-46

You can take advantage of SketchUp's double-sided faces to make a one-way window. In the interrogation room shown in Figure 8-46, the dividing window is painted translucent blue, so that the police and witnesses can view the suspect.

If the other side of the window face has the default material, it will become translucent, too (Figure 8-47)—which means the suspect can view his witnesses.

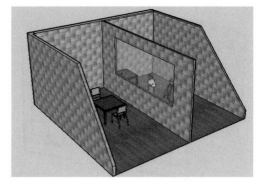

Figure 8-47

This is easily fixed: paint this side of the window with an opaque material (Figure 8-48). Now the suspect can't see out, but police and witnesses can still see in.

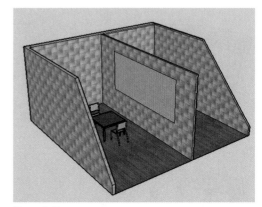

Figure 8-48

8.8 Painting Edges by Material

Problem

You want edges of a face to have the same material as the face.

Solution

Paint the edges and change the edge color to "By material."

Discussion

One way to achieve a more photorealistic look is to display edges in the same material as the faces they surround. Because edges can be common to multiple faces, SketchUp does not know which face material to match. Therefore, you have to paint edges just like faces. To display edges in the assigned materials, change the edge color to "By material" in the Styles window.

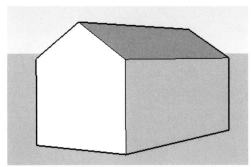

Figure 8-49

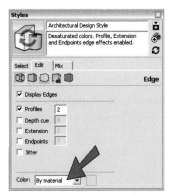

Figure 8-50

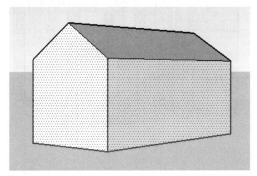

Figure 8-51

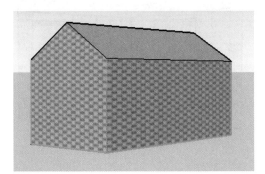

Figure 8-52

1. Start with a simple house with no faces painted (Figure 8-49).

2. Open the Styles window (Window→Styles) to the Edit tab, and click the Edge icon to open the Edge page. Change the edge color to "By material" (Figure 8-50).

3. Select the vertical faces of the house, plus all the edges of these faces except for those along the roof (Figure 8-51). The easiest way to do this is to hold Shift and double-click each face, which selects the faces and all edges, and then press Shift and click the edges along the roof to unselect them.

4. Pick a material and click any selected face or edge. All selected faces and edges get the new material (Figure 8-52).

5. Zoom in closely to see the material applied to the edge. The edges do not actually show the brick image, but rather get the material's base color.

—— **Note** ————————————————————

Another way to get a photorealistic look is to turn off edges altogether. To do so, uncheck the Display Edges and Profiles checkboxes in the Edge page of the Styles window. The look is similar to edges by material, but without the base-color outline.

————————————————————————

8.9 Positioning Textures: Fixed Pins

Problem

You want to adjust a material's location, angle, size, or skew.

Solution

Use texture positioning in Fixed Pins mode.

Discussion

If you need to make general adjustments to a material, such as overall size, aspect ratio, or color, you can simply edit the material (Recipe 8.5). If you need more specific adjustments, such as the starting location, angle, or skew, however, you can position the texture by using Fixed Pins mode.

The main example demonstrates how to adjust a tile backsplash so that tiles start and end in specific corners. In the "Other Uses" section, you'll see how fixed pins can be used to position bricks along a wall and make wallpaper with diagonal stripes.

1. Download my Backsplash model from the 3D Warehouse (Figure 8-53). The tile backsplash will be placed in the gray and white faces between the counter and cabinets.

Figure 8-53

2. Open the In Model folder of the Materials window and click the blue-and-gray tile material. Paint the two white faces with this tile (Figure 8-54).

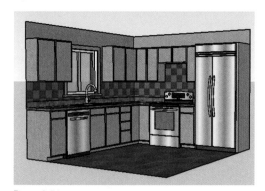

Figure 8-54

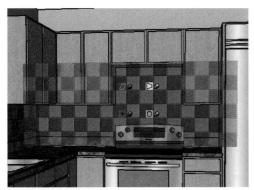

Figure 8-55

Figure 8-56

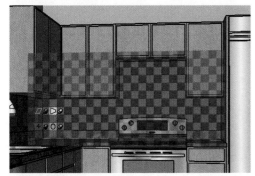

Figure 8-57

Figure 8-58

3. To start positioning, right-click on the backsplash wall next to the refrigerator and choose Texture→Position. Fixed pins are the red, blue, green, and yellow pins shown in Figure 8-55. These pins appear at the location on the face where you clicked to apply its material. (If you see four yellow pins, these are free pins. Right-click and choose Fixed Pins.) Each of the fixed pins has a purpose: red for moving, green for scaling and rotating, blue for shearing, and yellow for distorting.

Note

Free Pins mode, with four yellow pins, is used to fit an image to a face. This mode is described in Recipe 9.1.

---

4. You can move the tiles by clicking and dragging anywhere on the material, but the pins enable you to make more specific adjustments. To move the material so that a gray tile starts in the corner, click the red pin, keep the mouse button pressed, and drag this pin to the corner shown in Figure 8-56.

5. The green pin is used for adjusting both the scale and the angle. Drag the green pin straight to the left, maintaining the horizontal angle. This makes the entire material smaller (Figure 8-57).

6. The next step is to eliminate any partial tiles that appear on the right side of this face, close to the refrigerator. In addition to dragging pins, you can also place them in new locations. To "lift" the green pin, simply click it; do not keep the mouse button pressed. The green pin then becomes attached to your cursor. Click to "drop" the green pin at a point between two tiles (Figure 8-58).

7. Drag the green pin until it meets the edge close to the refrigerator (Figure 8-59). Now there is a neat row of whole tiles (no partial ones) along the backsplash.

Figure 8-59

8. Now look at one column of tiles. Your scale might be different, but Figure 8-60 shows about four tiles spaced between the counter and cabinet.

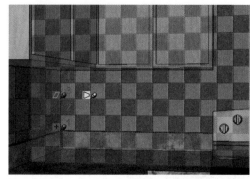
Figure 8-60

9. To get eight tiles instead of four, the image has to be sheared, or scaled in the vertical direction. To do this, lift the blue pin and place it just above the eighth tile in the column (Figure 8-61).

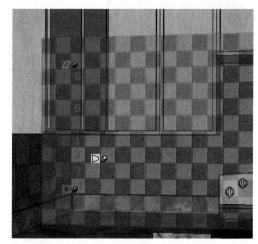
Figure 8-61

10. Drag the blue pin to the bottom of the cabinet (Figure 8-62). Now the tiles have half their original height.

> **Note**
>
> The yellow pin was not demonstrated here, but it is used for distorting the material: making the material appear to grow larger or smaller from right to left, or top to bottom.

Figure 8-62

Figure 8-63

Figure 8-64

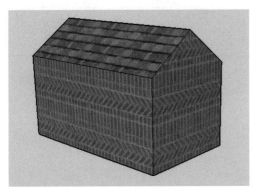
Figure 8-65

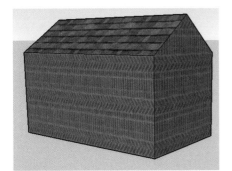
Figure 8-66

11. To end the positioning, right-click on the back-splash and choose Done.

    The face you positioned has the new scale, size, and location, but the other backsplash face, around the window, has the original material (Figure 8-63).

12. To apply the positioned material to the other back-splash, you first need to "sample" the new material. In Windows, click the eyedropper icon in the Materials window. On the Mac, press the Cmd key while the Paint tool is active (this also works in Windows if you press the Alt key).

13. The cursor should be an eyedropper symbol. Click the positioned backsplash and then click the original one. Now both backsplash faces have the positioned material (Figure 8-64).

Note

Positioning a texture does not change its definition in the In Model folder of the Materials window. If you apply the tile material to another face, it will appear at the original size.

Other Uses

Here are some other examples of positioning a material.

Figure 8-65 shows a house with the brick material applied to the walls, and Figure 8-66 shows the same walls after positioning. The red pin was used to start the diagonal bricks at the lower corner, the green pin was used to shrink the scale, and the blue pin was used to stretch the bricks so that there are three rows of diagonal bricks.

With fixed pins, redecorating is easy. Start with a room with vertical-striped wallpaper (Figure 8-67) and then use the green pin to rotate the material (Figure 8-68). Apply the positioned material to the other wall, and you have a whole new look (Figure 8-69).

> **— Note —**
>
> When using the green pin to rotate, you cannot specify a rotation angle. You can mark the angle in advance, however, by using the Protractor tool to create an angled construction line.

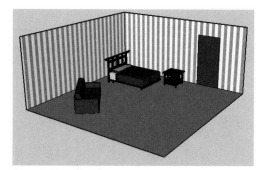

Figure 8-67

Figure 8-68

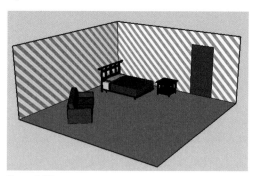

Figure 8-69

8.10 Positioning Texture on Round Faces

Problem

You want to position a material on a round face.

Solution

Show hidden edges, position the material on one segment, and then sample and apply this material to the rest of the face.

Discussion

Painting a material on a round face is easy: click the face, and the material wraps. Materials cannot be positioned on round faces, however, so if you want to make adjustments, you need to identify one segment and position the material on it. After the positioning is complete on that segment, you can sample the positioned material and apply it to the rest of the round face.

Figure 8-70

1. Download my Barber Pole model from the 3D Warehouse (Figure 8-70). A material with horizontal stripes is applied to the cylinder.

2. If you right-click on the cylinder, Texture is not on the pop-up menu. To position this material, you need to position it on one of the planar segments that compose the cylinder. To see these segments, display hidden edges (View→Hidden Geometry). The hidden edges are shown in dashed lines.

3. Right-click on one of the segments and choose Texture→Position. In Fixed Pins mode, drag the green pin to both rotate the stripes and make them larger (Figure 8-71).

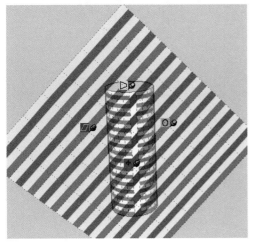

Figure 8-71

4. Right-click on the material and choose Done. Now the cylinder has the positioned material on one of its segments (Figure 8-72).

5. To apply the positioned material to the other segments, you first need to sample the new material. In Windows, click the eyedropper icon in the Materials window. On the Mac, press the Cmd key while the Paint tool is active (which also works in Windows if you press the Alt key). Click the segment with the positioned material.

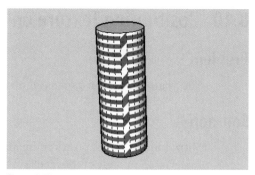

Figure 8-72

6. Choose View→Hidden Geometry again to turn off hidden edges. (You can also do this before sampling the positioned material.)

7. Click anywhere on the cylinder, and the new positioned material is applied to the whole cylinder (Figure 8-73).

8. Keep in mind that the positioned texture will become distorted if the size of the cylinder changes. To see what this means, make sure nothing is selected, activate Move, and click on the cylinder when you see a dashed vertical edge appear (Figure 8-74). You will probably have to move your mouse around the cylinder to get this vertical edge to appear.

 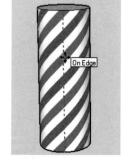

Figure 8-73   Figure 8-74

9. Drag this edge so that the cylinder radius increases or decreases. The material becomes distorted; within each segment, the material remains the same, but materials no longer align at the segments' edges (Figure 8-75).

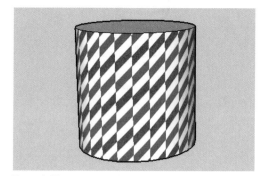

Figure 8-75

10. To fix this, just sample the material on any segment; you do not have to display hidden edges. Then click anywhere on the rest of the cylinder (Figure 8-76).

Figure 8-76

8.11 Creating and Editing a Unique Texture

Problem

You want to make changes to the material of a specific face.

Solution

Make a unique texture for that face and then edit the material.

Discussion

This technique is useful when you have more than one face with a specific material and you want to edit the material of only one of the faces. You make a unique texture for the face you want to change and then edit just that material.

The advantage to making a unique texture is that you can add detail to a particular face without changing all faces with the same material, and still keep the geometry simple. For example, you could edit a stone material to have different-colored stones, which would be difficult to achieve by adding extra geometry; you would need different materials for each new face.

In this example, you will use your graphics editor to add a sign and paint some of the bricks of just one building in a row of identical buildings.

Figure 8-77

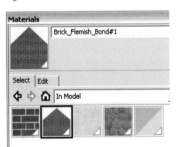

Figure 8-78

1. Download my Coffee Shop model from the 3D Warehouse (Figure 8-77). This is a row of shops. You will edit the material of the middle shop.

2. Right-click on the middle brick façade and choose Make Unique Texture from the pop-up menu. This adds a new material to the In Model folder of the Materials window, which has the exact shape of the face from which it was taken (Figure 8-78). The name of the new material is derived from the name of the original material, and you can change it if you want.

3. To edit this material, right-click either on the thumbnail in the Materials window (in Windows only) or on the material itself in the model. Choose Edit Texture Image from the pop-up menu.

4. The new material appears in your default graphics editor. Make some changes to the image. Figure 8-79 shows added text and some painted bricks.

Figure 8-79

5. Save the edited image and return to SketchUp. The middle façade now has the sign and painted bricks (Figure 8-80). Those yellow bricks would have taken more work to create within SketchUp and would have increased the file size.

Figure 8-80

—— **Note** ——

The thumbnail for the new material in the Materials window will reflect the changes you make in the graphics editor.

8.12 Using Alpha-Transparent Images

Problem

You want to paint with a material that has a transparent background.

Solution

Use an alpha-transparent image, position it to fit what you're painting, and hide edges if necessary.

Discussion

Images with alpha transparency have transparent backgrounds. Most graphics editors enable you to define a certain color as transparent. The .png file format is best for supporting this type of image. Alpha-transparent images are most commonly used for landscaping entourage (trees and plants), for images of people, and for objects such as fences and railings.

Alpha-transparent images can be used to paint faces just like any other image, and the transparent parts of the image will be transparent in SketchUp. Edges around alpha-transparent faces may appear to be hovering in space, but you can easily hide edges.

The greatest advantage of alpha-transparent images is that they enable you to reduce your file size by using graphics instead of geometry. A 3D tree has a much higher number of edges and faces than a 2D face painted with an alpha-transparent tree. A fence with repeated posts and pickets is much more complex than a 2D face painted with an alpha-transparent fence image.

Figure 8-81

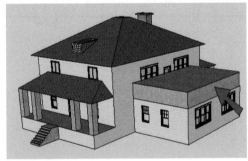

Figure 8-82

Figure 8-83

Note

You can use alpha-transparent images to create 2D Face Camera components, which are simple 2D cutouts that always face the same direction wherever you orbit, giving the look and feel of a 3D object. For more information and for a discussion of a problem with alpha images related to shadows, see Recipe 9.4.

The Fencing folder of the Materials window has a few materials with transparent backgrounds. To find more, you can search the 3D Warehouse for *alpha images* or its variations. The 3D Warehouse also has numerous models of alpha-transparent trees and plants.

In the main example, you will create a railing around a balcony by using an alpha-transparent image. In the "Other Uses" section, you'll see how a single alpha image can be used to simplify an Eiffel Tower model, and how to use an alpha image to make a ring of trees.

1. Download my Balcony House model from the 3D Warehouse (Figure 8-81).

2. The railing will be painted onto three vertical walls above the first floor. To make these walls, activate Push/Pull, press the Ctrl/Option key, and then pull up the first floor (Figure 8-82).

3. Erase the top face of this new box, which leaves just the three vertical walls (Figure 8-83).

4. Open the In Model folder of the Materials window and click the iron fence material. The background color of this image is defined to be transparent.

5. Paint one of the railing faces with the iron fence. You can see through the face, but the fence is the wrong size (Figure 8-84).

6. Use texture positioning in Fixed Pins mode, dragging the red pin to change the starting location, and dragging the green pin to change the scale, so that the image fits the face (Recipe 8.9). Right-click and choose Done when finished.

Figure 8-84

7. Sample the edited material (press the Alt key in Windows or Cmd on the Mac while the Paint tool is active, and click the positioned texture). Then paint the other two faces (Figure 8-85). Just like when you paint with translucent materials (Recipe 8.7), alpha-transparent images are applied to both sides of a face. (But you could override this by painting one side with a different material.)

Figure 8-85

8. To make the railing look more realistic, hide its vertical edges and top horizontal edges (select these edges, right-click on one of them, and choose Hide from the pop-up menu). Figure 8-86 shows the completed railing.

Figure 8-86

Figure 8-87

Other Uses

For a great example of how using an alpha-transparent image can reduce your file size, download Google's Eiffel Tower model from the 3D Warehouse (Figure 8-87). It looks complex, but it's actually a simple model painted with an alpha image. This model can be found in my 3D Warehouse collection for this chapter.

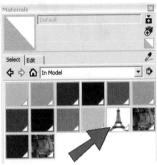

Figure 8-88

You can find the image in the In Model folder of the Materials window (Figure 8-88). This image was applied to all four sides, using material positioning in Free Pins mode to adjust the image to fit each face. Free Pins mode is described in Recipe 9.1.

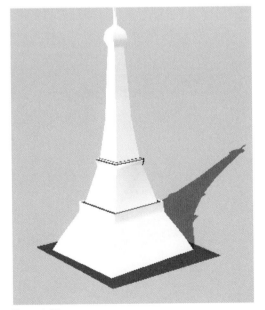

Figure 8-89

To see the unpainted model, switch from Shaded with Textures mode to Shaded mode (Figure 8-89).

You can also use a single alpha image of a tree to make a ring of trees. Figure 8-90 shows four vertical faces painted with a tiling tree image.

When the edges of the faces are hidden, it looks like a group of trees.

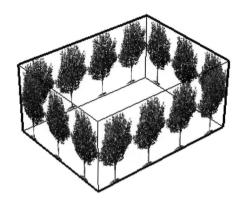

Figure 8-90

You can use Push/Pull on the faces to make a larger or smaller ring of trees (Figure 8-91).

Figure 8-91

CHAPTER 9

Modeling with Digital Photos

Continuing the discussion of painting and materials from Chapter 8, this chapter focuses on using digital photos to paint faces in your model, adding photo-realism and saving modeling time.

Using photos to paint faces can reduce the number of geometric elements you need to create. For example, you can take the time and effort to model geometrically accurate windows on the side of a building, or can you simply paint the face with a photo of the side of that building. (If you don't have an actual photo, a rendering works well, too.)

In addition to saving modeling time, using photos this way can greatly reduce file size. For this reason, Google encourages 3D Warehouse contributors to use digital photos on their models whenever possible. Many of the models in the 3D Warehouse are photorealistic, as are many 3D buildings in Google Earth. Some of these models represent extremely complex structures but are modeled in simple geometry painted with photos. To see some examples, open Google Earth with the 3D Buildings layer turned on, and explore any large city. Many buildings are plain gray, but a large number are painted. (For more information, see Chapter 13.)

This chapter covers all you need to know about painting with digital photos, including how to:

- Fit a photo to a face
- Use photos to make 2D components that look 3D
- Edit an imported photo
- Use photos to create 3D models
- Use Photo Match

—— **Note** ————————————

For the basics of where to find materials and images and how to get them into your model, see Recipes 8.1 and 8.2.

9.1 Positioning Textures with Free Pins

Problem

You want to fit a material to a face.

Solution

Use texture positioning in Free Pins mode.

Discussion

Free Pins mode is used to adjust a material so that it fits perfectly within a face. It is most commonly used to fit images, such as pictures of windows, doors, façades, or furniture. Free-pin positioning is essentially distorting an image by pulling its corners, to constrain the image to a face.

Note

The other positioning mode is Fixed Pins, which is used to adjust the location, scale, and skew of a tiling material. Fixed Pins mode is demonstrated in Recipe 8.9.

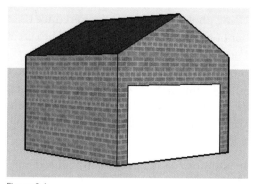
Figure 9-1

The main example demonstrates how to fit an image of a door to a face. In the "Other Uses" section, you'll see how fixed pins can fit images to the façade of a building or to faces of a bureau.

1. Download my Custom Door model from the 3D Warehouse (Figure 9-1). A picture of a custom garage door will be painted on the white face.

2. Open the In Model folder of the Materials window, which contains the photo of the door. Paint the door photo onto the face (Figure 9-2).

   The scale and location are not correct, and the lower edge of the door in the photo is not horizontal. You will need to adjust the photo to fit within the door face.

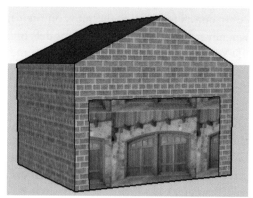
Figure 9-2

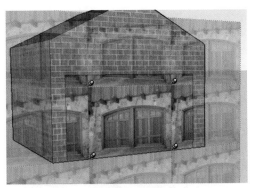

Figure 9-3

Figure 9-4

Figure 9-5

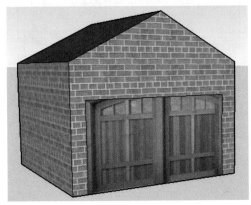

Figure 9-6

3. Right-click on the door and choose Texture→Position. If you see four multicolored pins (fixed pins), right-click again and choose Fixed Pins to deselect it. Free pins are all yellow and appear in each corner of one of the tiled images (Figure 9-3).

4. Free pins are free because they can be picked up and placed anywhere and then dragged into an exact position. To "lift" a pin, just click it. Then click again to "drop" it where you want it on the image. To place a pin accurately, you usually need to zoom in very closely to find the correct points on the photo. Using the Zoom window tool and the Previous View tool can speed this process up immensely. In Figure 9-4, one pin was placed at each corner of the rectangular part of the door, because these points are easy to find. (It would be harder to place a pin at the top of the arch.)

— **Note** ————————————————

When you lift and drop pins, look for dotted blue helper lines that indicate when a pin is horizontal or vertical from another pin.

5. Drag each pin to a corner of the door face in the model (Figure 9-5).

— **Note** ————————————————

Some users prefer to place all of the pins first and then drag all of them into place. Others prefer to place a pin and drag it, and then repeat for subsequent pins. Both methods work fine; it's a matter of preference.

6. If you need to tweak the image for a better fit, move and drag pins as needed. When the photo looks correct, right-click on the door and choose Done. The rectangular part of the door looks good, but the top of the photo is cut off (Figure 9-6).

7. Use the Move tool to move the top edge of the door up, passing the top of the door in the photo (Figure 9-7).

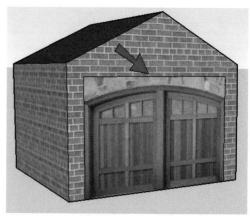

Figure 9-7

8. Use the Arc tool to trace the top of the door in the photo. Then use the Eraser to trim the rest of the door face. This results in a single door face with the correct photo (Figure 9-8).

Figure 9-8

9. For a more realistic garage door, use Push/Pull to push in the door slightly. The sides of the opening will have the same material as the door, so repaint them with the blue bricks (Figure 9-9).

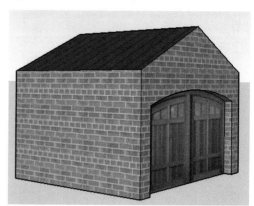

Figure 9-9

Figure 9-10

Figure 9-11

Other Uses

Free-pin positioning can be used for a multitude of models. For example, Figure 9-10 began as a simple box model, and then each face was painted with a photo of a building façade. Compare the file size of this painted box (about 2.5MB because the graphic files themselves are large) with the 5MB size of an actual geometric model including all of those windows, doors, and ornamentation. Using graphics of smaller file size can keep your file size quite low.

Figure 9-11 is a beautiful model of a Japanese bureau. Each face is painted with a photo taken of a real piece of furniture.

9.2 Editing a Photo

Problem

You want to make changes to a photo used in your model.

Solution

Use the Edit Texture Image option and make the changes in your graphics editor. The image will be updated in SketchUp automatically.

Discussion

If a material image in your model needs to be changed, you certainly could alter the original graphic file. But what if your changes are minor? Or what if the changes apply only to the current model? What if you want the image unaltered for other models? SketchUp provides a quick fix: the Edit Texture Image option exports the image to your default graphics editor, in which you can make your edits. Save the edited image, and the change appears in SketchUp automatically. The original image is untouched; the changes apply only to the image within the current SketchUp file.

In the main example, you'll see how to fix an image on a billboard. In the "Other Uses" section, you'll see how to make a change to a tiling stone image.

1. Download my Graffiti model from the 3D Warehouse (Figure 9-12). The antigraffiti billboard has been defaced with, well, graffiti. Also, the bottom of the photo has some green leaves sticking out.

Figure 9-12

2. Right-click on the billboard face and choose Texture→Edit Texture Image. (In Windows, this option is also available when you click on the image thumbnail in the In Model folder of the Materials window. On the Mac, when you edit a material, there is an icon for Edit Texture Image at the bottom of the Edit Material window.)

   The original photo used to make the billboard opens in your default graphics editor. (You can set the default editor in the Applications page of the Preferences window.)

3. Make the necessary changes to the photo. Figure 9-13 shows the word *Fun* removed, and the greenery at the bottom trimmed above the billboard's frame.

Figure 9-13

4. Save and close the photo you edited and return to SketchUp. The billboard now shows the improved photo (Figure 9-14).

   The image in the In Model folder is updated as well, but choosing Undo will bring back the original, unchanged image. The changes have not affected the source graphic file, only the graphic internal to the current SketchUp model.

Figure 9-14

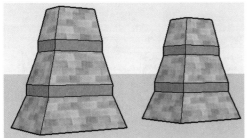

Figure 9-15

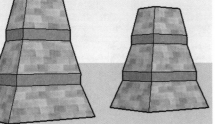

Figure 9-16

Other Uses

You can also edit a tiled image. Figure 9-15 shows two buildings with stone material. Edit Texture Image is used to add a blue and red stone. After you've saved the image and returned to SketchUp, the tiled image has been updated on all stone faces (Figure 9-16).

9.3 Adding Faces to Patch an Image

Problem

You want to patch over parts of an image in your model.

Solution

Draw a face over the area you want to patch, and position the texture within the new face.

Discussion

With the patching method, you do not edit the image you want to change; instead you add faces over the parts you want to patch, and position the materials within those faces. In the main example, you will see how to add faces to patch over some old windows, so that new windows can be inserted. The "Other Uses" section demonstrates how this technique can be applied to remove a logo from a truck.

Figure 9-17

1. Download my New Windows model from the 3D Warehouse (Figure 9-17). This is a renovation scenario, in which the windows on the wall indicated by the arrow will be removed and replaced with new windows.

2. Draw a rectangle around the first window, as shown in Figure 9-18.

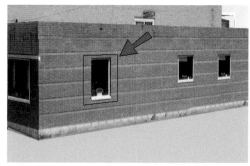

Figure 9-18

3. Position the material in this rectangle, using either Fixed or Free Pins. In either mode, click and drag the material itself (don't drag a pin) slightly to the left or right, so that the face contains only plain bricks, keeping mortar lines aligned (Figure 9-19).

Figure 9-19

4. Right-click on the positioned material and choose Done. Now the material looks seamless, and the window is removed, but you can still see the edges of the new face (Figure 9-20).

Figure 9-20

5. If you erase these edges, the window in the photo will return. So hide the edges instead. You can select the four edges, right-click on one of them, and choose Hide from the pop-up menu, or you can use the Eraser with the Ctrl/Option key pressed and click all four edges. Now you can't tell there used to be a window there (Figure 9-21).

Figure 9-21

Figure 9-22

Figure 9-23

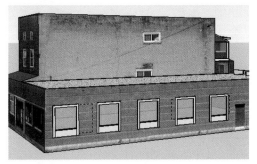

Figure 9-24

6. Repeat this patching technique for the remaining windows on the wall (Figure 9-22).

7. Insert new windows on this wall. The windows shown in Figure 9-23 are available in the In Model folder of this model's Components window. This demonstrates one of the problems you can encounter when using faces to patch an image: the wall is no longer a single face, and the windows do not cut the wall properly.

8. To fix the broken wall, first display the dashed lines indicating hidden edges (View→Hidden Geometry). The dashed lines indicate the patching faces you added.

9. Select the wall and all new windows, right-click on any selected face, and choose Intersect→Intersect Selected from the pop-up menu. This creates intersection edges on all faces where they meet the windows. Then you can erase the edges that fall within the new windows (Figure 9-24).

The patching method is a great quick fix for minor touch-ups, especially if you prefer not to edit your graphics. But if the patched face might be changed afterward, such as getting new windows, editing the image in advance (Recipe 9.2) might prove less work than repairing a patched face.

Other Uses

Figure 9-25

You can also use the patching method to remove a logo from a truck. In Figure 9-25, the blank space above the logo is narrow. So create a face around the entire logo and divide it in half, so that each half can be positioned with a new strip of "blank" truck.

Figure 9-26

Position the material in each narrow rectangle to cover the logo. Then hide the edges around each new rectangle (Figure 9-26).

9.4 Using Images to Make Face Camera Components

Problem

You want to use a 2D image to represent a 3D object.

Solution

Paint the image on a face. Trace a border around the image, trim away the rest of the face, and hide the remaining edges. Then make this face into a Face Camera component.

Discussion

Certain types of objects in your model can be represented by 2D images that give the "feel" of a 3D object, because they always face you no mater how you orbit the model. Good candidates are such objects as people, trees, plants, street lamps, trash bins—objects that look basically the same as you orbit around them (Figure 9-27).

In this example, you will create a Face Camera component of a tree. The tree image is an alpha-transparent image, which means its background is transparent (Recipe 8.12).

Figure 9-27

> **Note**
>
> *Face Camera* components are also sometimes called *Face Me* components. If you are searching the 3D Warehouse for models like these, try both terms in your search.

1. Download my Face Camera Tree model from the 3D Warehouse (Figure 9-28). The alpha-transparent tree is painted on a vertical face next to the house. Note that the shadow of the tree is a rectangle; SketchUp's shadows do not recognize transparent images.

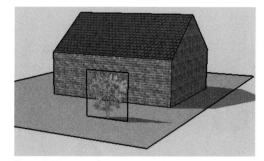

Figure 9-28

2. Orbit to a view like the one in Figure 9-29. The tree looks like a cardboard cutout at this angle. Plus you can see the face's edges.

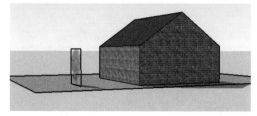

Figure 9-29

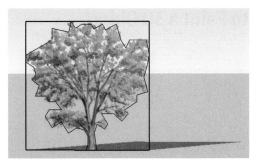

Figure 9-30

Figure 9-31

Figure 9-32

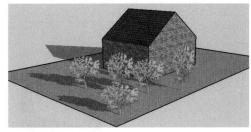

Figure 9-33

3. To get more accurate shadows, you need to trim the face to approximate the shape of the tree. Use the Line or Arc tool to trace around the tree (Figure 9-30). Accuracy is not important for shadows, because nobody notices the level of detail in a shadow, only its general shape. When tracing, be sure to look for the *On Face* inference. Otherwise, you may be drawing lines out of the plane of the face.

—— **Note** ——————————————

Because this image has a transparent background, you don't have to trace around it exactly; the transparent background means that extra space around the leaves won't be noticed. If you were trimming around an image with a visible background, you would want to trace the border more accurately, so that no background would show. If black edges are hard to see against the image, you can change the edge color in the Styles window (Edit tab, Edge page).

———————————————————————————

4. Use the Eraser tool to trim the corners of the rectangular face, so that only the tree shape remains (Figure 9-31). The shadow now looks tree-shaped.

5. The next step is to hide the edges around the tree. Activate Select and double-click the tree, which selects both the face and its edges. Then press and hold the Shift key to deselect the face, leaving only the edges selected. Right-click on an edge and choose Hide from the pop-up menu. The tree looks quite natural (Figure 9-32).

6. Now the tree can be made into a component. Activate the Select tool and double-click the tree, which selects both the face and its hidden edges. Right-click on the tree and choose Make Component.

7. In the Create Component window, select Always Face Camera, make sure Replace Selection with Component is selected, but leave Shadows Face Sun off to ensure that the shadows appear properly.

8. Now you can insert more trees, which cast proper shadows and always face you when you orbit around. Using various scales for the trees produces a nice, random look (Figure 9-33).

—— **Note** ——————————————

For details on how to use the Scale tool to make random-looking components, see Recipe 7.9.

———————————————————————————

9.5 Using Free Pins and a Single Image to Paint a 3D Object

Problem

You want to use a 2D image to paint an unpainted 3D object.

Solution

Paint the image onto one face, and use free-pin positioning to fit the image to the face. Then paint the remaining face based on the material of the first face.

Discussion

Recipe 9.1 demonstrates how to fit an image to a face. Based on that technique, you can create a photorealistic model by painting each face of the model with the appropriate photo. This means that, ideally, you should have one photo for each face (or at least one photo for each elevation and plan view), and your unpainted model should have accurate dimensions. But what if you have only one photo to work with?

If that one photo shows at least two faces of an object, you can use it to paint all faces that appear in the photo. With this technique, you first paint and position the image to one face of the unpainted model. If necessary, add or remove geometry to accommodate the picture. Then you can use that positioned material as a basis for painting the remaining faces that are shown in the photo.

Two examples are used to demonstrate this technique. In Example 1, you will paint a barn, and in Example 2, a truck.

Example 1: Barn with Free-Pin Positioning

In this example, you start with an unpainted box. After painting and positioning the front face, you will complete the model geometry. Then you will paint the rest of the faces based on the material of the front face.

1. Download my Barn model from the 3D Warehouse. It is an unpainted box in the approximate shape of a barn.

2. Open the In Model folder of the Materials window. This folder contains the image with which the barn will be painted. The photo shows three faces: the front, side, and roof of the barn. Paint the image onto the front face of the barn (Figure 9-34).

— **Note** —————————————

This technique requires an unpainted model to start. If you want to create your model from scratch based on a photo, use Photo Match as described in Recipe 9.6. You can also use Photo Match on an unpainted model as explained in Recipe 9.7.

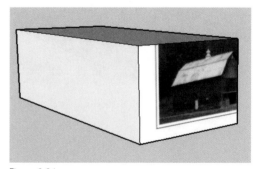

Figure 9-34

Figure 9-35

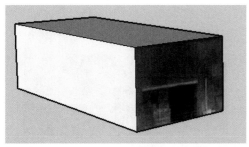

Figure 9-36

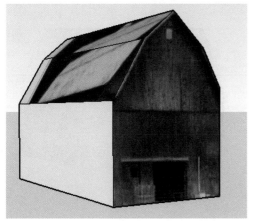

Figure 9-37

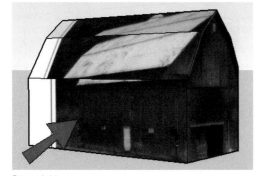

Figure 9-38

3. Position this material by using free pins, placing one pin at each corner of the rectangular part of the barn's front and dragging the pin to the corner of the model face (Figure 9-35).

4. Tweak the image if needed. Then right-click on the image and choose Done. The front face of the box is now painted with part of the front face of the barn (Figure 9-36).

5. To accommodate the rest of the front face, pull up the top of the box until it reaches the top of the roof in the photo. Trace the outline of the roof on the front face (there are four edges). Then push back the corners of the front face, to complete the roof faces (Figure 9-37).

   When tracing the roof, ideally the top of the roof in the photo would meet the midpoint of the top edge, and the roof itself would be perfectly symmetric. But it's hard to achieve that sort of accuracy with photos. You can base your tracing entirely on the photo and get slightly inaccurate geometry, or you can create accurate geometry and use free pins to tweak the photo so that it fits better. It's nearly impossible to get perfect results, but you can get pretty close. (If accuracy is important, it's ideal to start with a dimensionally accurate model on which to paint. Fitting the model to a photo works, too, but usually requires more steps and tweaking.)

6. Sample the material on the front face (press Alt in Windows or Cmd on the Mac while using the Paint tool, and click the front face). Then click the side face (Figure 9-38). This material is already correctly positioned along the edge shared with the front face, but the other two corners of the image need to be positioned.

7. Use free-pin positioning on this face and drag into place the two pins shown in Figure 9-39.

Figure 9-39

8. Paint the two roof faces the same way: sample the material either on the side or front and click the roof face (Figure 9-40). If you paint the lower roof face first, you will have to adjust only one pin per face.

Figure 9-40

9. To paint the other side of the barn, sample the painted side and then click the unpainted side. The resulting material is a mirror image of the original. Paint the roof faces on this side by sampling the side face below them. The finished barn is shown in Figure 9-41.

Figure 9-41

Example 2: Truck with Free-Pin Positioning

In this example, you start with an unpainted model of a truck and use a photo to paint the side and front. You will modify geometry at the front and bottom of the model to accommodate the whole photo.

1. Download my Truck model from the 3D Warehouse. It is an unpainted box in the approximate shape of a truck.

2. Paint the side of the truck with the image in the In Model folder of the Materials window (Figure 9-42).

Figure 9-42

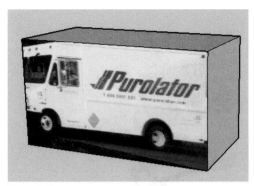

Figure 9-43

Figure 9-44

Figure 9-45

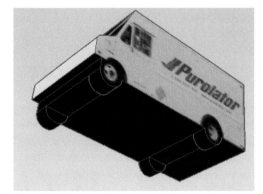

Figure 9-46

3. Use free pins to fit the rectangular part of truck to the side face.

4. Pull out the front of the box so that you can see the entire side of the truck in the photo, and pull down the bottom so that you can see the tires (Figure 9-43).

5. The next step is to trace edges around the tires and along the side, but if your default edge color is black, the tracing edges will be difficult to see against the image. To change the edge color, open the Styles window to the Edit tab and Edge page, and set a contrasting color for edges.

6. Use lines and arcs to trace around the side of the truck, including the tires. (You could also use the Circle tool for the tires.) The half-circles for the tires should be separate faces. Push back the extra faces (Figure 9-44).

7. To model the tires, use Push/Pull with the Ctrl/Option key on the half-circle faces. (The Ctrl/Option key creates a new face; without Ctrl/Option, you will just push the tires into the truck.) This creates the edges on the other side of the tire (Figure 9-45).

8. Repeat this Push/Pull operation for the other tires. Then trim the bottom of the truck to leave only the tires. Figure 9-46 shows the tires and truck bottom painted black.

9. To paint the front of the truck, sample the material on the side and click the front face (Figure 9-47).

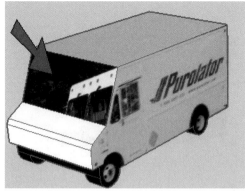

Figure 9-47

10. Adjust this face by using free pins, and paint the remaining faces by using the same technique. Figure 9-48 shows the completed truck with edges turned off.

Figure 9-48

9.6 Using Photo Match to Model a 3D Object

Problem

You want to use a 2D image to model a 3D object from scratch.

Solution

Import the photo as a matched photo. Use points on the photo to set the origin and axes for the model. Then draw your model based on the photo.

Discussion

Starting with a blank file (no existing geometry) and a photo that shows at least two faces of your model, you can use Photo Match to achieve the same results as you accomplished with Recipe 9.5's free-pin positioning technique. With Photo Match, you set the model's origin and axes based on data in the photo. After these are established, you can trace your model based on the photo, and then project textures from the photo onto faces in the model.

Photo Match is great for a quick, preliminary design, for which you have a photo but no accurate measurements or dimensions. It is not extremely accurate, however. If you are creating a serious photorealistic model, the ideal solution is to start with a geometrically accurate model for which each face (or elevation and plan views) has its own photo. In this recipe you'll re-create the barn and truck from the free-pin positioning examples, so you can compare the results.

Example 1: Barn with Photo Match

In this example, you will open the barn model used in Recipe 9.5's "Example 1: Barn with Free-Pin Positioning," and save its barn image to your hard drive. That image will be used to model the barn in a new file.

1. Download my Barn model from the 3D Warehouse. It contains one image in the In Model folder of the Materials window.

Figure 9-49

2. In Windows, right-click on this image and choose Export Texture Image from the pop-up menu. Save the image to your hard drive. On the Mac, edit the texture and click the Edit Texture Image icon. This opens the image in an external editor, from which you can save it to your hard drive.

3. Start a new SketchUp file and then choose File→Import from the main menu. Make sure you are looking for graphic file types and browse to the barn photo you saved. Import it as a new matched photo (Figure 9-49).

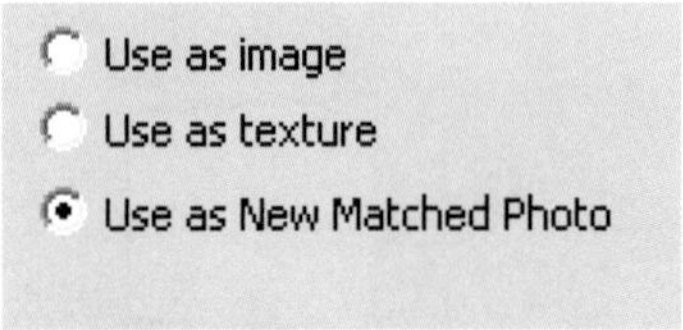

   Figure 9-50 shows the photo of the barn with two red and green axis bars, a blue axis to set the vertical direction, and a yellow origin point.

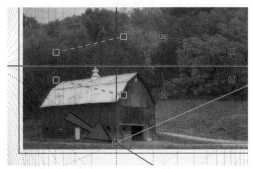

Figure 9-50

4. The origin should be placed at the corner nearest to the camera, on the ground. Click and drag the yellow origin point and place it on the ground where the front and side faces meet (Figure 9-51).

5. The red and green axis bars are used to define the red and green axes of the model. Use lines and points in the photo to place and orient these bars. To maximize accuracy, it's good practice to place the bars as far apart as possible, and to use the longest possible distance along each bar. Figure 9-52 shows the red bars along the top and bottom of the side, and the green bars at the top and bottom of the front.

Figure 9-51

Figure 9-52

6. Check to see that the blue axis is vertical. When the axes look right, right-click on the image and choose Done.

Figure 9-53

   There is now a scene tab at the top of your Sketch-Up window (Figure 9-53). If you orbit out of the current view, you will lose the barn picture. To get the picture back, you can click this tab.

7. The axes of your model are now aligned to the photo. Use the Line tool to trace over the rectangular part of the front of the barn, keeping the edges in the respective axis directions (Figure 9-54).

Figure 9-54

8. Push this face back to the back of the barn (Figure 9-55).

9. To pull the box up to add the roof, you first need to orbit out of the current view, which means the photo will disappear. Because you can no longer see the photo, push the top up by a large distance, higher than you know it needs to be.

Figure 9-55

10. Click the scene tab to return to the view that has the photo. The model covers the picture, so switch to X-Ray mode so that you can see the photo through the model.

11. Trace the roof lines on the front face (Figure 9-56).

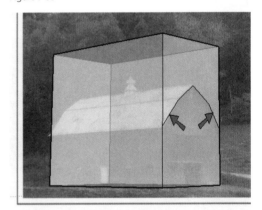

Figure 9-56

Figure 9-57

Figure 9-58

Figure 9-59

Figure 9-60

12. Push back the top of the box to complete the roof (Figure 9-57) and then switch back to Shaded with Textures mode.

Note

Here's another way you could complete the roof: starting from the initial box, orbit away from the photo and start the Push/Pull operation. Then return to the photo and complete the Push/Pull. Then you would trace the roof edges and push back faces as described in the preceding steps.

---

13. To paint all of the visible faces, click Project Texture from Photo, found in the Sketch Over window. (You can also paint an individual face by right-clicking it and choosing Project Photo.)

    The photo is projected on these faces, with more or less the correct positioning (Figure 9-58). If any faces need adjustment, you can position their material by using free pins.

14. Orbit out of the current view. The photo disappears, but the barn faces remain painted (Figure 9-59).

Example 2: Truck with Photo Match

In this example, you will open the truck model used in Recipe 9.5's "Example 2: Truck with Free-Pin Positioning," and save its image to your hard drive. That image will be used to model the truck in a new file.

1. Download my Truck model from the 3D Warehouse. It contains one image in the In Model folder of the Materials window.

2. Save the image to your hard drive as you did in step 2 of Example 1.

3. Import the truck image as a matched photo, and set the axes and origin (see steps 3 and 4 of Example 1 for tips). Figure 9-60 shows the origin set at the lower corner of the side of the truck, which is actually in the middle of the side face. It was placed here so that the blue axis could be checked relative to the top of the truck.

Note

You could also move the origin so that the side of the truck starts at the origin. As long as the red and green axes are set correctly, the origin can be anywhere, and the model geometry can be adjusted accordingly.

---

4. Trace the side of the truck, and push the face back to the edge of the truck in the photo (Figure 9-61). The resulting box will be too large, but you'll adjust it later.

Figure 9-61

5. Right-click on the side face and choose Project Photo from the pop-up menu. This paints the photo on the portion of the side face you modeled so far (Figure 9-62).

Figure 9-62

6. Following the same method outlined in Recipe 9.5's Example 2, pull the box to make more space where needed (front and bottom). Change the edge color, trace around the side of the truck, and then push back the extra faces (Figure 9-63).

Figure 9-63

7. To paint the rest of the truck, click the scene tab to return to the view with the photo. Select the faces that need correct photos, right-click on one of them, and choose Project Photo. Or you can click Project Textures from Photo on the Sketch Over window, which paints all visible faces at once. (You can overwrite the existing material or not, because the material for that face has not changed.) The front faces are now painted, but the model is too wide (Figure 9-64).

Figure 9-64

Figure 9-65

8. Orbit to a new view and push in the wide side to accommodate the photo (Figure 9-65).

9.7 Using Photo Match to Paint an Existing Model

Problem

You want to paint an existing model by using Photo Match.

Solution

Import a photo as a matched photo and set the axes and origin. Then scale the model to match the photo. If a second photo is available, orbit to the view in that photo, import the photo and set its axes, and size the model.

Discussion

In addition to creating models from scratch (Recipe 9.6), Photo Match can be used to paint existing models, producing similar results to free-pin positioning (Recipe 9.5). Photo Match is great for quick, preliminary designs, for which you have a photo or two plus a geometrically accurate model. Photo Match is not extremely accurate, however. If you are creating a serious photorealistic model, the ideal solution is to start with a geometrically accurate model for which each face (or elevation and plan views) has its own photo. But because accurate data is not always available, Photo Match is a great "quick fix" solution.

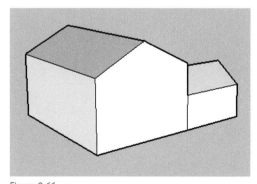

Figure 9-66

1. Download my White House model from the 3D Warehouse. This is a geometrically accurate model of a house. Orbit to the view shown in Figure 9-66.

> **Note**
>
> This example uses an unpainted model, but you can also use Photo Match to paint over a model's current materials.

2. Open the In Model folder of the Materials window, which contains two photos of the house. Save both of these images to your hard drive. (In Windows, right-click on each image and choose Export Texture Image. On the Mac, edit the texture and then click the Edit Texture Image icon. This opens the image in an external editor, from which you can save the image.)

3. Import WhiteHouse1.jpg as a matched photo (Figure 9-67).

Figure 9-67

4. It is easier to adjust the axis bars and origin when the model is out of the way. In the Match Photo window, deselect Model. The model is now hidden.

5. Adjust the red and green axis bars, and place the origin in the nearest corner (Figure 9-68).

Figure 9-68

6. Select the Model option in the Match Photo window to bring back the model. The model is now located at the correct corner (the origin) but is still the wrong size (Figure 9-69).

Figure 9-69

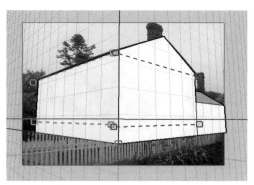

Figure 9-70

Figure 9-71

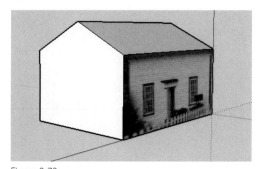

Figure 9-72

Figure 9-73

7. To adjust the model's scale to fit the photo, click and drag along any of the three axes on the photo (Figure 9-70).

8. When the positioning is complete, right-click on the image and choose Done.

9. In the Sketch Over window, click Project Textures from Photo, which paints the visible faces. When you orbit out of the view, the photo disappears, but the faces should be painted more or less correctly (Figure 9-71).

—— **Note** ————————————————————————

For minor adjustments to the photos, you can position the texture and tweak the free pins.

10. The second photo is of a different view of the house. Before you import this photo, it is important to orbit so that you are looking at approximately the same view as the second photo (Figure 9-72).

—— **Note** ————————————————————————

The origin you use for the first Photo Match photo will be used for the entire model. So for subsequent Photo Match photos, you must be able to see the origin in your model. This means you cannot use a front view and a back view, because you won't be able to see the origin from both views.

11. Import WhiteHouse2.jpg. This creates another scene tab, and there is a new set of axis bars to adjust.

12. Keep the origin in place, hide the model, and adjust the axis bars. Then bring the model back and scale it to match the photo (Figure 9-73).

13. Project the textures. If you overwrite the existing material on the side of the house, you will get a nicer view of the flowering bush in the corner (Figure 9-74).

Figure 9-74

CHAPTER 10

Modeling with Exact Dimensions

When SketchUp was first introduced, the idea behind it was that you could produce great-looking computer models representing your rough sketches, rather than scratch out your designs on the back of a napkin. Whereas most conventional CAD applications require you to know the exact sizes of all your model's objects, in SketchUp you can design "by eye."

What many SketchUp users don't take advantage of, however, is that the application also enables you to create entire models using exact dimensions, despite its deceptively simple tool set, meaning you can use SketchUp as a start-to-finish design tool. (SketchUp Pro provides even more sophistication with LayOut, an application that enables you to produce fully annotated and dimensioned drawings of your SketchUp model.) In addition, if you're handed a model that was created without regard to scale or dimension, SketchUp enables you to easily resize the entire model or only selected objects within it.

All of SketchUp's editing and drawing tools can be used with exact dimensions. You can enter a dimension's value before or after the tool's operation is complete, and you can enter new dimensions, repeatedly if necessary, to change the results after the operation is complete. After you start a new object or activate a new tool, you can no longer enter new dimensions for the existing object.

Dimensions appear in the Measurements field, located by default below the SketchUp window. The name of this field changes depending on the active tool (Length for line, Radius for circle, and so forth). To enter or change a dimension, just type the number, append a unit if necessary, and press Enter. There is no need to place your cursor in this field. In Windows, you can place the Measurements field anywhere on your screen by choosing View→Toolbars→Measurements. This displays the Measurements toolbar, which can be dragged or docked anywhere on your screen. On the Mac, you can add the Measurements field to your main toolbar by choosing View→Customize Toolbar and dragging the Measurements field to the toolbar.

— **Note** —————————————————

When you enter a value for a dimension or distance, SketchUp assumes the number is in the base dimensions of the model, which can be set in the Units page of the Model Info window. No matter which units you set for your model, you can enter dimensions in any other unit, as long as you append the correct unit symbol, such as *mm* for millimeters or *"* for inches.

For an example of using exact dimensions with editing tools, consider the Push/Pull tool. To do an exact pull, you can click the face you want to pull, move the mouse, type the distance you want to pull, and press Enter. Alternately, you can click the face to pull, click again to end the Push/Pull, and then immediately enter the distance you want. After the Push/Pull is complete, you can enter a new value to update the pull distance, as many times as you want, until you start a new operation. The other editing tools (Move, Scale, and Offset) can also take exact dimensions either before or after the operation is complete.

Some drawing objects (lines, circles, polygons, and arcs) can have their dimensions changed at any time via the Entity Info window. To open the Entity Info window, choose Window→Entity Info from the main menu, or right-click on an object and choose Entity Info from the pop-up menu. The information in Entity Info will reflect properties of the object or objects currently selected.

10.1 Working with Lines

Problem

You need to enter exact dimensions for a line.

Solution

Use the Length field or the Entity Info window.

Discussion

To set the exact length of a line, click the start point and move the cursor toward the endpoint. The length is indicated in the Length field (Figure 10-1).

You can type the length you want and press Enter, either before or after you click the endpoint of the line. Negative numbers can be entered.

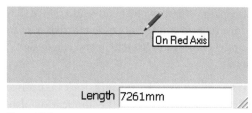

Figure 10-1

If you want to end the line at a specific coordinate, use the square bracket format. Start the line, and enter the coordinates in <red,green,blue> format (Figure 10-2) either before or after clicking the endpoint. If you are working in 2D on any standard plane, you still need to enter a value for all three directions, even if a value is zero. Figure 10-3 shows a line drawn in the red-green plane that starts at the origin and ends at the coordinate shown in Figure 10-2, entered using the square bracket format.

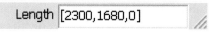

Figure 10-2

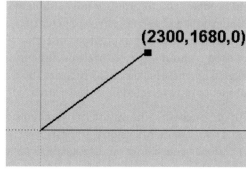

Figure 10-3

Length <1500,900,0>

Figure 10-4

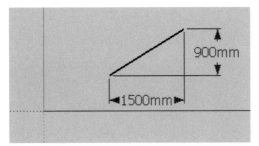

Figure 10-5

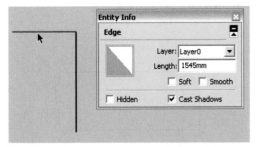

Figure 10-6

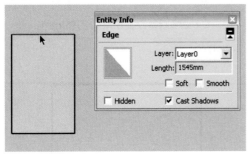

Figure 10-7

If you want the line to end at a distance relative to the start point, use the angle bracket format. Start the line, and enter the distances from the start point in the <red,green,blue> format (Figure 10-4) either before or after clicking the endpoint. Again, you still need to enter all three values, even if one is zero. Figure 10-5 shows a line that is 1500mm in the red direction and 900mm in the green direction from the start point, using the distances entered in Figure 10-4.

You can use more than one dimension method to create a line. For example, if you want to draw a line with a 2:1 slope and a length of 30mm, you would click the start point and enter *<2,1,0>* either before or after clicking the endpoint. This establishes the slope of the line. Then you would immediately enter *30mm* to set the correct length.

The Entity Info window will tell you a line's length (Figure 10-6). If the line has one endpoint free (not attached to another line or object), you can edit the Length field, which updates the line. If the line has no free endpoints, the Length field still informs you of the line's length, but the field is grayed out and cannot be edited (Figure 10-7).

If you select multiple edges, their total length appears in the Entity Info window, which is handy for calculating perimeters. If you select edges of arcs or circles, the total number of edges listed in Entity Info will include all of the arc or circle segments.

For an easy way to select all of the edges around a face, activate Select and double-click the face. This selects the face and its surrounding edges. Then press Shift and click the face again to deselect it, leaving only the edges selected.

10.2 Working with Rectangles

Problem

You need to enter exact dimensions for a rectangle.

Solution

Use the Dimensions field.

Discussion

To set the exact dimensions of a rectangle, click one corner point and move the cursor toward the other corner. The width and height are indicated in the Dimensions field (Figure 10-8).

You can type the dimensions you want and press Enter, either before or after you click the second corner. Be sure to separate the width and height by a comma. You don't need to include a space after the comma.

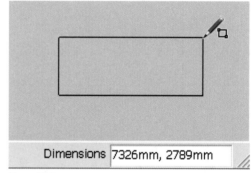

Figure 10-8

If you want to change only the height, enter new dimensions and leave the width blank. This means you enter a comma and the height (Figure 10-9).

Conversely, if you want to change just the width, leave the height blank, entering the width and then a comma.

> **Note**
>
> Rectangles are oriented to the face on which they are drawn or to one of the standard planes if drawn in blank space. If you want to create a rectangle with a different orientation, you can change your axes via the Axes tool (Tools→Axes). To reset your axes, right-click on any displayed axis (do not click on an object) and choose Reset. You can toggle your axis display via View→Axes.

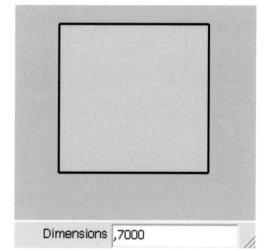

Figure 10-9

10.3 Working with Circles and Polygons

Problem

You need to enter an exact radius for a circle or polygon.

Solution

Use the Radius field or the Entity Info window.

Discussion

To set the exact radius of a circle or polygon, click the center point and move the cursor out toward the circumference point. The radius is indicated in the Radius field (Figure 10-10).You can type the radius you want and press Enter, either before or after you click the circumference point of the circle or polygon.

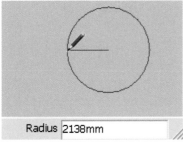

Radius 2138mm

Figure 10-10

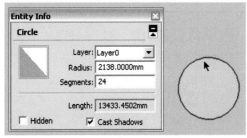

Figure 10-11

— **Note** —

You can also change the number of segments of a circle or polygon. Before you click the center point, enter the number of sides. After the center point is established, you can still change the number of sides by entering the number of sides followed by an *s*, either before or after clicking the circumference point. This applies to arcs as well.

The Entity Info window tells you the object's radius as well as its number of segments (Figure 10-11). It also tells you whether the object is a circle or a polygon, which can be useful if you don't know or remember how it was created. As long as the circle or polygon is intact (has not been exploded), you can change both the radius and number of segments by editing these fields.

Using the Entity Info window to change a circle works in 3D as well. For the top edge of the cylinder shown in Figure 10-12, you can edit the radius but not the number of segments. If you edit a radius this way, the center point remains the same and the circumference updates (Figure 10-13).

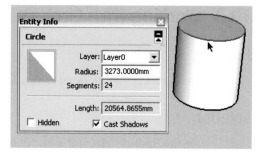

Figure 10-12

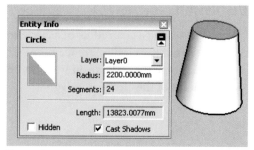

Figure 10-13

10.4 Working with Arcs

Problem

You need to enter an exact chord length or bulge for an arc.

Solution

Use the Length and Bulge fields or the Entity Info window.

Discussion

When creating an arc, the first two points you click establish the chord length, for which you can set an exact length as you would when creating a line. After the chord is set, you can set the arc's bulge, the perpendicular distance from the midpoint of the chord to the midpoint of the arc. This distance is indicated in the Bulge field (Figure 10-14). You can type the bulge you want and press Enter, either before or after you click the circumference point of the arc.

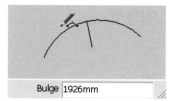

Figure 10-14

As for a circle and polygon, you can use the Entity Info window to change an arc's radius. If the arc is 2D and intact (not exploded), you can change both the radius and number of segments. If the arc is an edge of a 3D object, you can change only the radius (Figure 10-15).

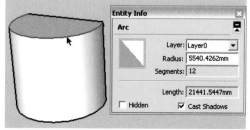

Figure 10-15

10.5 Importing Graphics

Problem

You need to add a graphic file with exact dimensions to your model, to use as a material or image.

Solution

Import the image and then use the Dimensions field for sizing.

Discussion

To import a graphic into your model, choose File→Import, find the graphic you want to use, and then select the Use as Image checkbox (if you plan the graphic to be used as an image) or the "Use as texture" checkbox (if you want to paint a face with it). Figure 10-16 shows a graphic that is imported as an image. Before you click to place the lower-left corner, the Dimensions field indicates the width and height of the graphic file.

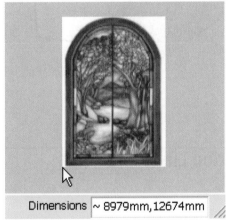

After you click the lower-left corner, you can size the graphic either by its width or height. If the cursor is anywhere along the top edge, the value that appears in the Measurements field is the height (Figure 10-17). If the cursor is anywhere along the right edge, the value that appears is the width (Figure 10-18).

Figure 10-16

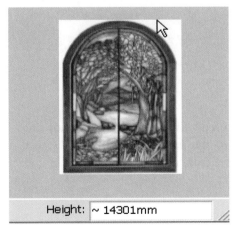

Figure 10-17

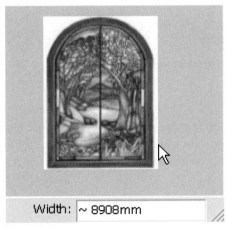

Figure 10-18

Decide which value you want to set, make sure that value appears in the Measurements field, and enter the value. Figure 10-19 shows the graphic with a width of 1000mm.

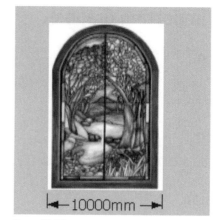

Figure 10-19

This also applies when you are importing a graphic as a texture. If you know the exact width of your material, such as the tiles shown in Figure 10-20, enter it when the Width field is displayed.

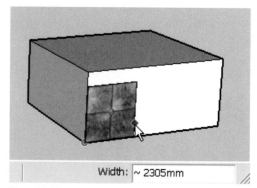

Figure 10-20

10.6   Using the Tape Measure for Construction Lines and Points

Problem

You need to create *construction lines* (temporary lines offset from existing edges) or construction points.

Solution

Use the Tape Measure tool.

Discussion

In addition to measuring, the Tape Measure tool can be used to make offset construction lines (sometimes also called *guide lines*). This is useful if you want to space objects at a set distance from other objects, or establish a line to which an object should be moved.

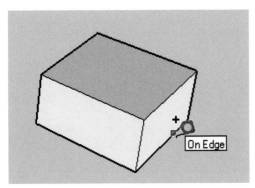

Figure 10-21

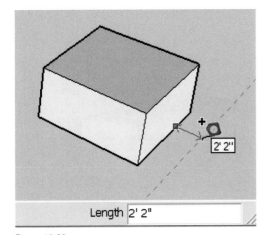

Figure 10-22

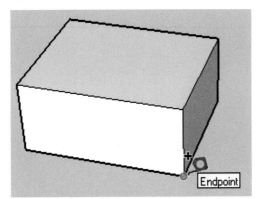

Figure 10-23

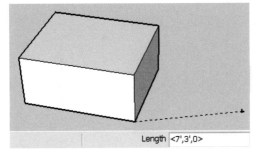

Figure 10-24

To make an offset construction line using an exact distance:

1. Ensure that the + sign appears next to the Tape Measure cursor. Tapping Ctrl/Option toggles this on and off.

2. Click the edge to which you want the construction line to be parallel (Figure 10-21). Do not click an endpoint.

3. Move the mouse away from the edge, and the offset distance appears next to the cursor and in the Length field (Figure 10-22). Type the distance you want and press Enter, either before or after clicking to create the construction line.

To make a construction point using an exact distance:

1. Ensure that the + sign appears next to the Tape Measure cursor. Tapping Ctrl/Option toggles this on and off.

2. Click the corner point from where you will measure the distance to the construction point (Figure 10-23).

3. For the distance to the construction point, use any of the methods you would use for creating a line with exact dimensions (explained in Recipe 10.1). Figure 10-24 shows a relative length of 7 feet in the red direction and 3 feet in the green, entered in the <red,green,blue> format.

Note ---

You can also use the Tape Measure to measure and resize objects, which is described in Recipe 10.10.

10.7 Measuring and Marking Angles

Problem

You need to measure an angle or create an angled construction line to mark an angle.

Solution

Use the Protractor tool.

Discussion

The Protractor tool can be used to measure angles and to create angled construction lines, such as for roofs.

To measure an angle:

1. Position the protractor in the plane or face you want. If you want to orient the protractor to a standard plane or to another face, set the orientation you want and hold the Shift key to lock the orientation. After you click to place the center of the protractor, you can release the Shift key.

2. Click the corner whose angle you want to measure (point 1 in Figure 10-25). Then click anywhere on one edge that defines the angle (point 2), and hover over a point along the other angle edge (point 3). The angle is listed in the Angle field.

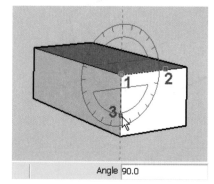

Figure 10-25

To create an angled construction line:

1. Position the protractor in the correct orientation, and click two points to set the baseline for the angle (Figure 10-26).

2. Move the mouse in the general direction you want for the line, type the angle you want, and press Enter (Figure 10-27). You can set the angle either before or after you click to create the construction line. Entering a negative angle places the construction line in the opposite direction from where you moved the cursor.

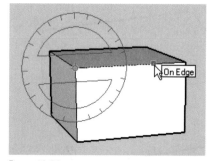

Figure 10-26

─── **Note** ───────────────────────────────

If you don't want to enter angle values manually, you can define snap values for the protractor. Open the Model Info window to the Units page and set the snap value under Angle Units. You can also enter an angle in *rise:run* format (such as 1:4)—for example, when defining a roof pitch.

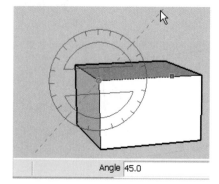

Figure 10-27

10.8 Finding the Area of Faces

Problem

You want to calculate the area of one or more faces.

Solution

Use the Entity Info window or the Area option.

Discussion

Area calculation can be important if you need take-off quantities for painting or surface finishing. Calculating the area of a simple rectangular face is not a problem if you know the length and width, but what if you have irregularly-shaped faces or need to calculate the total area of multiple faces? You can use the Entity Info window or the Area option in the pop-up menu.

Consider the model shown in Figure 10-28, a house with multiple materials. Right-click on a face whose area you want to calculate, and choose Area from the resulting pop-up menu.

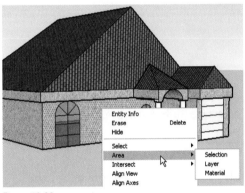

Figure 10-28

SketchUp offers three methods for calculating area: Choose *Selection* to calculate the area of the selected face or faces, *Layer* to calculate the area of all faces on the layer of the selected face, or *Material* to calculate the area of all faces with the same material as the selected face. If you select faces with different materials and then right-click on any selected face and choose Area→Material, the calculated area includes all faces of all selected materials. This applies to faces on multiple layers as well. No matter which type of calculation you choose, SketchUp displays the resulting area in a pop-up window (Figure 10-29).

Figure 10-29

— **Note** —————

Keep in mind that SketchUp faces are double-sided. If a face is painted with the same material on both sides, and you calculate area by material, the area of *both* faces is included. The exception to this rule involves translucent materials. If you paint window glass on a face, and that glass is automatically applied to the other side, the area calculation includes only one side of the face.

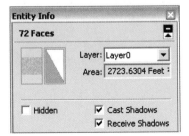

Figure 10-30

You also can calculate area by using the Entity Info window. Select the face or faces whose area you want to calculate; the Entity Info window then tells you how many faces are selected, as well as their total area (Figure 10-30).

If you want to use Entity Info to calculate the area of all faces with a specific material, you can select these faces in advance by using the pop-up menu option Select→All with Same Material. If you want to select faces with multiple materials (for example, all brick faces and all stone faces), select at least one face of each material. Right-click on either selected face and choose Select→All with Same Material, which will select all faces that have the selected materials.

Windows users can use the Materials window to calculate the area of all faces with a specific material. Find the material in the In Model folder, right-click on its thumbnail, and choose Area from the pop-up menu (Figure 10-31).

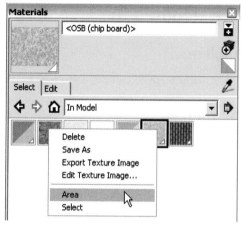

Figure 10-31

10.9 Creating a Grid

Problem

You want to use a grid to snap to points of set intervals.

Solution

Create arrays of construction lines at set intervals or create a sandbox surface.

Discussion

Although most conventional CAD programs have grids you can turn on and off, SketchUp does not. This is by design; SketchUp was never intended to be a "true" CAD program. You can make your own grid, however, by creating and copying a construction line or by setting up a sandbox.

1. Start with a horizontal line (or a line in the direction you want for your grid), and use the Tape Measure tool to create an offset construction line (Figure 10-32).

2. Make a copy of the construction line at a set interval (1 foot, 10mm, whatever you need).

3. Type *100x* and press Enter, or use whatever number you want, to create a set of construction lines separated by the distance you set for the first copy.

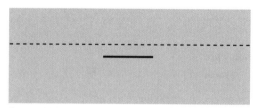

Figure 10-32

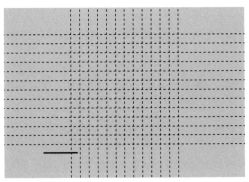

Figure 10-33

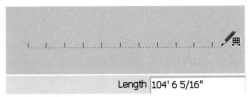

Figure 10-34

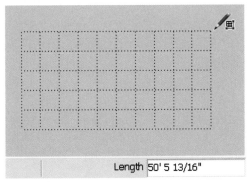

Figure 10-35

4. Select and rotate-copy all of the construction lines 90 degrees (Figure 10-33).

Although you won't have rulers to let you know exactly where you are in the grid, you can look at the Length field to see how long your lines are. You can snap to a grid point when you see the *Intersection* inference.

Another way to create a grid is to create a flat sandbox surface. Choose Draw→Sandbox→From Scratch. Set your grid spacing and click two points to define one side of the grid (Figure 10-34).

Then move your mouse in the perpendicular direction to define the other side of the grid (Figure 10-35).

The resulting grid is a group, which means that you can draw objects on it without the objects sticking to the grid.

10.10 Measuring Lengths and Resizing

Problem

You want to check a distance between two points. If this distance is too large or small, you want to resize your model.

Solution

Use the Tape Measure tool to measure a length between two points. To change this length, enter a new distance, which updates the size of the entire model uniformly.

Discussion

Picture this: you start a design without paying attention to scale and then realize later that your dimensions are off. Or maybe you receive or download a model that wasn't designed particularly carefully as far as numbers go. You can use the Tape Measure to measure a distance between any two points, and if the length is too large or small, you will want to resize the model. Right after measuring, entering a new length will resize the entire model to accommodate this new length.

Using Scale for Exact Sizing

It is possible to use the Scale tool for resizing, though it's a bit more difficult to get exact measurements with Scale than it is with Tape Measure. Scale values are ratios of a new length to a current length. So Scale is great if you want to change your model size by a scale factor, that is, make your entire model one-half or three times as big.

You can use the Scale tool for an exact resize, if you know the exact ratio of a desired length to a current length. You can apply this type of ratio in one, two, or three directions, depending on whether you drag a center, side, or corner handle. The Measurements field will indicate whether you are doing an overall (three-direction) scale, or a scale in one or two directions. Two-direction scale values must be separated by a comma. Pressing Shift enables you to toggle on and off the aspect ratio while scaling.

You can also enter exact measurements when using Scale, if you append a unit to the dimension you enter. For example, if the entire model is to be 10 feet tall, you would click the top-center drag handle to move in the blue direction, and then enter *10'*. The aspect ratio is lost, however, when you scale this way. If you know the overall model length in all three directions, you can enter the red, green, and blue measurements, separated by commas. Using Scale with exact dimensions requires you to know overall measurements of the entire model, not particular lengths between two points within the model.

Using measurements in inches while using Scale poses an interesting problem. The inch unit is entered as a quotation mark, which requires the Shift key. But if you press Shift while typing a value before the scale is complete, SketchUp assumes you're entering the number as a scale ratio. So if you want to scale to an exact inch value, complete an arbitrary scale first, and enter the dimension afterward with the quote symbol.

Figure 10-36

Figure 10-37

Figure 10-38

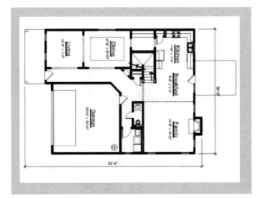

Figure 10-39

If you want to set an exact length and apply the factor between the old and new lengths to the entire model, use the Tape Measure tool.

Consider the model shown in Figure 10-36, which is of a dollhouse but was designed at the scale of a full-sized house.

If you know just one of the actual dimensions for the actual model, you can resize the entire model to match.

1. Activate the Tape Measure tool and make sure the + sign is *not* attached to the cursor. If it is there, the operation will result in an unwanted construction line. (Don't worry too much; you can always erase it.) Tap Ctrl/Option to toggle the + off and on.

2. In Figure 10-37, the known dimension is along the lower edge, along the front of the house. Click one endpoint and hover over the other endpoint. The measured length appears next to the cursor and also appears in the Length field. (If you needed to measure only this edge, you'd be finished, with no need to click anything else.)

3. Because this measurement is too large for a doll-house, the length needs to be resized. Click this endpoint, then enter the actual length you want for this edge. In the example, the front of the house should be 3 feet wide, so I entered *36* for 36 inches, using architectural units (Figure 10-38).

4. When you are asked whether you want to resize the model, click Yes. The entire model shrinks to accommodate the new dimension. When you resize this way, you may have to use the Zoom Extents tool to get the larger or smaller model back into view.

— **Note** —————————————————————

If there are components in the model that were imported from external files (components not created within the current SketchUp file), they will not be resized. Recipe 10.11 explains how to handle a situation like this.

————————————————————————————

Here's another example in which you would want to re-size a model: you have a graphic of a floor plan (Figure 10-39) and want to use it as a basis for your model. This could occur if you're renovating an old house for which there are scanned blueprints but no CAD drawings you can import.

1. Import the graphic as an image.

2. Use the Tape Measure tool to click two points at the extents of one of the existing dimensions (Figure 10-40), preferably the longest dimension so as to minimize scaling errors.

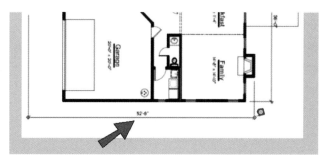

Figure 10-40

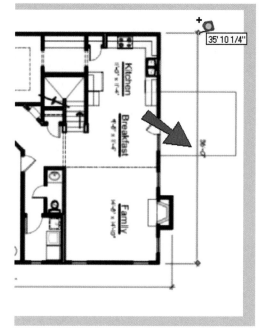

Figure 10-41

3. Enter the dimension listed on the graphic and resize the model. You can measure another dimension on the plan to check that the resizing was correct (Figure 10-41). It might not be exact, but you can get pretty close.

After your model is to scale, you can trace internal and external walls right on the image (Figure 10-42). Figure 10-43 illustrates how the walls look when pulled up to the correct height. Notice that in X-Ray mode, you can still see the graphic below.

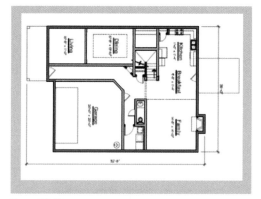

Figure 10-42

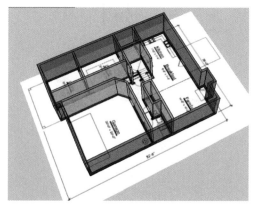

Figure 10-43

10.11   Resizing Models with Groups and Components

Problem

You want to resize your model, but some of its components will not resize.

Solution

Change the scale of the component in its original file, or resize it within the current file while editing the component.

Discussion

When you resize a model by using the Tape Measure tool, internal components (components that you create within the model) will resize, as will groups. Any components in the model that were imported from external files, such as models from the 3D Warehouse, will not resize. This is by design; if a manufacturer's window is 3 feet high, the window should keep its size even if objects around it change their size.

> **Note**
>
> If you use the Scale tool to resize, external components *will* resize. But this does not change the definition of the component; if you were to insert another component from the In Model folder, the new component would have the original size.

This example demonstrates how internal components, external components, and groups work while resizing with the Tape Measure tool.

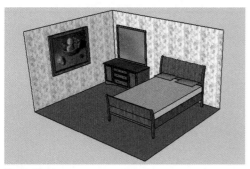

Figure 10-44

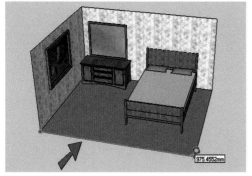

Figure 10-45

1. Download my Bedroom model from the 3D Warehouse (Figure 10-44). The walls and floor compose a group, and the bed is a component that was imported from an external file. The entire room has a very small scale.

2. Make the dresser into a component.

   You now have four types of objects: ungrouped (the painting on the wall), grouped (the walls and floor), internal component (the dresser), and external component (the bed).

3. Activate the Tape Measure tool, tap Ctrl/Option to toggle off Construction Line mode, and click the two endpoints of the edge indicated in Figure 10-45. The length of this edge is 975mm; the entire room is scaled too small.

4. Enter *4000mm* to resize the edge. You will see a warning message alerting you that external components will not be resized. Click Yes to resize everything else.

5. Use the Zoom Extents tool if your model disappears from view. The painting, room group, and dresser component are now larger, but the bed component has not changed (Figure 10-46).

There are three ways to resize this component. You could open the component in its original model file, resize it, save the file, and then reload it in the bedroom model (explained in Recipe 7.13). A second option is to use the Scale tool on the component, which is a bit complicated, as explained in the "Using Scale for Exact Sizing" sidebar earlier in this chapter. The third option, shown in the next steps, is to resize the component while editing it.

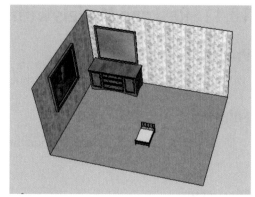

Figure 10-46

6. Open the bed component for editing. Activate Tape Measure and click two endpoints along the length of the mattress. The measured length is about 510mm (Figure 10-47).

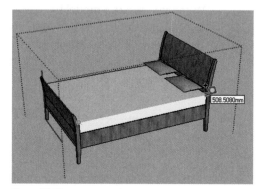

Figure 10-47

7. Enter the desired length of *1900mm* and confirm that you want to resize the component. You might have to move your resized bed into place within the room. The entire bed resizes, except for the pillows. The pillows are nested components within the bed component, so they retain their original size (Figure 10-48).

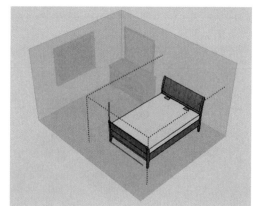

Figure 10-48

8. To resize the pillows, open either one of them for editing and use Tape Measure to make them both about 550mm long (Figure 10-49). Move them into place if necessary.

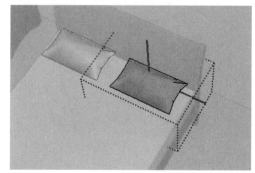

Figure 10-49

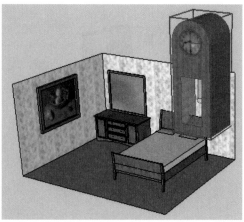

Figure 10-50

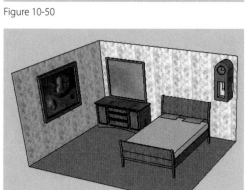

Figure 10-51

Now you know how to handle a problem you'll encounter frequently if you download models from the 3D Warehouse. Many models there are uploaded with inaccurate dimensions and need to be resized within your model. For example, you could find a wall clock that is larger than the bed (Figure 10-50). If the clock is a model you'll use in other models, it's worthwhile to save the model file to your hard drive and change the scale in that file. But if you are using the clock in only the current file, you can use the Scale tool, or edit the clock component and resize it by using the Tape Measure (Figure 10-51).

10.12 Resizing Parts of Your Model

Problem

You want to resize only certain objects within your model but not the entire model.

Solution

Make the objects you want to resize into a group, and use the Tape Measure tool while editing the group. (If the resized objects will be used repeatedly, make them into a component instead of a group.)

Discussion

In Recipe 10.11, you started with a model that had external components that needed to be resized separately. In this recipe, you start with a file that has no external components. The parts that you want to resize will be made into their own group, and resized while the group is edited without affecting the rest of the model.

In this recipe, you will start with a model of a desk that has several objects, one of which needs to be resized. In the "Other Uses" section, you'll see how separating objects into groups can be useful in making mosaic tiles.

1. Download my Office Desk model from the 3D Warehouse (Figure 10-52). The desk itself is an internal component (actually two mirrored half-components). The computer is a group, the vase is a group, but the clock is ungrouped. The clock is far too large and needs to be resized.

2. Make the entire clock into a group.

Figure 10-52

3. Edit the group and activate the Tape Measure. Click the two endpoints of the edge indicated in Figure 10-53 and resize this edge to 6 inches. Confirm that you want to resize the group to make the clock a more reasonable size (Figure 10-54).

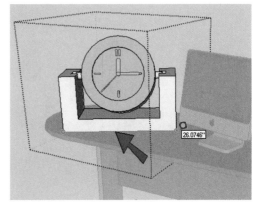

Figure 10-53

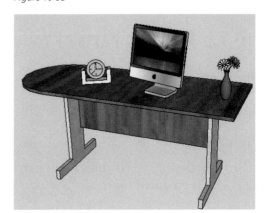

Figure 10-54

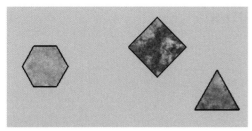

Figure 10-55

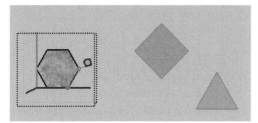

Figure 10-56

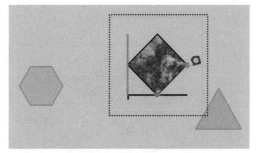

Figure 10-57

Other Uses

Separating objects into groups or components is a useful way to size tiles to make mosaics. Use the Polygon tool to make a flat hexagon, diamond, and triangle (Figure 10-55). For these tiles to be placed into a mosaic pattern, all edges of all shapes must be the same length, but you cannot specify edge length when creating a polygon.

Because the tiles will repeat, make each shape into its own component rather than a group. Then open one component for editing, and use the Tape Measure tool to set a specific length for one edge (Figure 10-56). Remember the length you set for the edge. Open the other components for editing, and resize them by using the same edge length as you used for the first shape (Figure 10-57). If you want to use Push/Pull to give the tiles some thickness, do this after the 2D shape is resized. Otherwise, the resizing will also change the tile thickness.

When all of the groups are edited and resized, their edge lengths will be the same, and you can arrange them in a mosaic pattern (Figure 10-58).

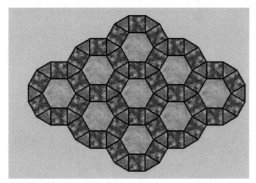

Figure 10-58

10.13 Resizing a Model in Multiple Directions

Problem

You want to resize a model by different factors in more than one direction.

Solution

Use the Tape Measure to resize based on a measurement in one direction. To make subsequent changes in scale in other directions, use construction lines to aid in resizing.

Discussion

Sometimes after you resize a model, you still want to change its scale in a particular direction. The trouble is that the Tape Measure tool resizes the entire model by the same factor in all directions. For example, say you used the Tape Measure to resize the picnic table in Figure 10-59, but decided it was still too narrow. If you use Tape Measure to resize the table for the correct width, the height and depth will also increase. The solution is to use a construction line to set the limits for the second resize, and edit the geometry to meet the construction line.

1. Download my Picnic Table model from the 3D Warehouse (Figure 10-59).

2. Use the Tape Measure tool to resize the height of the table. There are no points on the model that you can click to get this exact height, so click a point on the top of the table, press the up arrow or down arrow key, and click a point at the bottom of the table. This measures the vertical distance between the top of the table and the ground. The current height measures about 4 inches, a tad low for a real table (Figure 10-60).

3. Enter *27"* to resize the entire table.

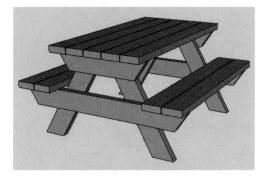

Figure 10-59

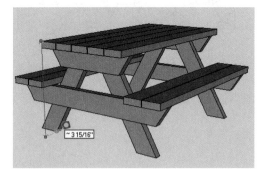

Figure 10-60

Figure 10-61

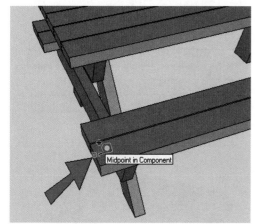

Figure 10-62

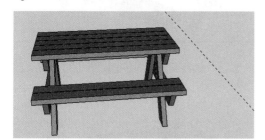

Figure 10-63

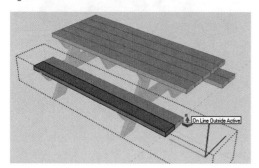

Figure 10-64

4. Use Tape Measure again to measure the width of one of the benches. It is about 4.5 feet (Figure 10-61), but the desired width is 6 feet.

5. If you enter 6 feet, the new table width will be correct, but the height will also increase, because resizing is uniform in all directions. So create a construction line that defines the 6-foot width. While Tape Measure is still active, make sure the + sign is displayed next to the cursor, and click anywhere on a left edge (not an endpoint) of the bench (Figure 10-62).

6. Place the construction line 6 feet to the right of this edge (Figure 10-63). You can enter 6' or 72", either before or after you click to place the construction line.

7. Each slat of this table is the same component. So open any one of them for editing, and use Push/Pull on the end you want to stretch. End the Push/Pull by clicking anywhere on the construction line (Figure 10-64).

8. The only object left to fix is the table support on the side you just lengthened. You could move it into place, but it's not clear where it should go because it is set back from the edges of the slats. The easiest way to fix this support is to erase it and start over, so remove it (Figure 10-65).

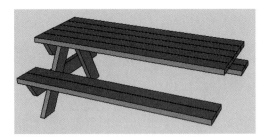
Figure 10-65

9. The new support will be a rotated copy of the original one. To establish the center of rotation, draw a temporary line halfway down the width of the table (Figure 10-66).

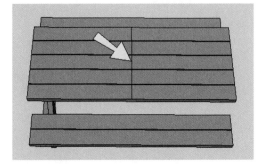
Figure 10-66

10. Select the table support and make a rotated copy of it 180 degrees away, using the center point of the temporary line as the center of rotation (Figure 10-67).

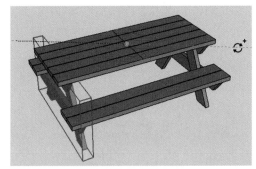
Figure 10-67

> **Note**
>
> Another way to fix the location of the support would be to move it *before* lengthening the slats. You would first select the support you want to move, and for the two move points, you would click an endpoint of one slat, move the mouse in the correct direction (or use the left arrow key), and click the construction line. Then you would use Push/Pull to lengthen the slats.

Another way to lengthen the table, after resizing the table to the correct height, would be to use the Scale tool. You would draw the same 6-foot construction line from the side of the table, select the entire table, and activate Scale. Then you would drag the center handle in the green direction until you meet the construction line (Figure 10-68). The results are slightly different using Scale, however, because the two supports would thicken a bit after the Scale operation.

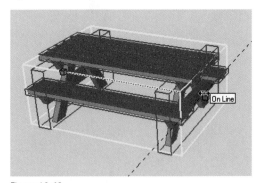
Figure 10-68

Yet another way to widen the table using Scale would be to click the center drag handle in the green direction and type 6' either before or after completing the scale.

CHAPTER 11

Presentation: Showing off Your Model

You've worked hard on your model, and now you want to show it to a boss, a client, a friend, or the whole world (if you upload it to the 3D Warehouse). It's easy enough to hand over your .skp file and walk away, but if you really want to knock their socks off and show them exactly what you want them to see, it's important to understand SketchUp's model presentation tools: layers, scenes, shadows, and sectioning. (Styles are also important, and they are covered in Chapter 12.)

Although some of these tools are not used exclusively for presentation, each can play a role in showing your model in exciting and interesting ways. When you understand each of these tools and learn ways to combine them, you'll become an expert at communicating your designs.

> **Note**
>
> The tools and techniques described in this chapter are available in the Free and Pro versions of SketchUp. SketchUp Pro users also have the benefit of the LayOut program, which is an application for presenting 3D models in a 2D format. LayOut has advanced features for view presentation and annotations such as dimensions and callouts. If you are not a Pro user, read about LayOut on SketchUp's website, and you may be convinced to become one.

11.1 Working with Layers

Problem

You want to control the visibility of certain objects in your model.

Solution

Use layers.

Discussion

Layers in SketchUp are used to control visibility of objects. For example, if you are designing a series of buildings, you can place each building on its own layer, and display only the buildings you need to see at any given time. For large models, placing objects on invisible layers can greatly increase the model's performance in SketchUp. For example, if you attempt to orbit around a model with lots of details, such as fully furnished rooms, SketchUp might need some time to redraw each object. If you don't need to see the furniture all of the time, place the furniture on invisible layers; the rest of the model will move much faster.

To create a new layer, choose Window→Layers to open the Layers window (Figure 11-1). Click the + icon (Add on the Mac) and assign a layer name. To hide, or *blank*, a layer, which hides all of the layer's contents, deselect the layer's Visible checkbox.

By default, Layer0 is the active layer, which means all new objects are created on that layer. To make another layer active and subsequently place all newly created objects on that layer, select the layer's radio button. (However, the best practice is to create all objects on Layer0 and move objects to different layers as needed.)

You can also display the Layers toolbar. In Windows, choose View→Toolbars→Layers; on the Mac, drag the Layers toolbar from the View→Customize Toolbar menu. If nothing in the model is selected, you can make a layer active by choosing it in the toolbar shown in Figure 11-2.

There are two ways to place an object on a layer. First, select the objects you want to place. If the Layers toolbar is displayed, you can choose the layer from its drop-down menu. Or you can open the Entity Info window (Window→Entity Info) and choose the layer from its Layer menu (Figure 11-3). Unlike in other CAD applications, in SketchUp an object can be placed on only one layer.

When layers are combined with scenes, you can save views that include only the objects you want to see, as you'll learn in Recipe 11.5.

It is important to note that you cannot draw objects directly on top of objects hidden on other layers. For example, if you create a box at a specific spot and place that box on a hidden layer, you cannot then draw another box of the same dimensions in the same spot. However, if the objects on the hidden layer are made into a group or component, you *can* place new objects in the same spot. This is shown in Recipe 11.6.

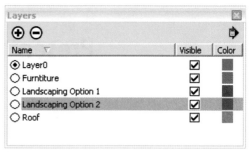

Figure 11-1

Figure 11-2

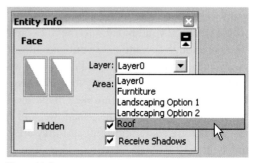

Figure 11-3

— **Note** ———————

The layer of a group or component can be different from the layers of the objects that compose it. So you can hide part of a group by blanking that object's layer, or hide the entire group by blanking the group's layer. In theory, this bends the "one layer per object" rule, because an object can exist both on its own layer and to the layer of its group. For an example of this, download my Layers Groups Components model from the 3D Warehouse and hide the various layers. Each object in the room resides on its own layer, as well as the layer of the room group.

11.2 Working with Scenes

Problem

You want to save the settings of the current model's display.

Solution

Create a scene.

Discussion

Creating scenes is how you save properties of the current model display. The most common use for a scene is to save the camera location (current view). This can be particularly helpful in large models when you need to repeatedly return to a hard-to-find spot. You can also use a scene to save the current style, shadow setting, visible layers, and more, which enables you to explore various design scenarios, animate sectioning, study moving shadows, and change the displayed style, to name only a few possibilities.

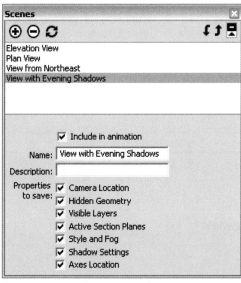

Figure 11-4

To save a scene, make sure the model is displayed with the properties you want to save (camera location, visible layers, and so on). Open the Scenes window (Windows→Scenes) and make sure only the properties you want to save are selected. Click the + icon and then assign a scene name. Figure 11-4 shows a model with four scenes. Scenes are listed in the order in which they are created, but you can rearrange the order via the arrow icons at the top-right corner of the Scenes window.

By default, a scene is saved with all of the properties selected. For any properties that are not selected, the scene will take on those properties from the scene that precedes it. For example, if you deselect Camera Location, the current scene will have the same camera location as the previous scene. (*Previous* does not necessarily mean the previous scene in the scenes list; it means any scene that was displayed before the current one.)

After each scene is created, it appears on a tab above the SketchUp drawing window (Figure 11-5). Click a tab to display the scene. Each scene tab has a pop-up menu that enables you to move, add, delete, or animate scenes.

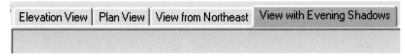

Figure 11-5

If you want to change or update a scene, first display that scene by double-clicking the scene name in the Scenes window or by clicking the scene tab. Make the change you want (orbit to a different view, change the properties to save, an so on) and click the Update icon in the Scenes window. (This is the icon with the two curved arrows.)

After you have two or more scenes, you can play an animation of the scenes. (If you want to omit a scene from the animation, you can set this property in the Scenes window.) To watch the animation, choose View→Animation→Play from the main menu, or choose Play Animation from any scene tab's pop-up menu.

To control the speed and smoothness of your animation, open the Animation page of the Model Info window (Figure 11-6). If scene transitions are enabled, the model will orbit smoothly from one scene to the next. You can adjust the time this transition takes, as well as the scene delay, which is the amount of time each scene is displayed.

To export your animation, choose File→Export→ Animation. There are several file formats to choose from, and you can click the Options button to see specific settings for your selected format.

—— **Note** ——————————————

This point is made elsewhere in this book but it bears repeating: If you want to download a model with scenes from the 3D Warehouse, do **not** download it directly into the current SketchUp file, or the scenes will not appear. Open the model in a new instance of SketchUp or save the model to your hard drive. Similarly, if you use File→Import to import a model with scenes as a component, the scenes will not appear.

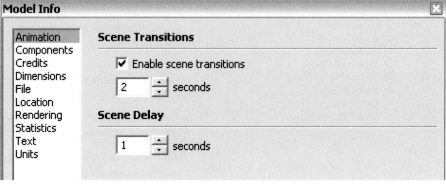

Figure 11-6

11.3 Working with Shadows

Problem

You want to cast shadows on your model.

Solution

Use Windows→Shadows to access the Shadow Settings window.

Discussion

Despite SketchUp's cartoonish rendering, its shadow calculations are extremely accurate. To cast shadows on your model, choose Window→Shadows to open the Shadow Settings window (Figure 11-7). Here you can control whether shadows are displayed, the time of day and year, the lightness of illuminated faces (Light slider) and the lightness of shadows (Dark slider), and which types of objects will receive or cast shadows.

Figure 11-7

Note

For large models, shadow display can slow down your model. Turning shadows off is a good way to maximize performance.

You can also display the Shadows toolbar: In Windows, choose View→Toolbars→Shadows; on the Mac, drag the Shadows toolbar from the View→Customize Toolbar menu. The toolbar is a smaller version of the Shadow Settings window (Figure 11-8), enabling you to toggle shadow display and set the times.

Naturally, the shadows cast depend on the location of your model. Model location is discussed in depth in Recipes 13.8 and 13.9, but basically there are two ways to define where your model is located. If you are working with Google Earth, you can use Get Current View to import a Google Earth snapshot and terrain into your SketchUp model, thereby setting the model's location internally. Otherwise, you can manually set the location in the Location page of the Model Info window. If your particular area is not listed on that page, you can enter your own latitude and longitude coordinates.

You can combine shadows with scenes to create an animation of shadows passing over your model. This technique is described in Recipe 11.7.

Figure 11-8

11.4 Sectioning Your Model

Problem

You need to show a cross-section of your model.

Solution

Use the Section Plane tool.

Discussion

The Section Plane tool (Tools→Section Plane) enables you to slice through your model to see what's inside. This is great for architectural designs (viewing floor plans), mechanical designs (viewing the inside of a machine), cabinet designs, mold making, and more.

Figure 11-9 shows a car with a section plane through the center.

When the section plane is active, half of the car behind the plane is hidden, and you can see inside (Figure 11-10).

To place a section plane, align the plane either to an existing face or to one of the standard planes. You can use the Shift key to lock the orientation of a section plane before you place it. Section planes can be erased, hidden, moved, copied, and rotated like other SketchUp objects. A section plane is infinite, so it can be placed anywhere and still slice through the entire model. Moving or copying a section plane always results in an offset (parallel) plane.

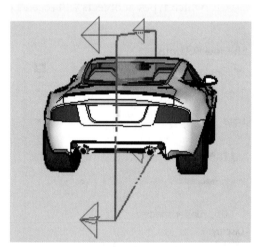

Figure 11-9

The pop-up menu for a section plane contains options to reverse the cut, activate the cut, and align the current view to the section plane. The option Create Group from Slice produces a group of objects where the model meets the section plane. For Pro users, this slice group can be exported into AutoCAD format by choosing File→Export→Section Slice.

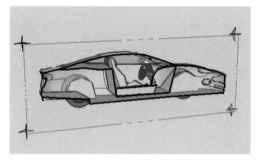

Figure 11-10

The View menu contains options for displaying section planes and section cuts. Turning off section cuts deactivates all section planes; the model appears intact, but you can still see the location of each plane. Only one section plane can be active at a time.

The Section Plane tool is available on the Large Tool Set toolbar. Windows users can also display the Sectioning toolbar (Windows: Choose View→Toolbars→Sections).

When you combine sections with scenes, you can create animated views of your model being sectioned, a great presentation technique that is described in Recipe 11.9. You can also use section planes within groups and components to create section animation in stages—an incredibly cool presentation technique that is shown in Recipe 11.10. (This technique also bends the "one section plane active at a time" rule.)

11.5   Using Layers and Scenes to Control Displayed Objects

Problem

You want to be able to turn on and off the display of objects in your model.

Solution

Place objects on separate layers and then control which layers are visible.

Discussion

You can control object visibility by creating layers and placing objects on them. When layers are made invisible, all objects on those layers are hidden. When you combine layers with scenes, you can create saved views with objects hidden or displayed, which can be a great way to present various elements of your model. To demonstrate, the main example shows how to use layers to produce various presentation views of a house. The "Other Uses" section shows how you can place text on different layers, to highlight specific features of a playhouse.

Figure 11-11

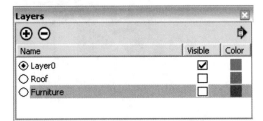

Figure 11-12

1. Download my Furnished Cottage model from the 3D Warehouse. It is a one-story house with furnished rooms (Figure 11-11).

2. Create a scene for this initial view (Recipe 11.2). Make sure all of the properties at the bottom of the Scenes window are selected. You can assign a scene name or accept the default, Scene 1. This is the first view your client would see in your presentation.

3. For the remaining scenes in the presentation, you want to show the rooms from above, with and without furniture. So the roof and furniture each need their own layer, in order to control their visibility. Create two new layers (Recipe 11.1), one for the roof and one for the furniture. Deselect the Visible checkbox for each layer, so that when you place an object on a layer, it automatically disappears from view (Figure 11-12).

The next task is to place the roof and furniture objects on their appropriate layers. You can do this in the Layers toolbar or the Entity Info window, so make sure one of these is displayed.

4. To select all of the roof faces, right-click on one of them and choose Select→All with same material. Place these faces on the roof layer. These faces disappear from view because they were placed on an invisible layer. What remains are some roof edges and ceiling faces (Figure 11-13).

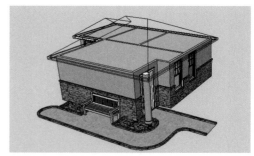

Figure 11-13

5. Add all of the roof edges and ceiling faces to the roof layer. (Do this in stages, because it is difficult to select all of the necessary objects at one time.) You can now see into all of the furnished rooms (Figure 11-14).

6. Select the pieces of furniture and place them on their own layer.

Figure 11-14

7. Now you are ready to create the next scene in the presentation. Switch to Top view and choose Camera→Parallel Projection, so that you have a true projection view (Figure 11-15), without the distortion you would see in Perspective view.

8. Create a new scene for this view of empty rooms and no roof.

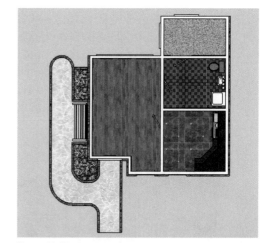

Figure 11-15

9. For the third scene, turn the Furniture layer back on by selecting its Visible checkbox. Switch back to Perspective view and then orbit to the view shown in Figure 11-16.

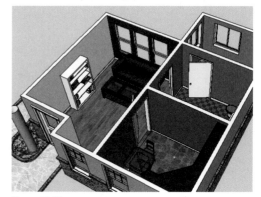

Figure 11-16

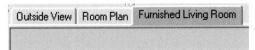

Figure 11-17

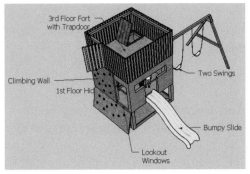

Figure 11-18

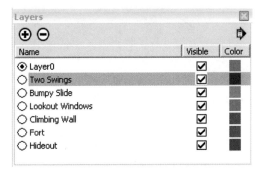

Figure 11-19

Figure 11-20

10. Create a third scene for this view.

   The three scene tabs are now at the top of your SketchUp window (Figure 11-17), and you can click each one to see the roof and furniture appear and disappear. You can also view the animation of these scenes.

Other Uses

If your presentation includes text, labels, or dimensions, you can use layers to control which annotations are displayed in a particular scene.

For an example, download my Play House model from the 3D Warehouse (Figure 11-18). If you turn on the visibility of each layer, you can see all of the labels marking various features of the playhouse. Using lots of labels can make your model rather cluttered.

A better approach is to display these labels one at a time by using layers and scenes. In this model, each label has its own layer, as shown in Figure 11-19. Each of the model's scenes (Figure 11-20) captures a different view with a single label; all other label layers are blanked. Click through the scenes or play the animation to see how this model presents the various features of the playhouse.

11.6 Using Layers, Scenes, and Groups for Different Design Scenarios

Problem

You want to try out different design ideas on a model, without being locked into specific camera views.

Solution

Place each design element as a group on its own layer and then create scenes to display each element. When creating the scenes, do not save the camera location.

Discussion

A typical scenario to illustrate this technique is a kitchen design for which you would like to try out different types of flooring. Each floor is placed on its own layer, and scenes are used to control which floor is visible.

When you create a scene, the default setting is to save the camera location, so that every time you click the scene tab, you return to the saved view. However, for this design scenario, you don't want to keep returning to the same view; you want to orbit to a view and stay in it, while trying out the different floors. In other words, you want to try out the floors when looking from above, when looking directly at the walls, and so on. The solution for this is to save each scene without its camera location, which means that the current view will not be saved with the scene.

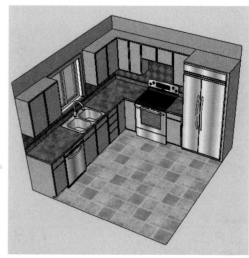

Figure 11-21

1. Download my Kitchen Floor model from the 3D Warehouse (Figure 11-21). The current floor has beige tiles, and you want to see how a different floor would look.

2. Create two new layers (Recipe 11.1), one for each floor, as shown in Figure 11-22.

3. Because the two floors will lie on the same plane, each must be made into a group so that they won't interfere with one another. (Without groups, you could not have two separate faces occupying the same spot.) Start by making the current floor a group: Activate Select and double-click the floor to select both its face and the edges around it, right-click on the floor, and choose Make Group.

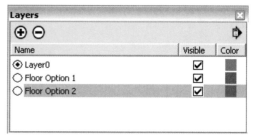

Figure 11-22

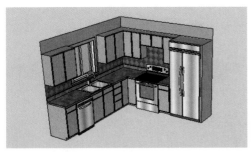

Figure 11-23

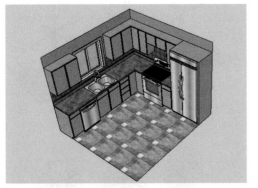

Figure 11-24

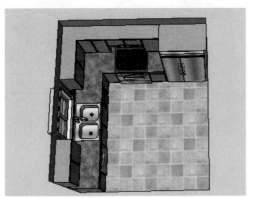

Figure 11-25

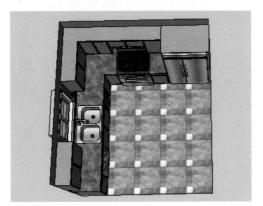

Figure 11-26

4. Place this floor group on one of the floor layers. Clear the Visible checkbox for this layer, which removes the entire floor from view (Figure 11-23).

5. Use the Rectangle tool to make a new floor in the same spot as the original floor. Apply a different material to this floor (Figure 11-24).

6. Make the new floor into a group and then place it on the other layer.

7. Create a scene for the floor currently displayed. When you create the scene, deselect the Camera Location property in the Scenes window, so that you don't return to the current view every time you click the scene tab.

8. Hide the current floor's layer, display the other layer, and create a new scene. The Camera Location property should still be deselected.

9. Now both floors are ready for you to examine. Because the camera view was not saved in either scene, you can orbit to any view, such as the plan view shown in Figure 11-25. Click the scene tabs to switch between floors (Figure 11-26).

Try out a few more views and see how each floor looks.

Other Uses

Another scenario for which this technique can be applied is landscaping. Download my Landscaping Options model from the 3D Warehouse (Figure 11-27). This landscaping model has three scene tabs, each of which shows a different landscape design. Orbit to any view and click each tab to see the landscaping change.

Another great use for this technique is to simulate moving or rotating objects. Download my Windmills model from the 3D Warehouse (Figure 11-28).

This model has eight scenes, representing increments of degrees that the blades are rotating. There are eight increments of 15 degrees for a total of 120 degrees, which is the angle between pairs of adjacent white blades or red blades.

There are also eight layers for the blades. If you display all layers, you'll see that there are eight copies of each set of blades (Figure 11-29). Each scene displays one set of blades, and the scenes proceed in rotational order. Play the animation to see the blades spin. In the Animations page of the Model Info window, you can see that there is no scene delay and a very short scene transition time (0.1 second). You can increase these values to slow the spinning. And because the scenes were not saved with camera properties, you can play the animation while in any view.

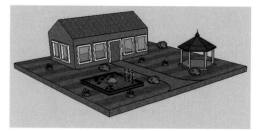

Figure 11-27

Figure 11-28

Figure 11-29

11.7 Studying Shadow Movements

Problem

You want to see how shadows move over a model during the course of a day, at various times of year.

Solution

Create a scene for each shadow's start and end time. When you click the start scene and then the end scene, the shadow will move as the scene transitions.

Discussion

The procedure to create a shadow study is simple: Set the shadow for the particular time of day and year (Recipe 11.3) and then create a scene. Adjust the shadows to another part of the day and then create a second scene.

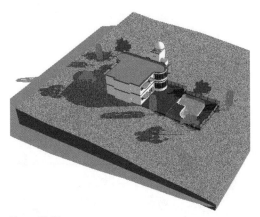

To see a model that has scenes for shadows, download my Shadow Study model from the 3D Warehouse (Figure 11-30).

Figure 11-30

This model has four scenes for morning and evening in summer and winter. Camera Location is not selected, so you can orbit to any view you want and check out the shadows without losing the view (Figure 11-31).

Click scenes to see how shadows move over the pool from a summer morning to a summer evening. Or see how shadows from the trees move over the house in the winter.

The model's location is Washington, D.C., but if you want to examine shadows in a more interesting part of the world (at least with respect to shadows), change the location to Svalbard, Norway. You'll have to enter the coordinates yourself: 78N, 20E. This town is close to the North Pole, so there is no sun in winter and no darkness in summer.

Figure 11-31

11.8 Walking Through Your Model

Problem

You want "real-world" views of your model.

Solution

Use the Position Camera, Look Around, and Walk tools.

Discussion

Often when presenting your model, you'll want to show exactly how one aspect of the model will look when a viewer is standing in a particular spot, at a particular height, looking in a particular direction. You can do just that with SketchUp's three walk-through tools: Position Camera, Look Around, and Walk.

Use Walk to simulate walking or running along your model. After you walk to where you want to stop and take a look, use the Look Around tool to turn your head or look up or down. For a view from a specific vantage point, use Position Camera. These tools are all available on the Camera menu, on the large tool set, and (for Windows users) on their own toolbar (View→Toolbars→Walkthrough).

The walk-through tools take a bit of practice. But after you get the hang of using them, you'll have no trouble producing informative animations of what can be found in your model.

Consider the model shown in Figure 11-32, which represents part of a three-story apartment building, located opposite a set of townhouses. (The townhouses are represented by an image stretched onto a wide face; think of the apartment residents looking across the street at a huge billboard rather than the actual houses of their neighbors.)

Imagine that a potential resident of the second-story apartment is curious about what sort of views he would see from his living room and balcony. By placing the SketchUp camera in strategic spots, you can simulate what can be seen in the actual apartment and then save scenes of these strategic views—a great marketing tool to show potential tenants.

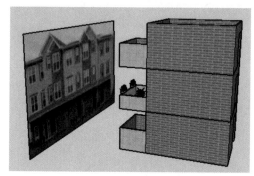

Figure 11-32

1. Download my Apartment Balcony model from the 3D Warehouse. Click the "Looking down on balcony" scene.

Figure 11-33

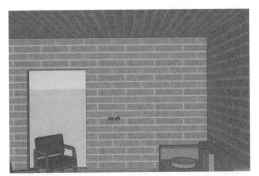

Figure 11-34

Figure 11-35

Figure 11-36

2. The first task is to place a camera that simulates a person standing on the balcony. Activate the Position Camera tool (Camera→Position Camera). Look at the Height Offset field, which should reflect a typical eye height (5' 6", in this case). If your field shows a different value, enter *5.5'* to set the correct height. Then click on the floor of the balcony, where indicated in Figure 11-33.

The camera is now 5' 6" above the floor, looking straight into the apartment (Figure 11-34). The cursor is a pair of eyes, indicating that the Look Around tool is now active.

3. To use Look Around, keep the left mouse button pressed and move the cursor. Moving up or down simulates looking up or down. Moving left or right simulates turning your head or spinning slowly in the same spot. Move directly to the right to turn halfway around, so that you are facing the townhouses across the street (Figure 11-35). This simulates what you would see when standing on the balcony.

4. Continue looking around until you are facing inside the apartment again.

5. The next view to examine is the view from inside the apartment. To simulate walking into the apartment, activate the Walk tool (Camera→Walk). The cursor is now a pair of feet (Figure 11-36).

6. Walk straight forward by keeping the left mouse button pressed and moving the mouse straight up. Moving the mouse higher will make you walk faster, so move up only slightly for now. You will get stuck almost immediately because you will run into the door (ouch). The cursor turns into a stick-figure person (Figure 11-37).

7. Break the collision detection by pressing the Alt key (Cmd on the Mac) and proceed into the apartment. While in the Walk tool, you can temporarily switch to the Look Around tool by holding the middle mouse button. By combining Walk and Look Around, you can peruse the entire space, viewing exactly what you would see from any vantage point.

Combining Walk and Look Around takes some practice, and you may find yourself backing out of the building altogether and ending up outside. It is helpful to save a scene at the point where you start walking, in case you get completely lost and want to easily get back to a familiar point. After you get used to these tools, you'll find that walking around is a powerful observation tool.

8. Walk to a point somewhere near the coffee table and look down at the couch (Figure 11-38).

9. The next view to examine is what you will see while sitting on the couch. Activate Position Camera again and enter a height of *2'*. This is approximately how far your eyes are above the seat of a couch while seated. Click the seat of the couch to place the camera there (Figure 11-39).

Figure 11-37

— **Note** —

While in the Walk tool, you can hold the Ctrl/Option key if you're in a hurry; this makes you run instead of walk. (Although running is convenient in a large space, it won't do much good in this small apartment.) You can also hold the Shift key to move straight up or down, simulating an elevator effect. If you try this while inside the second-floor apartment, you can examine the vacant apartments on the first and third floors.

Figure 11-38

Figure 11-39

Figure 11-40

Figure 11-41

10. Look around from this vantage point. You can see the room's furnishings (Figure 11-40) and the view outside the balcony (Figure 11-41). From the couch, you can see the underside of the third-floor balcony.

For purposes of a presentation, you would create a scene at each view of interest, making sure to save the camera location for each scene.

The 3D Warehouse collection for this chapter includes several other models that have animated presentations, both interior and exterior. The models Hacienda and Concept House each contain many scenes that guide you through nicely designed and furnished houses. Hameenlinna Castle contains scenes that include fog, so it appears that the castle is slowly appearing out of the fog (quite creepy). And Animated Mansion contains some nice illusion effects.

In some cases with these models, when the camera transitions from one scene to the next, it seems to pass through walls and floors. This is because SketchUp goes straight from one scene to the next without regard for objects that might be in the way. To avoid these "violent" transitions, you can simply add a scene or two in between, to guide the camera along a detour.

11.9 Creating Animated Sections

Problem

You want to animate the sectioning of your model.

Solution

Create section planes at the start and end of where you want sections cut. Save the start and end of each section as a scene.

Discussion

The Section Plane tool is a great way to peer inside your model, and when you add scenes into the mix, you can animate sections, making for a very cool presentation tool. Before creating each scene, activate the section for that scene. When you transition from a scene where the section starts to a scene when the section ends, the animation will appear to move the section plane from the start to the end location.

In this recipe, you will create animated sectioning from the front to the back of a house, and then from top to bottom. Finally, you will use diagonal section planes for an animation from one corner of the house to the other.

1. Download my Furnished Cottage model from the 3D Warehouse (Figure 11-42).

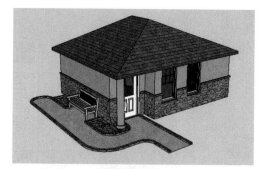
Figure 11-42

2. The first sectioning animation will slice the house from front to back. This requires two section planes: one at the front and one at the back. Activate the Section Plane tool (Tools→Section Plane) and click the long, narrow vertical face at the bottom of the roof (Figure 11-43).

Figure 11-43

This plane cuts a section along the face on which it was placed, so the narrow vertical face of the roof is no longer visible (Figure 11-44).

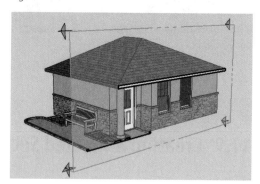
Figure 11-44

3. Select the section plane and move it just slightly away from the house (Figure 11-45), so that the entire roof is visible.

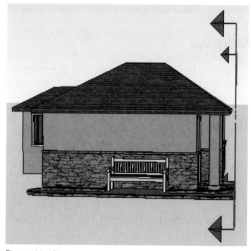
Figure 11-45

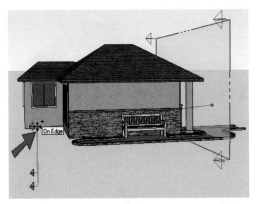

Figure 11-46

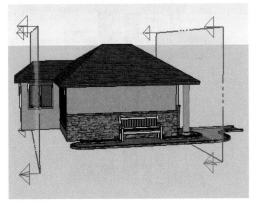

Figure 11-47

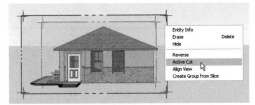

Figure 11-48

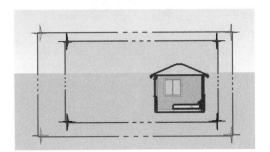

Figure 11-49

4. With the section plane still selected, the next task is to copy near the back of the house. For the first move point, click anywhere on the section plane. (Because section planes are infinite, it does not matter where you click on it.) For the second move point, click where indicated in Figure 11-46.

This creates two parallel section planes, one at the front of the house and one toward the back (Figure 11-47).

5. Orbit so you are facing the front of the house, which is the view you want to see during the front-to-back sectioning. The first scene will use the section plane in front of the house, so that the initial view of the house will be whole (not sectioned). To make this section plane active, right-click on it and choose Active Cut (Figure 11-48).

6. Create a scene of this view. In the Scenes window, make sure that all options are checked. The Active Section Planes option ensures that the sectioning will appear in the scene, and Camera Location ensures that the scene will record the current view.

7. For the second scene, activate the section plane at the back of the house. You should see only one small chunk of the back of the house; the rest of the house is in front of the section plane (Figure 11-49).

8. Save this view as the second scene.

9. The next task is to create the two section planes for the top-to-bottom animation. You need the entire house to be displayed again, so turn off the display of section cuts (View→Section Cuts). Then select and hide the two existing section planes, to clear the display.

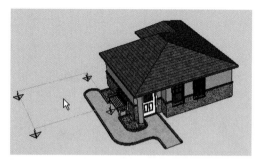

Figure 11-50

10. The next section plane will be horizontal and sit at the very top of the house. The roof faces are sloped, so none of those faces can be used to align the section plane. Activate Section Plane, place the cursor in blank space on the ground (Figure 11-50), and hold the Shift key to lock this horizontal orientation.

11. With Shift pressed, click the top of the roof to place the section plane there. Then move the plane up slightly so that the roof remains unsectioned (Figure 11-51).

Figure 11-51

12. Copy this section plane approximately halfway down the wall (Figure 11-52).

Figure 11-52

13. As before, orbit to the view you want to see for a top-to-bottom sectioning (Figure 11-53).

14. Activate the top section plane and create the third scene. Then activate the bottom plane and create the fourth scene.

15. Turn off section cuts and then hide the two section planes.

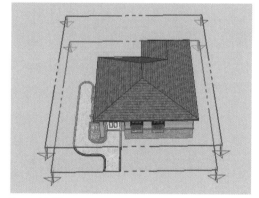

Figure 11-53

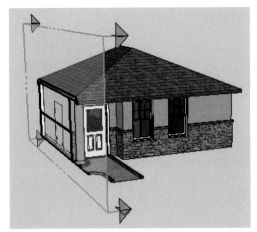

Figure 11-54

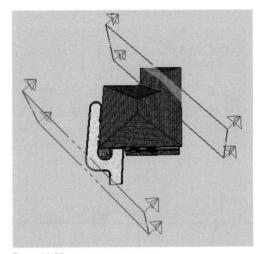

Figure 11-55

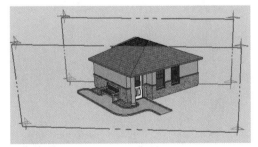

Figure 11-56

16. The next two section planes will be diagonal. Create the first plane by clicking the side or front of the house (Figure 11-54). This plane will be rotated into place.

17. Select and rotate the section plane, and then move it away from the house so that no part of the house is sectioned. Create a copy toward the other corner, leaving a small part of the house behind the section plane (Figure 11-55).

18. Orbit to a view as shown in Figure 11-56 and create the fifth and sixth scenes.

19. Click the start and end scene for each pair of section planes. Assuming your scene transitions are enabled, you will see the planes invisibly slicing through the house. The transition between pairs of scenes (back to top, bottom to corner) are especially fun to watch.

You can download my Furnished Cottage Animated model from the 3D Warehouse, which contains the six scenes created in this recipe.

— Note —————————————

The 3D Warehouse collection for this chapter also includes a model called Concept House. This model has dozens of scenes, some of which use section planes. Play the animation; it is a great walkthrough of an interesting model.

11.10 Creating Staged Sectioning Animation

Problem

You want to animate sectioning of your model in stages, showing only certain sections appearing at a time.

Solution

Separate each design element into groups or components, and place section planes in the group or component while editing it.

Discussion

This technique takes a bit of planning and organization, but the results are well worth the effort. The most important tasks, and the ones that require the most work, are to figure out the order in which you want design elements to appear, and to separate each design element into groups or components. Although layer display is not needed for scene creation, it is extremely helpful to place each element on its own layer, because by turning layers and off, you can verify that each element is grouped correctly.

After groups and components are established, the section planes are placed within the group or component *while it is open for editing*. The easiest way to set up the animation is in the "reverse" direction: Start by animating the last design element you want to appear and then work backward. As you create scenes for each element, you are displaying less and less of the model, until you are left with the first scene you want to display.

Although the preceding explanation sounds quite complicated, this technique is not so difficult. Work through the following example, and you'll get the hang of it.

Figure 11-57

1. Download my Castle model from the 3D Warehouse (Figure 11-57).

2. Take a few minutes to look through the layers of this model. The Towers layer contains four identical components, and the remaining layers each contain a single group. Turn on one layer at a time to see the design element that resides on that layer.

The animation will be created in reverse order. So the first element to be animated will be the outer walls, then the towers, then the steps, then the palace, and finally the plaza. The last scene (which will actually become the animation's opening scene) is the plot of grass. This makes a total of six scenes.

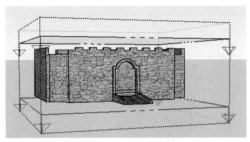

Figure 11-58

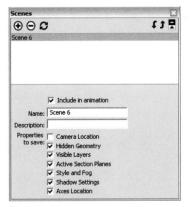

Figure 11-59

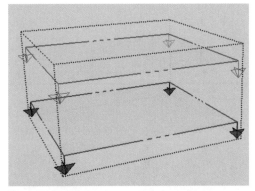

Figure 11-60

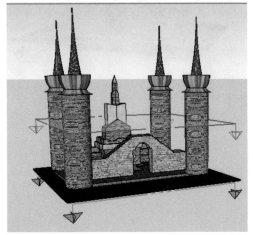

Figure 11-61

3. Open the Outer Walls group for editing. (This model is set to hide everything but the group or component being edited, which is helpful when placing section planes. This setting is found in the Components page of the Model Info window.) Place a horizontal section plane just above and just below the walls, making sure each plane extends a bit past the top and bottom of the walls (Figure 11-58).

4. Activate the top section plane, in which the walls are still visible, and create the first scene. Because the scenes are created in reverse order, this will actually become the last of six scenes; I named the scene Scene 6 (Figure 11-59).

— **Note** —————————————————————

In this example, I save each scene without its Camera Location, so that the animation can be viewed from any angle. If you do save your camera location, which can also produce great results, make sure you are facing the walls the way you want them to appear in the scene. Also keep in mind that the rest of the model will appear in the animation, so leave room in your view for the towers.

5. Activate the bottom section plane, which hides the entire wall group (Figure 11-60). Save this as Scene 5.

6. Close the group, and the rest of the model returns to the view. You can still see the wall group's section planes, the lower of which is still active. Because this section plane is active, the outer walls remain hidden (Figure 11-61).

7. The next design element to animate is the four towers. Each one is an identical component, so open
   any one of them for editing (Figure 11-62).

   For this and the remaining design elements, only
   one section plane is required. Because the previous
   group (comprising the outer walls) is already hidden, you need only to place a section plane at the
   bottom of the tower component, which will simulate the tower disappearing from top to bottom.
   (When played in reverse order, of course, the tower
   will grow from bottom to top.)

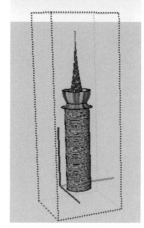

Figure 11-62

8. Place a section plane at the top of the tower, and
   move it down past the bottom, so that no part of
   the tower is visible (Figure 11-63). Save this as
   Scene 4.

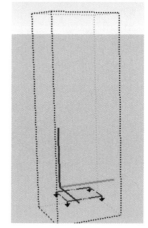

Figure 11-63

9. Close the tower component, and now the first two
   design elements (the outer walls and towers) are
   both hidden (Figure 11-64).

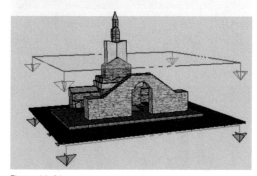

Figure 11-64

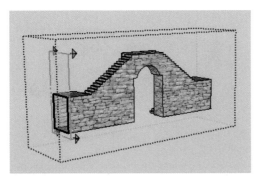

Figure 11-65

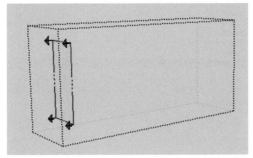

Figure 11-66

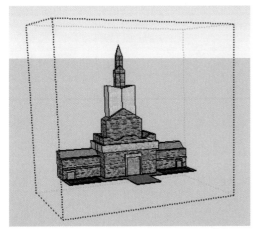

Figure 11-67

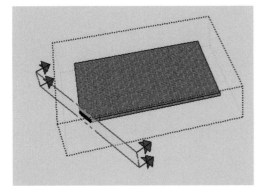

Figure 11-68

10. The next element is the steps. Place a vertical section plane at the side wall (Figure 11-65). The steps are still visible because the plane is facing the wrong way.

11. Right-click on the section plane and choose Reverse. Then move the plane away from the wall slightly, so that the group disappears completely (Figure 11-66). Save this as Scene 3.

12. Close the wall group and open the palace group (Figure 11-67).

13. Place a downward-facing section plane below the bottom of the palace, so that the palace is completely hidden, and save Scene 2.

14. For the last scene, open the plaza group. Spice things up by using a diagonal section plane (Figure 11-68).

15. Move the plane past the opposite corner so that the plaza disappears, and save Scene 1.

16. Close the plaza group, and all that is visible is the plot of grass upon which the castle will be built, as shown in Figure 11-69. To hide the section planes that are cluttering the view, choose View→Section Planes.

Figure 11-69

17. That's it! If you play the animation as is, the tower will "decompose," with each element disappearing one by one, until just the grass remains. If you want to grow your castle instead, move the scenes into the correct order, using the up and down arrow icons at the top-right corner of the Scenes window (Figure 11-70).

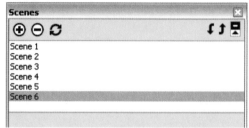

Figure 11-70

You can download my Castle Staged Animation model from the 3D Warehouse, which contains the six scenes created in this recipe.

───── **Note** ─────────────────────────────

The 3D Warehouse collection for this chapter also includes a model called Animated Garage. This model has eight scenes that show stages of creating a garage, and these scenes have saved camera locations. Also in this collection is Animated Car, which contains scenes for building a car.
───

CHAPTER 12

Displaying Your Model

You know the basics of changing the way your model is displayed: You routinely change the face display from Shaded to Hidden Line to X-Ray, as well as turn off edges and profiles when appropriate. You may not know that you can control even more display aspects, such as default face colors, backgrounds, watermarks, and edge styles. Showing your model in a variety of styles enables you to tailor your model display to your personal taste. And, if you work for a company, you can establish your own standard styles for presenting designs to clients and colleagues.

In this chapter, you will learn how to change, create, and save your own styles, combine features of various styles to create new styles, produce attractive watermarks, use sketchy edges, and use styles as part of an animation.

12.1 Hiding and Softening Edges

Problem

You want to remove some edges from the model display.

Solution

Use the Eraser tool or the Soften/Smooth Edges window to hide or soften edges.

Discussion

Hiding all edges in your model is easy (deselect Display Edges and Profiles in the Edge page of the Styles window); but what if you want to remove the display of only certain edges in your model? There are two ways to "blank" selected edges: hiding and softening. *Hiding* edges simply removes them from the display, while *softening* smoothes the corner where the edge was, resulting in a single face.

Consider a polygon pulled into a cylinder-like shape. To hide its vertical edges, you can use the Hide tool (available on an edge's pop-up menu or on the Edit menu), or you can use the Eraser tool while holding the Shift key. In either case, when the vertical edges are hidden, you can still see the facets between faces, and each vertical face remains a single face (Figure 12-1). Also note that when the vertical edges are hidden, there are no vertical profile edges to mark the limits of the cylinder.

To soften these edges, use the Eraser while holding the Ctrl key (Option on the Mac). Softening the vertical edges results in a smooth vertical face. As you can see in Figure 12-2, the facets are not visible, and the face can be selected as a single face. When edges are softened, there are still profile edges on either side of the vertical faces.

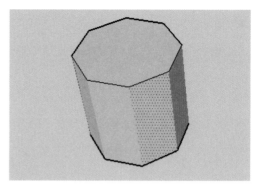

Figure 12-1

— **Note** ————————————————

If edges are softened within a planar face, the face can be selected as a single face. SketchUp does not consider it geometrically to be a single planar face, however; you cannot use Push/Pull on it or select it as a path for Follow Me.

———————————————————————

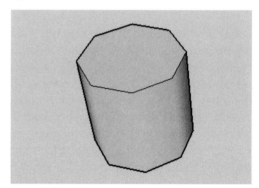

Figure 12-2

To locate edges that are hidden or softened, you can display indicators that mark where they are. Choose View→Hidden Geometry from the main menu. The dotted line on the left side of Figure 12-3 indicates a hidden edge, and the dashed line on the right side indicates a softened edge.

To unhide or unsoften an edge, right-click the edge and choose the relevant option from the pop-up menu, or use the Eraser with both Shift and Ctrl pressed (Shift and Option on the Mac).

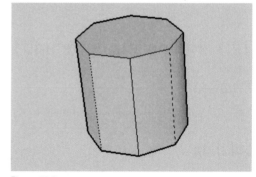

Figure 12-3

Another way to soften edges is via the Soften/Smooth Edges option. For example, consider a Sandbox surface. (A sandbox is created as a group, so to soften its edges, you need to edit the group or explode it.) To soften the edges between each square, select the entire surface, right-click on it, and choose Soften/Smooth Edges. (You can also open this window via the Window menu.) As the slider value increases, more edges are smoothed. When Smooth Normals is not selected, the surface looks faceted. And when Soften Coplanar is not selected, there are still edges between faces on the same plane (such as the flat part of the surface in Figure 12-4).

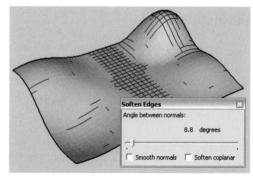

Figure 12-4

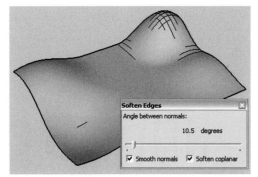

Figure 12-5

Selecting "Smooth normals" removes the faceting, and "Soften coplanar" removes edges from faces in the same plane (Figure 12-5).

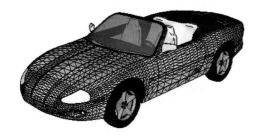

Figure 12-6

Softening edges is essential for organic shapes, such as a car body. Figure 12-6 shows the triangulation needed to make such surfaces; edges separate each of the small triangles that compose the surfaces.

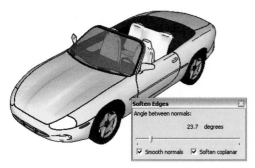

Figure 12-7

Softening these edges produces sleek-looking surfaces (Figure 12-7).

After edges are smoothed, you can use View→Hidden Geometry to see where they are.

12.2 Changing the Style

Problem

You want to change how model elements (faces, edges, and such) are displayed.

Solution

Use the Styles window to set the display properties you want.

Discussion

Your model's style controls the display of nearly all model elements: face color, axis display, edge thickness, background colors, and so on. SketchUp comes with several sample styles to choose from, and you can create and save your own styles as well.

The model shown in Figure 12-8 was created by using the Simple template, which is one of the default templates you can choose when you open SketchUp. Except for the painted door and window frames, all faces have the default color: The front faces are showing on the sides of the house, and the back faces are showing on the roof. There is a blue sky and green ground, and the axes are displayed.

The Styles window (Window→Styles) for this model lists the current style name and description at the top of the window. From here, you also can access folders with several other sample styles (Figure 12-9).

To make changes to the style, click the Edit tab. This tab contains five pages of categories you can change: Edge, Face, Background, Watermark, and Modeling settings. Figure 12-10 shows the Face page, on which you can change the default front and back colors for faces, and control how faces are displayed (Shaded, X-Ray, and so on).

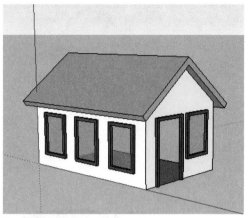

Figure 12-8

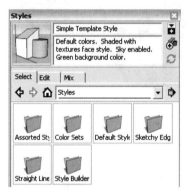

Figure 12-9

--- **Note** ---

Many of the style-changing options are also available on the View menu, such as hiding the axes, changing the face or edge style, and displaying hidden geometry.

You can also change the style name by editing the name field at the top of the Styles window.

When any change is made to a style, such as the new face colors shown in Figure 12-11, the style thumbnail in the Styles window will feature a double-arrow symbol indicating the style has changed but has not yet been saved.

To update the style, click the thumbnail or click the Update icon near the top-right corner of the Styles window. The double-arrow symbol will disappear from the thumbnail. Note that this does not change the original definition of the style; it changes the style in the current file only. You can find the updated style in the In Model folder of the Styles window. If you open the style folder that houses the original style, you'll see that version has not changed. If you click the thumbnail of the original, unchanged style to apply it to your model, the original style will then appear in the In Model folder, in addition to the style you changed and updated.

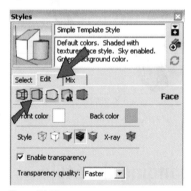

Figure 12-10

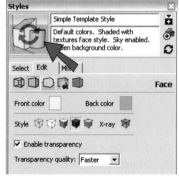

Figure 12-11

12.3 Creating a New Style

Problem

You want to create a new style for your model.

Solution

Create a new style based on an existing style.

Discussion

Suppose you want to create a new style that won't overwrite the one currently in use. The solution is to create a new style based on an existing one.

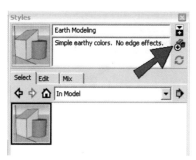

Figure 12-12

Consider a model with one style in its In Model folder. To create a new style, click the Create a New Style icon, indicated in Figure 12-12.

Figure 12-13

This creates an identical style whose name is the same as the original, with a 1 appended to it. This new style becomes the active style. Use the Edit tab to set the new parameters for the new style and update it. Figure 12-13 shows a copy of the Earth Modeling style, renamed as "Earth Modeling at Night," which has darker sky and ground colors.

12.4 Saving Styles

Problem

You have one or more styles that you want to be able to use in other files.

Solution

Create a new collection and add to it the styles you want to save.

Discussion

Saving styles works in the same way as saving materials and components: You create a collection and then save it as a favorite for future use.

When you have the styles you want in the In Model folder, click the Details arrow, indicated in Figure 12-14.

Figure 12-14

Choose to save the collection; you'll have to browse to the location where you want the collection saved. The collection name appears as the folder name (Figure 12-15). If you want the collection to be easily accessible in future files, click the Details arrow again and choose Add Collection to Favorites. (Mac users can choose to add a collection to their favorites at the time the collection is created.)

Figure 12-15

You can easily add and remove styles from this, and any other, collection. Click the Secondary Pane icon indicated in Figure 12-16, which opens a second styles folder below the top one. You can now move styles back and forth by dragging and dropping.

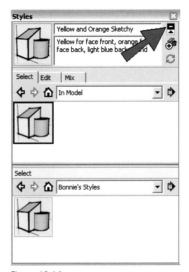

Figure 12-16

12.5 Saving a Style As a Template

Problem

You want a certain style to be the active style when you open a SketchUp file.

Solution

Make the desired style active and save the SketchUp file as a template.

Discussion

If you have a style that you want to be active whenever you open SketchUp, activate the style and save the SketchUp file as a template. Everything in that file, including all objects, in-model materials, components, layers, and styles, will also be included in the template.

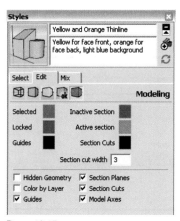

Figure 12-17

For example, consider a model in which the style shown in Figure 12-17 is active. In addition to yellow and orange faces and thin edges, the Modeling page is set to highlight selected objects in magenta.

Figure 12-18

This file itself contains one person component standing on the origin (shown in Figure 12-18 as selected, and therefore in a magenta bounding box). The camera angle is showing a front view.

To save this file as a template, choose File→Save as Template from the main menu. Enter a name and a description; SketchUp assigns it a filename automatically based on the name (though you can change it). There is also an option to save this template as the default (Figure 12-19). The next time you open SketchUp, the template will be available (Figure 12-20). If you open a file using this template, it will contain the same component and camera view as the file you saved.

While in SketchUp, there are two ways to choose a new template. You can open the Welcome to SketchUp window via the Help menu, or choose Window→Preferences (SketchUp→Preferences on the Mac) and open the Template page. Choosing a new template will not affect the current model; the template will take effect when you open a new file.

As you've seen, any SketchUp file can be made into a template. So if your company has a standard template, make sure that everyone has a copy of the SketchUp file to be used as the template and that everyone saves the file by using File→Save as Template.

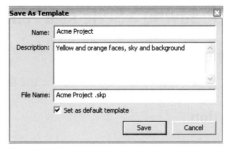

Figure 12-19

Figure 12-20

Everything Goes into Your Template

When you save a file as a template, be aware that any objects in your model are saved as part of the template, so you might not want to leave any extra edges or faces lying around. Also be sure that your In Model folders contain exactly what you want to save. Any unpurged components, materials, and styles will be saved as part of the template. This can be useful, for example, if you want to save a template with colors or styles that you want to access easily. It can also be useful to save a template that has ready-made layers. On the other hand, you could accidentally leave in some unpurged components or materials that could bog down your file. Take stock and then save.

12.6 Mixing Styles

Problem

You want to create a style that takes certain properties from other styles.

Solution

Create a mixed style by using the Mix tab of the Styles window.

Discussion

Each page of the Styles window's Edit tab (Face, Edge, and so on) has a set of related properties. When you mix styles to produce a new style, you are assigning to the new style sets of properties from various existing styles.

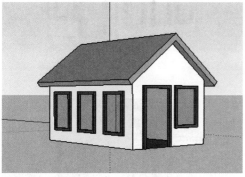

Figure 12-21

Figure 12-22

The following steps demonstrate how to mix a new style by using properties of other styles.

1. Download my Mixing Styles model from the 3D Warehouse. It is a basic house with the Simple style active (Figure 12-21).

2. The In Model tab of the Styles window shows four styles, whose properties will be used for the new style. To avoid overwriting the active style, create a new style based on the Simple style (Recipe 12.3). SketchUp names the new active style Simple Style 1.

3. Click the Mix tab, which is next to the Edit tab. The top pane shows a list of property categories, and the bottom pane shows the current styles folder. Open the In Model folder in the bottom pane.

4. The first properties to change will affect edges. Click the Marker Loose style in the bottom pane (Figure 12-22); its edge properties will be used for the new style.

5. Windows users: click Edge Settings in the top pane (Figure 12-23) or drag the Marker Loose thumbnail onto Edge settings. On the Mac, drag the Marker Loose thumbnail onto Edge settings.

Figure 12-23

This style now has the sketchy edge properties from Marker Loose, but no other properties have changed (Figure 12-24).

Figure 12-24

6. The next properties to update are for faces. Click the Google Colors style and apply it to Face Settings. This changes the front and back face colors of the style (Figure 12-25).

Figure 12-25

7. Background settings will remain as they are. For watermark settings, use the style Scribble on Masonite. This will overlay a texture onto the entire SketchUp window, as shown in Figure 12-26.

Figure 12-26

8. Return to the Select tab. Assign a new name and description for this style, and update it. You should now have five styles in the In Model folder: the four you started with and the new mixed one (Figure 12-27).

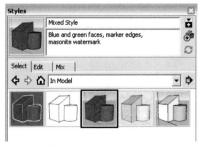

Figure 12-27

12.7 Adding a Watermark

Problem

You want to add a watermark to a style, either as a background image or a positioned image.

Solution

Add background or overlay images to your style via the Watermark page of the Styles window.

Discussion

There are two main types of watermarks: images that fill the entire SketchUp window and images that are in specific positions. You can add either type of watermark as a background (behind the model) or an overlay (above the model).

Figure 12-28

1. Download my Watermark Style model from the 3D Warehouse. It has a beige canvas overlay that fades toward the edges of the SketchUp window (Figure 12-28).

   The easiest way to understand how this watermark was created is to deconstruct and reconstruct one. The style contains the watermark images, so you can export them and use them to build the watermark from scratch.

2. Click the Edit tab and open the Watermark page. For each of the three images (Gradient Mask, Canvas, and Beige Underlay), right-click on the thumbnail and choose Export Watermark Image. Save them to a folder you will remember.

3. To remove the watermark, highlight each image and click the minus-sign icon indicated in Figure 12-29.

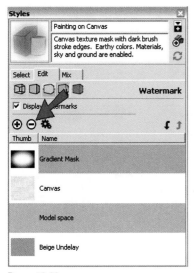

Figure 12-29

The watermark is now gone (Figure 12-30).

Figure 12-30

4. To rebuild the watermark, click the + icon and import the Canvas image. This should be an overlay (Figure 12-31) so that the canvas texture can be seen on the faces of the model. Otherwise, the texture will appear in the background only. Click Next.

Figure 12-31

5. The next window is used to set the texture's blend. Set the Blend slider between Model and Image so that the model faces will be clearly visible but the canvas texture can also be seen (Figure 12-32). Click Next.

Figure 12-32

6. The last window is used to position the watermark image. This image should be tiled, and the scale should be increased so that the texture will be clear (Figure 12-33). Click Finish.

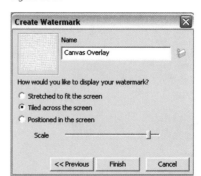

Figure 12-33

Figure 12-34

Figure 12-35

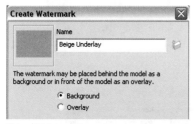

Figure 12-36

Figure 12-37

The Canvas image appears on the Watermark page. It is located above Model Space, which indicates that it is an overlay rather than a background (Figure 12-34). The canvas texture can be seen on the model itself (Figure 12-35).

7. For the next image, import the beige underlay. Make this one a background (Figure 12-36), because as an overlay the beige color would darken the faces of the model. As a background, the beige color will be visible only on the canvas in the background.

8. Adjust the blend and set the positioning. Now the canvas looks beige, but the faces of the house are still bright (Figure 12-37).

9. Finally, import the gradient image as an overlay, so it will affect the entire window. On the window shown in Figure 12-38, select the Create Mask checkbox. This means that brighter areas of the image are read as transparent, and darker areas of the image will use the style's background color.

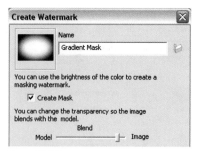

Figure 12-38

10. The gradient image should be stretched across the screen. Deselect the Lock Aspect Ratio checkbox so that the image can adjust slightly to fit the screen (Figure 12-39).

The resulting watermark is the faded canvas look shown earlier in Figure 12-28. The Watermark page should show the gradient and canvas images above the model space, with the beige underlay below the model space. To edit any of the images, you can click the Edit Watermark Settings icon, which is next to the minus-sign icon.

Figure 12-39

Another common use for watermarks is logos and stamps. For an example of this, download my Watermark Logo model from the 3D Warehouse. It is a simple model with an overlaid logo (bottom right of Figure 12-40) and Approved stamp (top left).

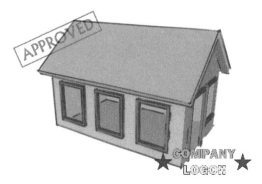

Figure 12-40

Both of these watermark images are .png files with transparent backgrounds, and both are overlays; each always appears above the model. You can use the Watermark page to change an overlay to a background (and vice versa). For this example, highlight the Approved image and click the down arrow indicated in Figure 12-41.

Figure 12-41

Figure 12-42

Now the Approved stamp is below the model, as you can see in Figure 12-42.

12.8 Creating a Sketchy Edge Style

Problem

You want to customize your style with edges other than straight lines.

Solution

Create a sketchy style, either manually or via the Style Builder (Pro users only).

Discussion

Sketchy edges are a great way to give your model a customized look. To see what they look like, open the Sketchy Edges style folder and try out some of the samples.

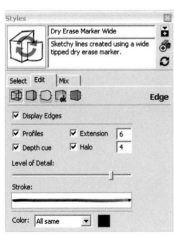

Figure 12-43

A sketchy style's Edge page has different settings than you'd see for normal, uniform edges (Figure 12-43).

The unique settings here are Depth cue (closer edges are thicker), Halo (the blank space surrounding each edge), and Level of Detail (the distance at which the smallest edges will not appear). The Stroke field shows a sample prototype graphic for an edge.

Sketchy edges are in essence a compilation of graphics of various lengths. A sketchy style typically contains several prototype edges for each length. To see what this means, look at Figure 12-44, which is a house drawn in the Twigs style. This style has three prototype edges for lengths varying from short (32 pixels) to long (512 pixels). Look specifically at the six horizontal lines drawn within the roof; each prototype appears twice, but the overall look is random (if you don't look too hard).

If you were to zoom in or out, the prototypes used for those six lines would be replaced with the prototypes assigned to longer or shorter lengths. This way, no prototype has to be stretched or squashed too much to fit the edge length, and all edges will appear to have the same approximate thickness.

Style files are located in the Styles folder of your Sketch-Up installation. Each file has a .style extension, which is equivalent to a .zip extension. To see how a style is set up, copy one of these files and change the copy's extension to .zip, and then open or extract the compressed file.

Each style contains a folder called *ref*, which contains the graphics that represent each edge prototype. The Twigs style has 15 graphics in its *ref* folder (Figure 12-45), three graphics for each of the five lengths (32, 64, 128, 256, and 512 pixels).

The file document.xml contains the meat of the style: its name, description, edge settings such as thickness and halo, and most important, the names of the graphics files in the *ref* folder. The file documentProperties.xml also contains a style name—this is the name that appears in the Styles list, and as the style's tooltip name.

If you're looking to build your own sketchy edge style, start with scanned or drawn prototypes for your edges, a few for each of the lengths. Darker colors in these prototype graphics represent the edges themselves, and lighter areas will be read as transparent. Gray areas of the graphic will produce blurry or faded edges, which can be a nice effect. Prototype graphics are usually gray-scale, but you can use color, keeping in mind that only light and dark will be read.

Figure 12-44

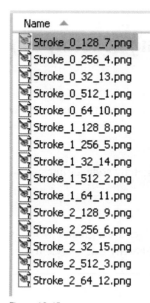

Figure 12-45

The easiest way to create a new style using your edge prototypes is to copy an existing style. Rename the style file, change the .style extension to .zip, and extract the files and folder. Replace the graphics in the *ref* folder and modify the document.xml and documentProperties.xml files. (You don't have to be a programmer to do this; just open the .xml file in a text editor and change the edges settings and graphic names.) Zip it all back up when you are finished, and change the .zip extension back to .style.

To use this style in SketchUp, click the Details arrow in the Styles window and open a collection, which is the folder where your new style file is saved. (If your style is saved in one of SketchUp's provided style folders, it will automatically appear with the other styles in the folder.)

Pro users don't have to go through this rigmarole; they can use the Style Builder application (Figure 12-46). This is an application external to SketchUp, located in the same folder in which SketchUp Pro is installed.

In Style Builder, you load the prototype graphics in the left pane by using options on the Strokes menu. In the top-right pane, set the lengths you want to include and the number of strokes for each length. To populate each stroke, simply drag the prototype graphic from the left pane and drop it into the correct slot in the top-right pane. Empty slots will be interpreted as blank edges. The bottom-right pane shows a preview of the style; you can use the default model or change the model by using the Preview menu.

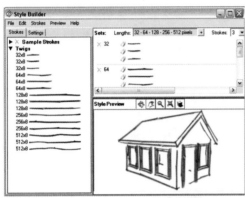

Figure 12-46

12.9 Using Styles in a Presentation

Problem

You want to show different styles in your model, without having to choose them from the Styles window.

Solution

Save the style as part of a scene.

Discussion

Chapter 11 showed numerous ways to save aspects of the model in a scene, so that you can return to a particular display with a simple click. With two or more scenes, you can create an animation—an impressive way to show off your model. Among other properties, the active style can be saved in a scene, which adds to the many ways you can wow your clients (or teachers or family or friends).

This recipe shows how to use styles as part of an animation that showcases a house in a variety of camera angles and styles.

1. Download my Styles Presentation model from the 3D Warehouse (Figure 12-47). This house will look familiar if you read Chapter 11. (If you haven't, you should read it now; for this recipe, you need to be familiar with the concepts in that chapter, including section planes.)

Figure 12-47

   The In Model folder of the Styles window contains three styles; the active one is the Simple style.

2. Create the first scene from this initial view and include all scene properties.

3. Switch to Front view and activate the Pencil Edges style (Figure 12-48). Save this as the second scene.

Figure 12-48

4. The third scene will be a floor plan view of the rooms, so a section plane is needed. Place a horizontal section plane right below the roof (Figure 12-49).

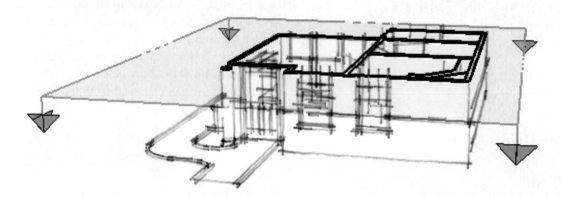

Figure 12-49

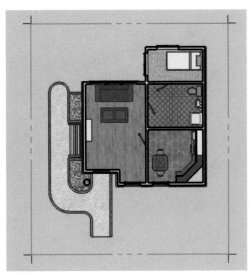

Figure 12-50

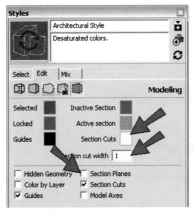

Figure 12-51

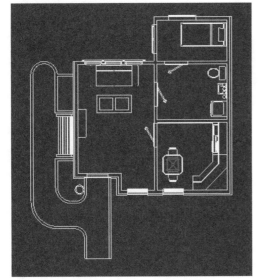

Figure 12-52

5. Switch to Top view and choose Camera→Parallel Projection. Activate the Architectural style (Figure 12-50). This scene is to have more of a blueprint feel, so the style needs some changes.

6. Edit this style and change the color on the Edge page to white. Also deselect Display Profiles. While you are making these changes, do not update the style; you will save it later as a new style.

7. On the Face page, switch to Hidden Line mode (or you can choose View→Face Style→Hidden Line).

8. On the Background page, remove the sky and change the background color to dark blue.

9. Finally, on the Modeling page, change the Section Cuts color to match the edge color (white). Reduce the section cut width, and deselect Section Planes so that the section plane will not be visible (Figure 12-51).

Your model now looks like Figure 12-52.

10. Save this as the third scene. When you see the Scenes and Styles warning, save the current style as a new style, so that the original Architectural style will not be changed.

11. For the last scene, activate the Architectural style again. Return to Perspective view and then orbit to a view like the one in Figure 12-53. Hide the section plane, and turn off edges and profiles. On the Modeling page, lower the section cut width.

12. Save this as the fourth and last scene. This time you can update the style, because the original Architectural style will not be used again.

13. The scenes are all created, but there is one more task. Click Scene 1, and the section plane returns (Figure 12-54). This is because the Simple style is set to display section planes.

Figure 12-53

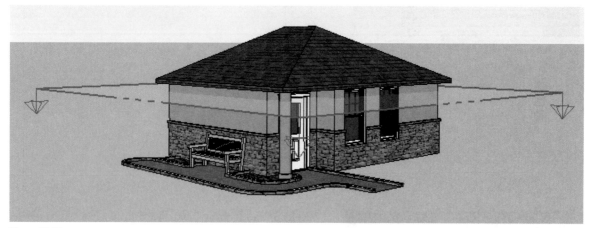

Figure 12-54

14. Edit the style to hide section planes and update the style. The same change is needed for the Pencil Edges style in Scene 2.

Now the animation is ready to play. Note how the style transitions smoothly from one scene to the next—a very nice effect.

For a completed model with these four animation scenes, download my Styles Presentation Animated model from the 3D Warehouse and see how your version compares.

CHAPTER 13

3D Warehouse and Google Earth

The potential for seamless integration between SketchUp models and Google Earth is what prompted Google a few years back to buy @Last Software, the original creators of SketchUp. Google wanted a simple, intuitive content engine to produce the models that would populate Google Earth, and SketchUp fit the bill. By creating the 3D Warehouse, Google then made it easy to share your work with the world. Google Earth and the 3D Warehouse often work in tandem: You can georeference a SketchUp model by importing location data from Google Earth, and place that same model in the 3D Warehouse for all (or for specific people) to see.

This chapter takes a closer look at these two resources. Recipes 13.1 through 13.7 cover the various ways you can use the 3D Warehouse, how you can place your own models and collections there, and how to control the privacy of your work. Recipes 13.8 through 13.13 move on to Google Earth, teaching you how to georeference a model, place a model in Google Earth, remove or replace location data, and download specific models found in Google Earth.

Before getting started, you should be familiar with the Google Tools icons (Figure 13-1) in the Getting Started toolbar, which runs by default horizontally above the SketchUp window. (Mac users can display these tools via View→Tool Palettes→Google.) From left to right, the tools are as follows:

Figure 13-1

- **Get Current View**. Imports into SketchUp a snapshot of the view plus a model of the terrain currently displayed in Google Earth.

- **Toggle Terrain**. Toggles between the snapshot (flat) view from Google Earth and the terrain (3D) view from Google Earth.

- **Place Model**. Places everything currently visible in your SketchUp model into Google Earth.

- **Get Models**. Opens the 3D Warehouse for a model search.

- **Share Model**. Enables you to upload the current model to the 3D Warehouse.

You'll be using these five tools throughout this chapter.

13.1 Finding Models in the 3D Warehouse

Problem

You want to find and download a model in the 3D Warehouse.

Solution

Search the 3D Warehouse from your Components window, use Get Models, or open the 3D Warehouse from your Internet browser (*http://sketchup.google.com/3dwarehouse*).

Discussion

You can access models in the 3D Warehouse via three routes. From within your SketchUp file, you can search the 3D Warehouse directly in the Components window or you can use Get Models. You can also search the 3D Warehouse outside of SketchUp, by opening the 3D Warehouse in your Internet browser.

---- **Note** ---

You do not need to be signed in to Google or to even have a Google account to search and download models from the 3D Warehouse. However, you will need to be signed in if you want to upload your models (Recipe 13.3).

Figure 13-2

Method 1: Use the Components Window

The Components window is the most convenient way to search for 3D Warehouse models: Simply enter the search keywords in the search field at the top (Figure 13-2), and SketchUp displays thumbnails of the models it finds. The Components window displays up to 12 models at a time, so if you don't see what you want at first, use the scroll arrows at the bottom of the window to keep looking.

To insert a model directly into the SketchUp file, click the model's thumbnail and click again to place it in your model. SketchUp inserts the model as a component with a bounding box around it and adds it to the In Model folder of the Components window.

If you want more information about the model before you download it, such as a larger view, descriptions, or reviews, click the model name to open the model's 3D Warehouse page, shown in Figure 13-3. (If the name doesn't appear as a link in the Components window, click the View Options icon to the left of the house icon and then choose Details.)

Figure 13-3

Figure 13-4

Figure 13-5

If you click the Download Model button on this page, you will be asked whether you want the model loaded directly into your SketchUp model. If you click Yes, SketchUp imports the model as a component. If you click No, you can either open the model in a new instance of SketchUp (Windows only) or save the model to your hard drive.

Method 2: Use the Get Models Option

Another way to find 3D Warehouse models from within SketchUp is to click the Get Models icon, or choose File→3D Warehouse→Get Models. This opens a 3D Warehouse search page, in which you can enter your search keywords. In the search results (Figure 13-4) you can click Download Model, or click the model name or thumbnail to open its larger, descriptive page (which also has a Download Model option).

When you use Get Models, the download options are identical to using the Components window: you can import the model directly into your SketchUp file, and if you choose not to import directly, the options are to open the model in a new instance of SketchUp (Windows only) or save it to your hard drive.

Method 3: Open the 3D Warehouse in Your Internet Browser

If SketchUp is not open, or if you prefer to find models independently of SketchUp, you can open the 3D Warehouse from your Internet browser. The URL is *http://sketchup.google.com/3dwarehouse*. The interaction is the same as when you use the Get Models icon: there is a search field at the top of the web page, and each model thumbnail has a download link. You cannot place a model directly in an open SketchUp file, but you can open the model in a new instance of SketchUp (Windows only), or you can save the model to your hard drive.

An advantage to using an Internet browser is that you can search directly for collections, in addition to models. Figure 13-5 shows a collection search that will yield collections of 3D people.

Note ────────────────────

You can also search for collections by using the Components window or Get Models, but this is an advanced search feature (see Recipe 13.2).

13.2 Refining Your 3D Warehouse Search

Problem

You want to refine your model search in the 3D Warehouse by adding search criteria.

Solution

Use the Advanced Search option, or enter search operator syntax in the 3D Warehouse Search field.

Discussion

If you enter a generic word such as *tree* or *house* in the 3D Warehouse Search field, you will turn up far too many results to comb through. The Advanced Search web page and search operator syntax enable you to whittle down your search results to meet specific criteria, such as location, author, descriptive terms, and so on. You can also use an advanced search to look for collections instead of models.

The Advanced Search link appears on the initial 3D Warehouse page, next to the Search field (Figure 13-6). You can access this page when using Get Models or when searching the 3D Warehouse from within your Internet browser.

Figure 13-6

Figure 13-7 shows the advanced search options available when you click the Advanced Search link. In this example, the search will turn up all models that have the word *house* in the title, *beach* in the description, and are located. (*Located* models, also called *georeferenced* models, are saved and uploaded with a specific location, as explained in Recipes 13.8 and 13.9.)

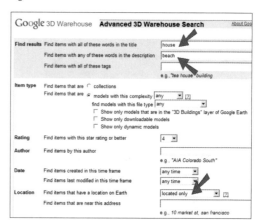

Figure 13-7

— **Note** —————————————————————

As you know, the quality of 3D Warehouse models can vary greatly. If you want to search only for well-crafted models, you can specify the author, search for ratings of at least four or five stars, or search for models located on the 3D Buildings layer of Google Earth.

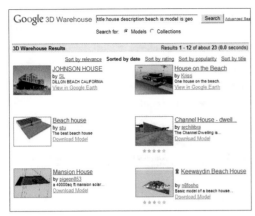

Figure 13-8

Figure 13-8 shows the models found by the search for located beach houses. There are two things to note on this page: the model links and the Search field syntax.

Note that some models have a link for View in Google Earth instead of Download Model. This means that those models were uploaded as .kmz files, which is native to Google Earth. Opening a .kmz file will take you directly to the model at its specified location in Google Earth. (You can still download these models as SketchUp files; the Download Model button on the model's description page has options for downloading in different formats.)

The syntax in the Search field is *title:house description:beach is:model is:geo*. Here's a breakdown of what these terms mean:

- **title:house**. The word *house* appears in the model title.

- **description:beach**. The word *beach* appears in the model description.

- **is:model**. The search is for a model, not a collection.

- **is: geo**. The model is georeferenced.

Here are some other common search operators:

- **author:smith**. The name *smith* will appear somewhere in the author's name.

- **author:"john smith"**. The model author's exact name is *John Smith*.

- **tag:tea tag:house**. The search will be for models that are tagged with the term *tea* or *house*.

- **tag:"tea house"**. The exact term *tea house* appears in the model's tags.

- **is:best-of-geo**. The model has been accepted into the Best of Warehouse collection and appears in Google Earth.

- **is:dynamic**. The model is a dynamic component (described in Chapter 14).

- **near:Denver**. The model is in the vicinity of Denver.

If you learn the syntax for the search operators you need, you can simply enter the necessary syntax in the Search field and not bother with the lengthy Advanced Search page. A list of all search operators can be found in the SketchUp Help Center. From SketchUp choose Help→Help Center. Search for the phrase *advanced search operators*. From the resulting web pages, open "How do I use Advanced Search in the 3D Warehouse?"

If you are using the search field in the Components window, the Advanced Search link is not available. But you can (and should) use search operator syntax in the search field. Figure 13-9 shows models that meet two search criteria. First, they are located at or near 1600 Pennsylvania Avenue in Washington, the address of the White House. (In the Advanced Search window, you would enter this address in the "Find items that are near this address" field. A zip code can also be entered in this field.) Second, these models are all *best-of-geo*, which means they were accepted onto the 3D Buildings layer of Google Earth. (In the Advanced Search window, this is equivalent to selecting the checkbox labeled "Show only models that are in the 3D Buildings layer of Google Earth.")

The advantage of using search operator syntax in the Components window search is that all resulting models appear right in the Components window, and you can click them one at a time to import them into your SketchUp file. When you search by using Get Models or your Internet browser, you can download or import models only one at a time.

For example, if you want to place all buildings of a college campus in your SketchUp model, you could search in the Components window with operator syntax for title (name of the college) or location (street address or zip code). After clicking a model thumbnail to import the first building, you would click thumbnails for the subsequent buildings you want to import, preserving their location each time. Figure 13-10 shows a monochrome view of how these imported models might look, each imported with its slice of terrain from Google Earth, and placed at the correct location.

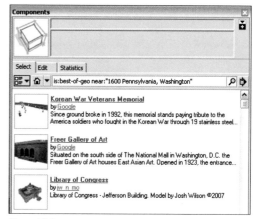

Figure 13-9

Note

When using the **near** syntax, you can include the **within** syntax to find models within a certain radius. For example, you can use **near:94116 within:5000** to get models within 5 km of zip code 94116.

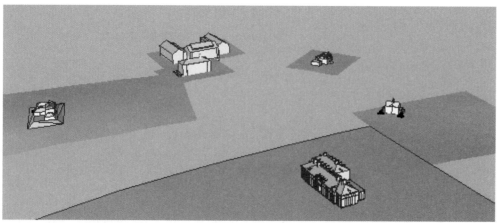

Figure 13-10

13.3   Uploading Models to the 3D Warehouse

Problem

You want to upload your model to the 3D Warehouse.

Solution

Use Share Model.

Discussion

The 3D Warehouse enables you to share your model with the world. All you need is a Google account, which is free and easy to set up.

Figure 13-11

Note ---

A word about hidden objects: objects hidden using Edit→Hide will be included with your uploaded model, and will not appear when the model is downloaded or inserted. But you can use Edit→Unhide to display them. You can also place objects on hidden layers; layers are preserved when uploading..

Figure 13-11 shows a model of a banana tree that is to be uploaded to the 3D Warehouse. Note that it is located at the origin, which is good practice: The origin location will be the model's *grab* point—the point by which it is grabbed and inserted into another model. The model should also be at the correct scale before uploading.

1. Click the Share Model icon, or choose File→3D Warehouse→Share Model.

2. If you are not already signed in to your Google account, or if you don't have a Google account, the Sign In window will appear. Either enter your Google username and password in this window, or click Create an Account Now to create a Google account.

Note ---

When you are signed in to your Google account, the G icon at the lower-left corner of the SketchUp window will be bold. Clicking this icon will also open the Sign In window, or it will open the Sign Out window if you are already signed in.

---

3. When you are signed in, the Upload page appears (Figure 13-12). Enter a model name and a description (these are mandatory). If you want, you can also enter tags: These are keywords people can use to find your model. For the banana tree model, tags could include *landscaping* or *tropical*. If the model is georeferenced (saved with a specific location), you will also see the Google Earth Ready option, which is described in Recipe 13.10. If you click the + sign next to "Additional content," you will see additional options for adding a logo, adjusting privacy settings (Recipe 13.5), and so on.

Upload your model to 3D Warehouse

Banana Tree.skp (171 kb)

> Banana Tree

> Model of a banana tree

> banana,tree,landscaping,fruit,tropical

⊞ **Additional content** *(includes url, logo, configuration and share settings)*

[Upload]   [Cancel]

Figure 13-12

If your model has materials or components that are not in use, you will be asked whether you want to purge them. Purging is not mandatory, but it's good practice to upload a model with a file size as small as possible.

When the model has completed its upload process, it will appear on its new 3D Warehouse page (Figure 13-13). There are links here to edit, share, or remove the model from the 3D Warehouse. If you have collections in your account (Recipe 13.4), you can use the "Add this model to a collection" link to place it inside a collection.

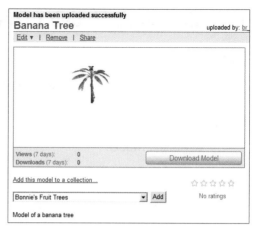

Figure 13-13

> **Note**
>
> Use the Edit link to edit a model if you want to change 3D Warehouse information such as title, description, or privacy settings after the model has been uploaded. If you want to change the model itself, go back to SketchUp and edit the model you originally uploaded, then re-upload by using Share Model. All of the 3D Warehouse information should be saved with the file, so you shouldn't have to reenter it.

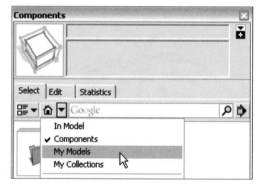

Figure 13-14

4. Save your model, so that all of its 3D Warehouse data will also be saved.

As long as you are signed in, all models you have uploaded will appear when you click the My Models link, either in the Components window (Figure 13-14), or at the top-right corner of the opening page of the 3D Warehouse.

13.4 Creating Collections in the 3D Warehouse

Problem

You want to place your own collections of models in the 3D Warehouse.

Solution

Go to My Collections and create a new collection.

Discussion

Because the 3D Warehouse has unlimited storage space and can be accessed from anywhere, it is the perfect place to store collections of models. These could be collections of entire projects you are working on, collections of "entourage" people or plants used to populate models, collections of furniture models used for interior decorating, collections of windows and doors used for renovation projects, and so on. Models in your collections can be models you have uploaded yourself (Recipe 13.3) or models found elsewhere in the 3D Warehouse. (You can even create your own collection that includes the collections of models used in this book.)

Figure 13-15

Figure 13-16

Figure 13-17

1. Open the 3D Warehouse, either via Get Models or with your Internet browser. If you are not signed in or don't have a Google account, click the Sign In link at the top-right corner of the 3D Warehouse Web page. Either enter your username and password, or click the link to create a new account.

— **Note** —————————————————

You can also sign in to your Google account by clicking the G icon at the lower-left corner of the SketchUp window.

————————————————————————

2. After you are signed in, click the My Collections link (Figure 13-15).

3. Click the Create link (Figure 13-16).

4. Each collection must have a name and description (Figure 13-17). This example is a general landscaping collection that will contain other collections for trees and shrubs, so Other Collections is selected under Collection Will Contain.

— **Note** —————————————————

When creating collections, it's a good idea to set up a hierarchy of collections within collections. A logical collection structure makes it easy to locate models later. Keep in mind that a collection can contain *either* other collections or models, but not both.

————————————————————————

Farther down on the collection creation page is Sharing Settings (Figure 13-18). The default setting is Publicly-viewable, which means anyone can find your collections. If you want to control who can find your collection, see Recipe 13.5.

5. There are also optional fields for adding a logo, URL, and so on. After filling in all the required fields, and any optional fields you want, click Save Changes. Your collection then appears on its new 3D Warehouse page. There are links here to edit, share, or remove the collection.

6. Because the collection in this example was set to contain other collections, there is an option for creating a *child collection* (Figure 13-19), which means a collection within this collection. Click this link to create a child collection.

7. This child collection will be for flowering shrubs and is set to contain models (Figure 13-20).

   When a collection is set to contain models, you will see the Google Earth Ready option shown in Figure 13-21. Select this checkbox *only* if you plan to georeference all models in this collection and have them considered for acceptance into the 3D Buildings layer of Google Earth (see Recipe 13-10). For collections such as landscaping or furniture, this option is irrelevant.

8. You can also create a child collection without using the "Create a child collection" option. Figure 13-22 shows a new collection for fruit trees, using the Create option. This collection is set to contain models.

9. After this new collection is created, click the option "Add this collection to another collection" (Figure 13-23). All of your collections will appear in the drop-down menu. In this example, the fruit tree collection is added to the general landscaping collection.

Sharing Settings What's this?

⊙ **Publicly-viewable** - Anyone can view this collection and see it in search results.
○ **Private/Share** - This collection won't be publicly-viewable, but you will be asked if you wish to add viewers or collaborators.

Figure 13-18

Bonnie's Landscaping Collections
by br_design62
All sorts of trees, shrubs and plants
Updated 1 minute ago

No collections

☆ ☆ ☆ ☆ ☆
No ratings
You can edit, share, or remove this collection, and find out how to add or remove items.

Add this collection to another collection...

Create a child collection...

Figure 13-19

Collection Name   Add or edit translations... ▼

Bonnie's Flowering Shrubs

Description   Add or edit translations... ▼

Flowering shrubs, what else?

Have a website with more info on this collection?
Paste in your web address (URL) (optional)   Add or edit translations... ▼

Collection Will Contain

⊙ Models ○ Other Collections

Figure 13-20

Google Earth Ready ⓘ

☐ This 3D Collection will contain only real, current, and correctly-located models.

Figure 13-21

Bonnie's Fruit Trees

Description   Add or edit translations... ▼

Trees that grow apples, pears, and oranges.

Have a website with more info on this collection?
Paste in your web address (URL) (optional)   Add or edit translations... ▼

Collection Will Contain

⊙ Models ○ Other Collections

Figure 13-22

Bonnie's Fruit Trees
by br_design62
Trees that grow apples, pears, and oranges.
Updated 1 minute ago

No models

☆ ☆ ☆ ☆ ☆
No ratings
You can edit, share, or remove this collection, and find out how to add or remove items.

Add this collection to another collection...

Bonnie's Landscaping Collections ▼ Add

Figure 13-23

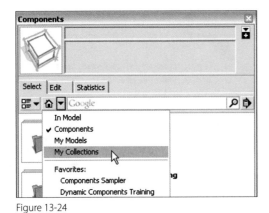

Figure 13-24

As long as you are signed in to your Google account, all of your collections will appear when you click the My Collections link, either in the Components window (Figure 13-24) or at the top-right corner of the opening page of the 3D Warehouse.

13.5 Controlling Model or Collection Privacy

Problem

You want to control who can find your models and collections, or invite collaborators to work on your models.

Solution

Change the Share settings.

Discussion

Say you are working on a project for a design company and want your 3D Warehouse models available only to certain coworkers. Or say you are uploading models for a class project and want your work visible only to the instructor. By default, all models and collections are viewable by anyone, but the Share options in the 3D Warehouse enable you to control who can find your models and who (if anyone) can make changes to it.

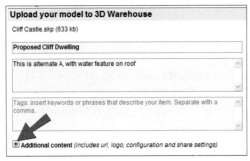

Figure 13-25

When you upload a model (Recipe 13.3) or create a collection (Recipe 13.4), you can access the Share options by clicking the + sign next to "Additional content" (Figure 13-25).

To limit who has access to your model, first deselect the checkbox labeled "Allow anyone to view this model and see it in search results" (Figure 13-26).

After the uploading begins, you will see the page with privacy settings (Figure 13-27). For existing models and collections, you can access this page by clicking the Share link.

You can toggle public viewing and editing on and off, and invite people to access your models as either collaborators (who can make edits) or viewers (who cannot make edits). Click "as collaborators" (or "as viewers" as the case may be) under "Invite people," and then enter the email addresses of your coworkers. You can also choose to send them invitations to your model. Figure 13-27 shows two colleagues added as collaborators; the entered addresses are the addresses the colleagues use to access the 3D Warehouse. (If your collaborators or viewers use Gmail or Google Mail email addresses for the 3D Warehouse, you need to enter only their usernames and not their full email addresses.) After your collaborators or viewers are established, click Done at the top-right corner of the page.

Figure 13-26

Figure 13-27

13.6 Adding Models or Collections to Your Collections

Problem

You want to add models or other collections to a collection.

Solution

Use the "Add this model to a collection" or "Add this collection to another collection" link.

Discussion

To add a model to a collection, you need to have already created the collection (Recipe 13.4), the collection must be set to contain models (as opposed to other collections), and you need to be signed in to your Google account. If you are not signed in, click the G icon at the lower-left corner of the SketchUp window.

To add your own model to a collection, upload it to the 3D Warehouse (Recipe 13.3). After you upload, the "Add this model to a collection" link appears, and all of your available collections are listed in the drop-down menu.

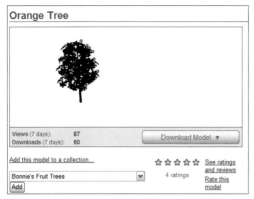

Figure 13-28

Figure 13-29

You can also search the 3D Warehouse for models to add to your collections. On the page for any model, the "Add this model to a collection" link appears under the model picture. Figure 13-28 shows a 3D Warehouse model of an orange tree that has been added to a fruit tree collection.

> **Note**
>
> When you add someone else's model to your collection, be aware that the model's owner may at some point remove the model from the 3D Warehouse, thereby removing it from your collection as well.

If you have created a collection that is set to contain other collections, you can add collections to it. When searching via Get Models, a component search is available in the Advanced Search options, or you can enter this syntax in the search field: *is:collection*. Find the collection you want to add, such as the collection for this book (Figure 13-29), and the link below the collection's thumbnail will read "Add this collection to another collection."

13.7 Taking Credit for Your Model

Problem

You want your name attached to your models in the 3D Warehouse.

Solution

Use the Credits option.

Discussion

Until version 7, your models in the 3D Warehouse would appear under your username, but after someone downloaded one of your models and used it in their own model, your model was no longer "your own." Version 7 makes it possible to keep your name with your model after it has been downloaded.

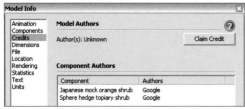

Figure 13-30

To claim credit, click the person icon to the left of the G icon at the lower-left corner of the SketchUp window, or choose Window→Model Info and open the Credits page (Figure 13-30). If you have any components already in your model downloaded from the 3D Warehouse, their authors will appear on this page. To claim credit for the entire model, click the Claim Credit button.

The nickname associated with your Google account will then appear under the model credits.

13.8 Manually Georeferencing Your Model

Problem

You want to manually assign a location to your model.

Solution

Set the location in the Model Info window.

Discussion

A SketchUp model can have three georeferencing states, as indicated by the lightbulb icon at the lower-left corner of the SketchUp window.

- **No location**. This option is for models such as furniture, electronics, and so on.

- **Manual location**. The location is set in the Model Info window, as discussed in this recipe.

- **Location from Google Earth**. Data from Google Earth is imported into the SketchUp model, thereby setting the model location (Recipe 13.9).

To manually georeference a model, open the Model Info window by clicking the lightbulb icon at the lower-left corner of the SketchUp window or by choosing Window→Model Info. On the Location page of the Model Info window (Figure 13-31), make sure that the "Use georeferencing" checkbox is selected, and then use the Geographic Location list to choose the city in which you want your model set. To set a more specific location, click the Set Custom Location button and then enter latitude and longitude coordinates. When a model is georeferenced by using the Location page, the lightbulb icon turns bold.

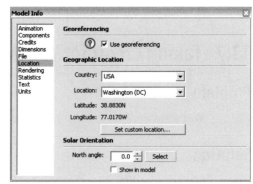

Figure 13-31

Using the Location page to manually set the model's location is fine for a general placement, as you might need for a shadow study. But if you need a more accurate placement, relative to existing landmarks or streets, use the Get Current View method described in Recipe 13.9.

13.9 Georeferencing Your Model by Using Google Earth

Problem

You want to place your model in an exact spot on Google Earth.

Solution

Use Get Current View to bring a Google Earth snapshot and terrain into SketchUp, and locate your model based on the Google Earth data. Then use the Place Model option to place the model in Google Earth.

Discussion

The seamless integration between SketchUp and Google Earth makes it easy (and rather fun) to place models directly in Google Earth. After your model is placed in Google Earth, you can save it in either SketchUp's or Google Earth's native formats. If your model is accurately placed and well modeled, it could be accepted into the 3D Buildings layer of Google Earth (Recipe 13.10).

When modeling for Google Earth, you can start with either the model or the data from Google Earth. If you start with the model, you then import the Google Earth snapshot and terrain faces, and move or rotate the model into place relative to the Google Earth faces. If you start with the Google Earth faces, you would build the model on top of them.

Of course, you don't have to create a model from scratch; you can download one from the 3D Warehouse. The following example demonstrates how to place a downloaded model on a cliff top, both in SketchUp and in Google Earth.

Figure 13-32

Figure 13-33

──── Note ────

If you don't have Google Earth, you can download it for free from *http://earth.google.com/*. (You also can purchase versions with more features, but these features are not necessary for working with SketchUp.)

1. In Google Earth, enter the latitude and longitude coordinates *34.088136 -19.057294* in the Fly To field, to the left of the Earth window (Figure 13-32).

2. This flies you to a cliff above Point Mugu, California—a rather isolated spot and the perfect location for a castle overlooking the sea. Make sure Google Earth's terrain layer is displayed. (Layers are listed in the lower part of the window, to the left of the Google Earth window.) Use the tilt, pan, and zoom controls to get to the view shown in Figure 13-33.

Note ────────────────────────────────

The Fly To field can also take an exact address; a city, state, or country name; a zip code; a landmark; or coordinates in degrees, minutes, and seconds.

---

3. When importing data from Google Earth into SketchUp, it's best to display a plan view in Google Earth, at an appropriate scale for placing your model. Get to a view as shown in Figure 13-34, close enough to see some shrubs and rocks.

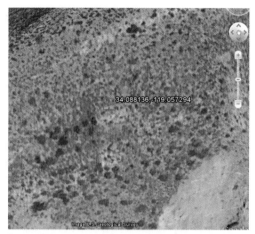

Figure 13-34

4. In SketchUp, click the Get Current View icon, or choose Tools→Google Earth→Get Current View. The snapshot and terrain based on what's visible in Google Earth are imported into SketchUp (Figure 13-35).

   The two faces imported into SketchUp from Google Earth are a snapshot (flat) view and a terrain (3D) surface. To see both of these, open the Layers window and change the layer visibility. Each Google Earth face is a locked group; you cannot edit or move them. (Well, you can if you unlock them, but that's strongly discouraged.)

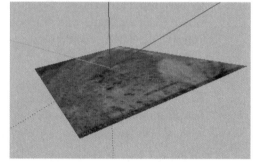

Figure 13-35

Note ────────────────────────────────

When creating a SketchUp model for Google Earth, you may want to use one of SketchUp's Google Earth modeling templates (Windows→Preferences→Template). These templates have no extra components to get in the way, and edges are displayed with no profiles.

---

5. Take a look at the lightbulb icon at the lower-left corner of the SketchUp screen. After Google Earth terrain is imported, the icon changes to a bulb with a Google Earth background. If you open the Model Info window to the Location page, you'll see the coordinates you entered in Google Earth.

6. When placing the SketchUp model onto the Google Earth faces, displaying only the snapshot view makes the process easier. Download my Cliff Castle model from the 3D Warehouse, inserting this model directly into the current SketchUp file (Figure 13-36).

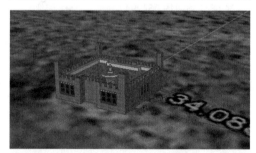

Figure 13-36

Figure 13-37

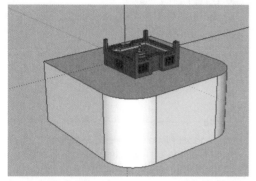

Figure 13-38

Figure 13-39

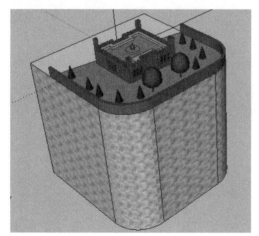

Figure 13-40

Note ———————————————————————

If you prefer to create a model from scratch, you can, of course. If the Google Earth faces get in the way, hide their layers.

---

7. Now display the terrain view, either by adjusting the layer visibility or by clicking the Toggle Terrain icon. Now you can see the cliff slope. Move the model so that its lower-back edge is against the cliff (Figure 13-37).

8. Hide the terrain, and build a huge support to hold up the castle (Figure 13-38).

9. To bring the castle model into Google Earth, click the Place Model icon or choose Tools→Google Earth→Place Model. The castle and its support are sitting pretty on the cliff in Google Earth (Figure 13-39).

10. To make changes to the model, go back to Sketch-Up. Figure 13-40 shows some landscaping, added materials, and a parapet wall around the grounds. You could also move the model to a new location.

Note ———————————————————————

If you want to change the model's scale by using the Tape Measure tool, be sure to scale the model within a group or component, as described in Recipe 10.11. Otherwise, you will be scaling not just the model, but the Google Earth faces as well.

---

11. Click Place Model again, and you will be asked whether you want to reload the model. Click Yes. The changed model replaces the previous model in Google Earth.

Figure 13-41

The model and its location appear in Google Earth in the Places list, below Temporary Places (Figure 13-41). If you move away from this location, you can double-click the placemark's name to return to it. If you want to save this placemark in Google Earth, right-click on the name and choose Save to My Places. This means that you can return to the castle the next time you open Google Earth; the place is no longer temporary. Or you can right-click and choose Save Place As, which enables you to save the model as a .kmz file. This is a Google Earth native format that saves both the model and location data. If you don't plan to have this model accepted into the 3D Buildings layer of Google Earth (sadly, this one would be rejected), you could still send the .kmz file to a colleague or upload the .kmz file to the 3D Warehouse.

The 3D Warehouse collection for this chapter contains the georeferenced version of the castle. Open the 3D Warehouse through your Internet browser (not from within SketchUp) and find the model named Cliff Castle Georeferenced. The default download for this model is View in Google Earth, which means Google Earth will open the .kmz file. If you open the model's 3D Warehouse page and click the Download Model option, you can download either the .skp or .kmz format.

When you place a model into Google Earth by using Place Model, that model appears in your copy of Google Earth only; other Google Earth users cannot see it (unless they have your .kmz file). Buildings that appear in Google Earth's 3D Buildings layer were uploaded to the 3D Warehouse and placed into a queue for screening before acceptance (Recipe 13.10).

Note

You cannot upload .kmz files directly into the 3D Warehouse from either SketchUp or Google Earth, but you can do it "manually" from within the 3D Warehouse. When you open the 3D Warehouse from your Internet browser, the initial page has an Upload link at the top-right corner. Click this link, and you can upload either .skp or .kmz files.

13.10 Getting Your Models into the 3D Buildings Layer

Problem

You want to have your model added to the 3D Buildings layer of Google Earth.

Solution

Create a well-crafted model in the correct location, and upload it to the 3D Warehouse so that it goes in the 3D Buildings acceptance queue.

Discussion

If you're not familiar with how 3D buildings appear in Google Earth, make sure the 3D Buildings layer is turned on, Then fly to a major city and zoom in on its center. Some buildings are gray boxes, which means they are estimates of models based on surveying data; others have colors and textures, indicating that they were modeled in SketchUp and uploaded to the 3D Warehouse. Figure 13-42 shows some of the 3D buildings in St. Louis, Missouri.

Figure 13-42

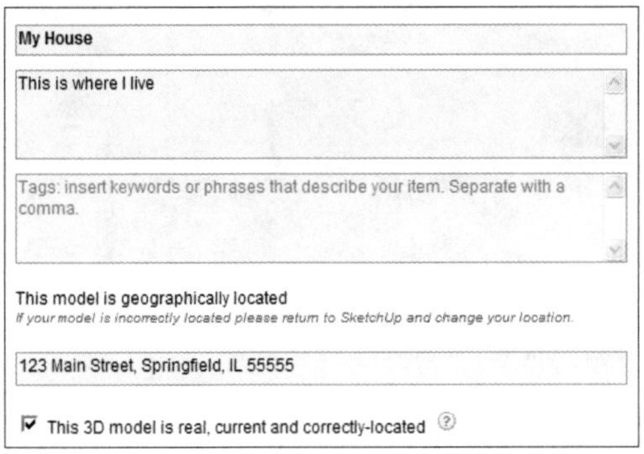

SketchUp models that appear in Google Earth were accepted by judges who check for accuracy and location. If you want your model to be considered, here are some guidelines:

- Models should be as simple as possible. Don't include any interior furniture, outside landscaping, or other extraneous detail.

- Rather than model every feature on the façade of a building, paint faces by using graphic images. Chapter 9 contains techniques for painting with digital photos.

- Keep round objects minimal. Arcs and circles are composed of small segments, and each segment counts as a separate edge. Rather than use a 24-segmented arc or circle, you can usually get by with six or so segments, because the level of detail is not easily visible in Google Earth.

- Correctly georeference your model by importing data from Google Earth into SketchUp (Recipe 13.9).

When you upload your model to the 3D Warehouse (Recipe 13.3), give it an accurate name, description, and address (Figure 13-43). Keep the checkbox labeled "This 3D model is real, current, and correctly-located" selected. (This checkbox is selected by default; if you are modeling something you know is *not* accurate, or does not yet exist, make sure to *deselect* this box.)

My House

This is where I live

Tags: insert keywords or phrases that describe your item. Separate with a comma.

This model is geographically located
If your model is incorrectly located please return to SketchUp and change your location.

123 Main Street, Springfield, IL 55555

☑ This 3D model is real, current and correctly-located ⑦

Figure 13-43

When the model is uploaded, it is placed in the queue for checking. The estimated wait time is generally a few days. At the time of this writing, you are not notified by Google if your model is accepted, but you can see the model's status on its 3D Warehouse page.

13.11 Creating a Placemark in Google Earth

Problem

You want to save a location and view it in Google Earth.

Solution

Create a placemark.

Discussion

Using the Search field in Google Earth can get you to a lot of places. You can enter a city name (Milan, Italy), exact address (1600 Pennsylvania Avenue), or landmark (Eiffel Tower). But what if you are working on a SketchUp project that is to be placed somewhere where there are no easy landmarks nearby, or you want to save a certain viewing angle? The solution is to create a *placemark*. This example shows you how to place a placemark with a specific location and viewing angle.

1. In Google Earth, fly to the approximate location you want to save. Figure 13-44 shows a plan view of part of the campus of Johns Hopkins University (my alma mater). You can get to this spot by entering *johns hopkins homewood* in the Fly To field and then zooming in. The 3D Buildings layer is turned on in this example.

2. Choose Add→Placemark. The pushpin is placed at the center of the view, but you can drag it to the spot you want (Figure 13-44).

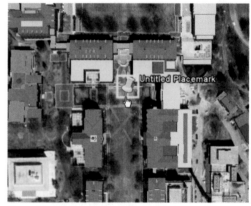

Figure 13-44

3. In the New Placemark window (Figure 13-45), enter a placemark name. You can also see the exact latitude and longitude coordinates here, and change them if needed. Do not click OK yet. (If you do close the New Placemark window, you can right-click on the pushpin and choose Properties to reopen it.)

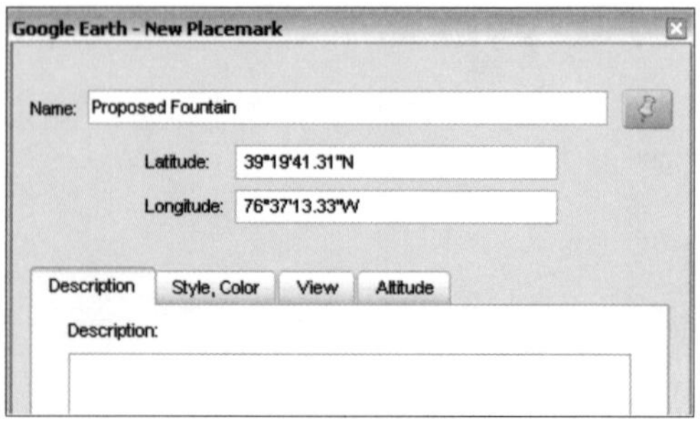

Figure 13-45

Figure 13-46

4. Get to the exact view you want to save (Figure 13-46).

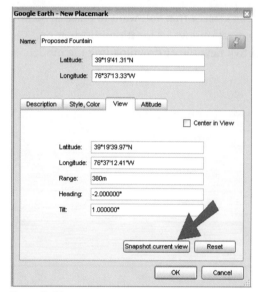
Figure 13-47

5. On the View tab of the New Placemark window, click "Snapshot current view" (Figure 13-47). Then click OK.

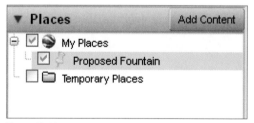
Figure 13-48

The placemark with the location and its viewing angle is saved under My Places, as shown in Figure 13-48. To return to this spot, just double-click the placemark name. To save the placemark as a .kmz file, right-click on it and choose Save Place As.

13.12 Relocating a Georeferenced Model

Problem

You want to place a georeferenced model in a new location.

Solution

Save the model to a new file without its location data, or download it from the 3D Warehouse without preserving its location.

Discussion

Say you have a georeferenced model of a beach house in Greece that you want to place in Spain instead. Before you can place the house in Spain, you must remove its location information. There are two ways to do this: saving only the model to a new file or downloading the model from the 3D Warehouse with new location data.

Method 1: Save the Model Without Georeferencing

This method involves downloading the georeferenced model and saving it to your hard drive. It's a good method to use if you're not yet ready to place the model into another model.

1. Find a georeferenced model in the 3D Warehouse whose location you want to remove, and download it into your current SketchUp file or to a new instance of SketchUp.

2. If the model itself is not already a component, make it one. Then right-click on the component and choose Save As. This saves just the model, without any other objects or terrain faces, into its own file. Save the model to your hard drive.

3. Now the model is ready to import into a new file, and it can be placed anywhere.

Figure 13-49

Figure 13-50

Figure 13-51

Figure 13-52

Method 2: Download the Model with a New Location

In this example, a scaled-down model of the Eiffel Tower will be placed on the front lawn of the White House in Washington, DC. This is a good method to use if you have a georeferenced SketchUp model open, into which the georeferenced model will be imported.

1. In Google Earth, fly to the White House (enter the phrase *white house* in the Fly To field) and zoom in to a plan view as shown in Figure 13-49.

2. In SketchUp, use Get Current View to bring the Google Earth faces into SketchUp.

3. Use the Components window or the Get Models option to find the Eiffel Tower. Download the one by Google (you can use the syntax *Eiffel Tower author:google* in the Search field).

4. In the pop-up message that appears, click Choose New Location.

5. Place the tower and its Google Earth faces in some blank space next to the White House land (Figure 13-50).

6. This step is not necessary, but to clean up the tower model, you can remove its Google Earth faces. Open the tower component for editing. Use the Layers window to control the visibility of the Google Earth faces, and erase them both. (The terrain face will have to be unlocked before it can be erased: Right-click on the face and choose Unlock.) The reason this step is not necessary is that the terrain that appears in SketchUp is not included in what's placed in Google Earth. But it looks neater in the SketchUp model to remove unnecessary or irrelevant terrain.

7. Use Scale to shrink the tower, and move and rotate it into place (Figure 13-51).

8. Use Place Model to bring the tower into Google Earth. Turn on the 3D Buildings layer to see the new addition to the White House surroundings (Figure 13-52).

13.13 Downloading Buildings That Appear in Google Earth

Problem

You want to download models that appear in the 3D Buildings layer of Google Earth.

Solution

Click the building in Google Earth to find the model's name or other identifying features, and use that information in your 3D Warehouse search.

Discussion

In this recipe, you are proposing a new hotel for the main street (the Strip) in Las Vegas. You can see the site's surrounding buildings in Google Earth, and want to download them into your SketchUp model so that you'll have a reference for the new structure. Clicking a 3D building in Google Earth opens a page containing some information about the model. Athough you can't download directly from Google Earth into SketchUp, you can get enough information from Google Earth to use in your 3D Warehouse search.

1. In Google Earth, fly to the Bellagio hotel (you can enter this name in the Fly To field). Make sure the 3D Buildings layer is turned on, and get to a view as shown in Figure 13-53. The three hotels indicated by the arrows are the ones you want to download into SketchUp. The proposed new hotel will be placed in the middle of these three.

Figure 13-53

2. Click the hotel indicated in the lower-right corner of Figure 13-53. This opens an info page that describes the model, whose name is Aladdin Casino and Resort (Figure 13-54). If you click the model picture on this info page, your Internet browser will open the model's 3D Warehouse page.

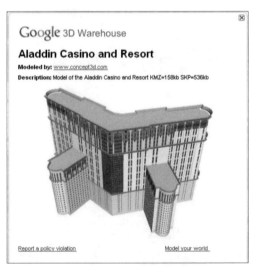

Figure 13-54

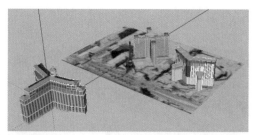

Figure 13-55

Figure 13-56

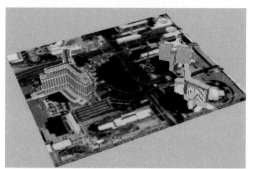

Figure 13-57

Figure 13-58

3. You can download the model from the browser, which will open a new SketchUp instance. Or you can search the 3D Warehouse from within Sketch-Up, using the Components window or the Get Models option, and enter the name Aladdin Casino to find the correct model. To show only the specific model that appears in Google Earth, you can use an Advanced Search, or use this syntax in your search: *aladdin casino is:best-of-geo.*

4. Import the Aladdin model, and from within the same SketchUp file, search for the other two hotels: the Paris Las Vegas and the Bellagio. For each of these, choose to preserve their location, so that they will be imported in the correct position and location. Some models include Google Earth faces, and some do not (Figure 13-55).

5. Some of the land between the hotels is missing, so it must be filled in by returning to Google Earth and taking a new snapshot. In Google Earth, get to a view as shown in Figure 13-56.

6. Return to SketchUp and use Get Current View to fill in the missing land (Figure 13-57).

7. On the Google Earth snapshot, create your new hotel model. The one shown in Figure 13-58 is an enormous, tacky arch with windows that spans over the Strip and nicely frames the Paris hotel's mini Eiffel Tower.

8. This is an important step before placing your new model into Google Earth: erase or hide the three other buildings (Figure 13-59). Everything that is visible in SketchUp, except for the Google Earth faces, is brought into Google Earth, and Google Earth already has the three existing hotels. If you don't want to remove these models permanently, hiding is a good solution; it will keep the models out of Google Earth but they can easily be redisplayed in SketchUp.

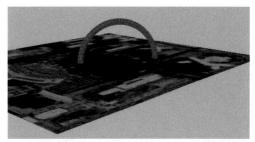

Figure 13-59

9. In SketchUp, use Place Model to bring the new hotel into Google Earth (Figure 13-60).

The 3D Warehouse collection for this chapter contains the georeferenced version of this hotel. Open the 3D Warehouse through your Internet browser and find the model Vegas Arch. The default download for this model is View in Google Earth, which means Google Earth will open the .kmz file. If you open the model's 3D Warehouse page and click the Download Model option, you can download either the .skp or .kmz format.

Figure 13-60

CHAPTER 14

Dynamic Components

Dynamic components are the major new feature of SketchUp 7. In essence, a *dynamic component* is a component that has attributes: features that can be adjusted, toggled on and off, moved, replaced, resized, and so on. A simple dynamic component could be a box that you click to change its color or click to open and close the box top. A more complex example would be a dining set in which you can adjust the number of chairs, choose various finishes and table tops, scale to adjust the length, and then see the calculated price for the current configuration. Another common type of dynamic component is one that self-copies when scaled, such as a fence that will adjust its number of pickets to accommodate the fence length.

Dynamic components are free and available for all SketchUp users to download. However, only users of the Pro version can create their own dynamic components and change attributes of existing ones. For this reason, and because creating dynamic components is a topic that requires an entire book of its own, this chapter covers only the basics of where to find dynamic components, and the various things you can do with them.

—— **Note** ——————————————

If you are a Pro user interested in learning how to create dynamic components, you can find online videos and self-paced tutorials on SketchUp's website and via the Help Center (choose Help→Help Center).

Before getting started, display the Dynamic Components toolbar (Figure 14-1). In Windows, choose View→Toolbars→Dynamic Components. On the Mac, choose View→Tool Palettes→Dynamic Components.

Figure 14-1

From left to right, these tools are as follows:

- **Interact**. This tool is used on dynamic components that have attributes that can be changed with a mouse click. For instance, you can click to swing open a door, to change a material, or to move an object from one point to another.

- **Component Options**. For dynamic options that have descriptive attributes or user-defined attributes, the Component Options window lists each available option or description.

- **Component Attributes**. For Pro users only, this window enables you to add or change attributes of a dynamic component.

14.1 Finding Dynamic Components

Problem

You want to find and import dynamic components.

Solution

Find the dynamic components provided in the Google collections in the 3D Warehouse, or perform an advanced search for dynamic component models or collections.

Discussion

When looking for dynamic components in the 3D Warehouse, keep in mind that they work only when they are imported directly into your SketchUp model via either the Components window or Get Models. (Searching the 3D Warehouse is explained in Recipe 13.1.) If you open a dynamic component in a new SketchUp instance, it will open as its own model and won't function as a component.

> **Note**
>
> If you have a dynamic component on your hard drive, you can use File→Import to import it, as you would for a nondynamic component.

Figure 14-2

When searching for models and collections in the 3D Warehouse, those that are dynamic are identifiable by the green square-and-triangle icon shown to the right of the fence thumbnail in Figure 14-2.

The Google collections, such as Architecture, Landscaping, and People, which can be opened directly from your Components window, contain both dynamic and nondynamic collections. For example, the Architecture collection contains a collection called DC Cabinets and another called DC Doors and Windows.

When using Get Models, you can use the Advanced Search feature to find only dynamic models, or you can use the *is:dynamic* search operator syntax in the search field. For example, entering *window is:dynamic* will yield all models that have the word *window* in the title or description, and are dynamic (Figure 14-3).

> **Note**
>
> Advanced search and operator syntax are described in Recipe 13.2.

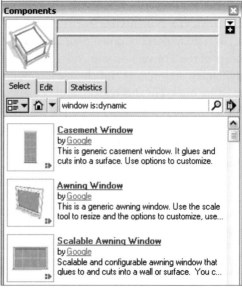

Figure 14-3

If you want to find entire collections of dynamic components, use the syntax *dynamic is:collection*.

14.2 Interacting with Dynamic Components

Problem

You want to see how dynamic components interact.

Solution

Use the Interact tool.

Discussion

The Interact tool lets you activate dynamic attributes that are enabled by a mouse click. For dynamic components that have mouse-click attributes, clicking on certain parts of the dynamic component will cause something to happen: a change of material, movement, rotation, and so on.

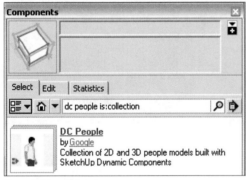

Figure 14-4

Figure 14-5

Interact is available via the hand icon on the Dynamic Components toolbar (View→Toolbars→Dynamic Components), or you can choose Tools→Interact.

For a simple example of Interact, find the DC People collection in the 3D Warehouse. You can access this collection by clicking the Navigation arrow in the Components window and opening the People collection and then the DC People collection. Or you could use the search syntax *dc people is:collection* (Figure 14-4).

Open DC People and import Sang into your model. (Sang might already be in your model; he's the default component for some SketchUp templates.)

With the Interact tool active, move your cursor over the various parts of Sang. When the cursor is over Sang's hair, shirt, or pants, the cursor symbol's pointer finger radiates little yellow lines, indicating that the cursor is on something you can interact with (Figure 14-5).

Click Sang's shirt, pants, or hair to scroll through a preset list of colors. The component attributes are defined so that Interact will scroll through just a few colors, but you can choose different colors. Open Sang's Component Options (right-click on Sang and choose Dynamic Components→Component Options) to see an interactive window in which you can manually choose colors, either by name, RGB value, or hexadecimal value.

For another fun example of using Interact, import the Dynamic Art Frame by Google (search for *art frame is:dynamic*). Place two of these frames on walls, and while Interact is active, click each painting to scroll between three other works of "art." The frame size automatically adjusts to meet the extents of the painting. In the Component Options window, you can also adjust the frame color and size (Figure 14-6).

Figure 14-6

—— **Note** ————————————————————————

When you import more than one instance of a dynamic component, copies of the component are listed in the In Model folder. If you import one dynamic component and use the Move tool to make copies of it, the In Model folder will reflect only one component. But as soon as you make changes to any of the copies, a new dynamic component will appear in the In Model folder. This is explained in Recipe 14.5.

———————————————————————————————————

The Interact tool can also be used to animate. Figure 14-7 shows a house with two dynamic awning windows and three dynamic double-hung windows. (To find dynamic windows, search for *window is:dynamic*.) Clicking on a double-hung window slides it open; clicking it again closes it. Clicking on an awning window rotates it open and shut. Dynamic doors work the same way.

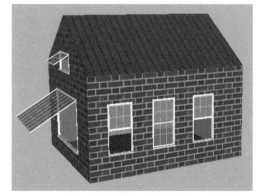

Figure 14-7

For an example of a dynamic component with several types of interactions, download Google's dynamic delivery truck (search for *truck is:dynamic*). While Interact is active, you can click the front wheels to turn them, click the doors to open and close them, click the cab to scroll through various colors, and click the bed to scroll through various configurations (Figure 14-8).

Figure 14-8

14.3 Investigating Dynamic Component Options

Problem

You want to see all of the possible changes you can make to a dynamic component.

Solution

Open the Component Options window to see what options are available.

Discussion

There are infinite possibilities for modifying dynamic components: using the Interact tool, changing component options, scaling, and more—all at once or in any combination. A well-crafted dynamic component provides an explanation of all its possibilities in its description in the Component Options window. You can open this window by right-clicking on the component and choosing Dynamic Components→Component Options. The Component Options window is akin to the Entity Info window; you can keep it open all the time if you want, and options will appear for whatever component is selected.

For some examples of what component options can look like, open Google's Dynamic Component Catalogs collection (search for *dynamic catalog is:collection*). This catalog includes several collections by manufacturers such as Smart Furniture, Marvin Windows and Doors, and KitchenAid. Many more collections are expected to be added in the future.

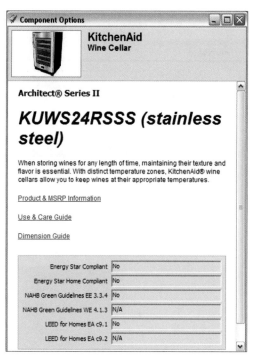

Open the KitchenAid collection and import the under-counter wine cellar into your model. Its Component Options are shown in Figure 14-9. This is one of the simplest types of dynamic components; it has nothing to change or interact with, but you can view its features and link to various web pages for more information.

Figure 14-9

Figure 14-10 shows the options for Smart Shelves by Smart Furniture. In addition to being able to link to the company's online store, you can configure your shelves within SketchUp and see the resulting price.

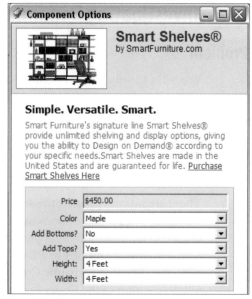

Figure 14-10

Figure 14-11 shows the options for a Marvin window. The description informs you that you can use the Interact tool to open the window. The window's dimensions are grayed out, because they depend on the model number you select from a list. You can choose to include a grille or jamb extension. This is a great way to condense a large number of possible window configurations into a single component, as opposed to providing hundreds of nondynamic components representing each window model. And you can try out different configurations by simply changing options, rather than searching for different components to load.

Figure 14-11

14.4 Scaling Dynamic Components

Problem

You want to change the size of a scalable dynamic component.

Solution

Select the component, activate Scale, and resize the component by using the available drag handles.

Discussion

When you scale a nondynamic component, all objects in the component are stretched or squashed by the same proportion. So if you want to widen a nondynamic couch, its arms and supports will widen as well. Dynamic components can be set to maintain dimensions of certain objects, such as the arms of a couch, and allow the size to change only for other objects, such as the couch cushions. A dynamic component can also be set to add or remove objects when the size gets too large or small. So a widened dynamic couch would take on extra cushions after the cushions exceed a set width. Finally, dynamic components can have certain scale handles hidden, limiting you to scale only in certain directions. So a dynamic couch can be scalable in width but can have scaling restricted in height or depth.

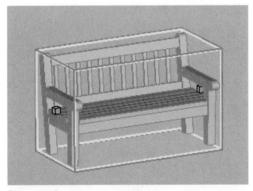

Figure 14-12

To see what this means, import Google's wood high-back bench (search for *highback bench is:dynamic*). Its Component Options window informs you that scaling is the only way to change this model; there are no other options or interactions. When the Scale tool is activated, you will see drag handles only in the width direction, not height or depth (Figure 14-12).

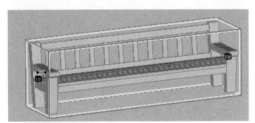

Figure 14-13

Drag one of the handles to make the bench wider. While you are dragging the mouse, all parts of the bench appear to grow wider, including the arms, legs, and slats (Figure 14-13).

As soon as you click to complete the scale, the bench regenerates. The arms, legs, and slats maintain their original sizes, and more slats are added to accommodate the new width (Figure 14-14).

For another example, draw a wall and insert Google's dynamic scalable casement window. In its Component Options window, the width and height are grayed out, because the only way to set the window size is via the Scale tool, as stated in the description (Figure 14-15).

Drag handles are available only to change either the height or width; you cannot scale in both directions at once. To scale the window to a specific width or height, start dragging the mouse in the relevant scale direction, and then type the dimension you want, followed by the unit symbol, and press Enter. Grilles are added or removed as needed, to keep the window panes from exceeding a set dimension (Figure 14-16).

— **Note** —————————————————————

At the time of this writing, you cannot use double-quotation marks while specifying a set length via the Scale tool. So if you are working in inches, enter the length in feet instead, using the single-quote foot symbol. For example, you can't enter *18"* but you can enter *1.5'* or *1'6*. Alternatively, you can create a "dummy" rectangle to represent the final window size, and scale the window to meet the edges of the rectangle.

————————————————————————————————

When the window is resized, its new dimensions appear in the Component Options window.

For a final scaling example, import several copies of Google's dynamic pine tree. You can scale this tree in the height direction only, and the groups of needle clusters will adjust accordingly (Figure 14-17). This is an example of a dynamic component that can be modified in several ways. Aside from scaling, you can change various tree features in the Component Options window and use the Interact tool to tweak the individual needle clusters.

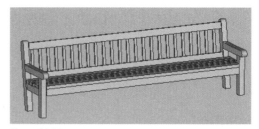

Figure 14-14

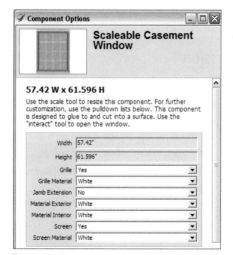

Figure 14-15

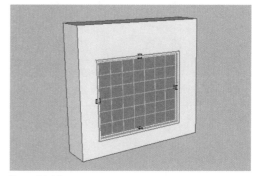

Figure 14-16

Figure 14-17

14.5 Modifying and Replacing Dynamic Components

Problem

You have several copies of a dynamic component. You want to modify one of them and then replace the remaining dynamic components with the one you modified.

Solution

Modify one dynamic component, which automatically creates a new component. Then use Replace Selected in the Components window to replace all of the original components with the new one.

Discussion

When you have copies of a dynamic component, making changes to one of them is equivalent to using the Make Unique option on a nondynamic component. A new component is created, which can be seen in the In Model folder. In this example, involving lengthening dynamic fence components, you will see when and how new components are created as a result of modifying dynamic components. You will also see how to replace components with other components, and how to use the Component Options window to change multiple dynamic components at once.

Figure 14-18

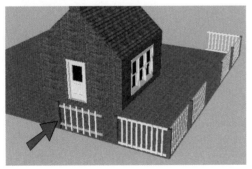

Figure 14-19

1. Download my Dynamic Fenced Yard model from the 3D Warehouse (Figure 14-18). If you import this model directly into your SketchUp model, explode the model before continuing.

    The fence components around the yard are dynamic, and one component is placed at each fence post location. These components are identical copies, so only one fence component appears in the In Model folder of the Components window. To fill in the missing rails and pickets, each fence component will be scaled to meet the next post.

2. Select one of the fence components and use its Component Options window to widen the picket spacing and offset the rails. Then open the modified component for editing, and paint the rails (Figure 14-19).

    The fence components started out as identical, but when you changed the options for one of them, a new fence component was created. The In Model folder will show a new component: Dynamic Fence#1. So when that modified component was opened for editing and you painted the rails, the changed materials did not affect any other components.

3. Replacing all of the original fences with the new one, as shown in Figure 14-20, can be done entirely in the In Model folder of the Components window. Right-click on the thumbnail for the original fence component and choose Select Instances. Then right-click on the thumbnail for the modified fence and choose Replace Selected.

Figure 14-20

4. Use Scale on each fence to extend it to meet the next fence post (Figure 14-21). Now that each fence component has been modified, each one is a separate component.

Note

To remove the overhanging rails and pickets on the last fence component, you could explode that last component and erase the rails and pickets. Or you could make it unique and edit it.

Figure 14-21

The picket spacing is set in the Component Options, but each fence component has a different length. So where does the difference in spacing appear? Look at the pickets on either side of a post; only the spacing here is not uniform (Figure 14-22).

5. Even though each fence is a separate component, you can still change the options for all of them at once. Open the Component Options window, select all of the fences, and change one of the options, such as picket spacing. All of the fences will update.

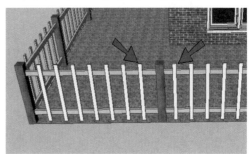

Figure 14-22

14.6 Sizing by the Reference Point

Problem

You want to import a dynamic component at the correct point in your model.

Solution

When you bring the component into your model, pay attention to the point by which you grab the component. This is the *reference point*, and changes in dimension are made relative to this point.

Discussion

The reference point is one of the most important aspects of a dynamic component, because changes in scale and location are done relative to this point. When you use the fields on the Component Options window to change dimensions, the component's reference point will remain in place. For example, if you drag in a dynamic window by its lower-left corner and place that corner at point A, the window's lower-left corner will remain at point A unless you manually move it. When you enter a new window height or width, the resizing will be relative to point A.

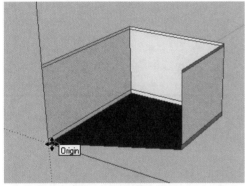

Figure 14-23

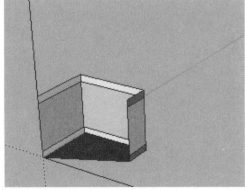

Figure 14-24

Note ─────────────────────────────

The reference point *can* move when you use the Scale tool, depending on which scale handle you drag.

In this example, you will see how a component's reference comes into play when resizing a room and its floor.

1. Import Google's Angled Wall Room dynamic component (search for *angled room is:dynamic*). Place the reference point at the origin of the SketchUp model (Figure 14-23).

2. In the room's Component Options window, change the width to 126", the length to 102", the height to 8', and make the base trim 12". The resulting room in Figure 14-24 also shows some changed colors. The corner of the room at the origin remains in place, and the walls adjust accordingly.

3. Import my Floating Floor component from this chapter's 3D Warehouse collection. This is a tiled floor whose tiles will self-copy when the floor is resized. The tiles are to start at the corner farthest from the origin, so the floor's reference point should be placed there. Click the bottom point of that corner (Figure 14-25). The tiles themselves are set to start 12" above the point by which they are placed (this is, after all, a floating floor). This is why the floor aligns with the top of the 12" base trim. (The floating distance is one of the options that can and will be changed.)

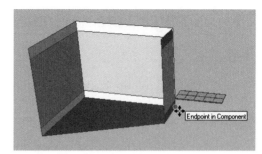

Figure 14-25

4. Scale the floor to meet the other corner of the room (Figure 14-26).

5. Use the Component Options to reduce the floor height to 3" (so the base molding will be visible), and change the tiles to 12"×18". You can also change the floor material if you like. The resulting floor should look like Figure 14-27: the tiles extend past the corner at the origin. This is because the 12" x 18" tiles don't fit perfectly in a 126"×102" room.

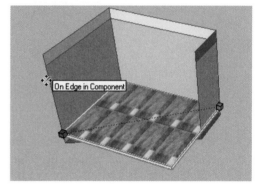

Figure 14-26

To trim the tiles to fit the room, you would have to explode them, which means the floor will no longer be a component. So in the real world, this is a step best saved for the last minute, after you know that your room dimensions will not change.

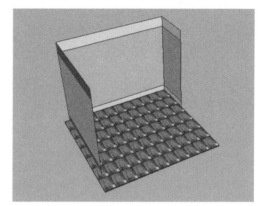

Figure 14-27

If you want to trim the tiles, here is the procedure: Open the Component Options for the room itself and display wall A, the only wall not currently displayed. Then explode the floor, which reduces the floor to its individual tile components. With all of these tiles selected, explode them, too. (This also changes the scale of the material.) Next, right-click on the room component and choose Intersect→Intersect with Model. With the intersection edges thus created, you can trim away the parts of the tiles that extend past the floor. Then you can hide walls again via the room's Component Options (Figure 14-28).

If you then wanted to change the scale of the material, you would use the Fixed Pins method described in Recipe 8.9. After the position of the material in one tile is set, use the eyedropper to "sample" the material. Then right-click on any tile and choose Select→All with same material, and click any selected tile, which applies the new positioned texture to all of the tiles.

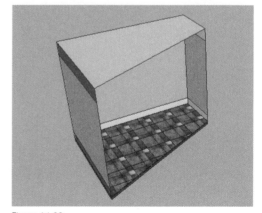

Figure 14-28

Translucent Materials model, 205
trash bin, 44
trees
  2D versus 3D, 166
  ring of, 222
Trimmed Rails model, 56
trimming components with
    themselves, 73–78
trimming objects, 54–56
trimming rails to meet curved
    face, 56
truck
  painting with free-pin
    positioning, 236–238
  removing logo, 231
  using Photo Match to model,
    241–243
Truck model, 236, 241
Twigs style, 312
two-sided coloring, 148–150

U

Umbrella model, 129
ungluing faces, 135–137

ungrouping components, 37
ungrouping (see Explode)
ungrouping (see exploding
    components)
Unhide, 55
units, 3
  Architectural, 5
  Imperial, 5
unsticking edges, 137–141
Use Offset, 177
Use Texture Image, 195

W

Walkthrough, 284
Walk tool, 284–287
walls
  protecting from edits, 141–143
  Push/Pull, 142
Watermark Logo model, 310
watermarks, 307–311
  Blend slider, 308
  Create Mask checkbox, 310
  Lock Aspect Ratio checkbox,
    310

Watermark Style model, 307
Wavy Windows model, 64
White House model, 243
Windmills model, 282
windows
  curved, 105
  decorative trim around, 40
  in 3D walls, 172–178
    known thickness, 177–178
    unknown thickness, 173–176
  octagonal, 169
  one-way, 207
  stained-glass, 101
  three-paned, 101
Wireframe view, 147

X

X-Ray mode, 262
X-Ray view, 146

Z

Z-fighting, 143, 197
Zoom Extents tool, 264
Zoom window tool, 225

About the Author

Bonnie Roskes has been writing SketchUp books since 2002, and has a loyal customer base that loves her books. She frequently hears that her books are clearer and easier to understand than any other software book out there. She also has a great relationship with the SketchUp folks, who have been very supportive of her work. Bonnie has a degree in structural engineering and several years of experience in bridge design, so she approaches design from a practical standpoint, not a theoretical one.

Colophon

The animal on the cover of *Google SketchUp Cookbook* is a golden pheasant (*Chrysolophus pictus*). Native to mountainous forests of western China, this gamebird has been recorded in Chinese culture and art for centuries and is also known as the Chinese pheasant. Very little is known about the birds' natural habitat, as the mountain slopes and ledges they occupy are often rocky and treacherous and therefore inaccessible to humans.

Golden pheasants are striking birds. Males are more distinctive than females, and are characterized by a golden crest tipped with red, a bright red body, and a deep orange "cape," which, when spread during the courtship display, creates a fanlike shape of alternating black and orange. Females, by contrast, have mottled brown plumage with accents of beige on the face, throat, and abdomen. The tail of the female accounts for about half of her total body length, whereas the male's is proportionally longer, comprising about two-thirds of an average 40-inch body length. Both sexes have yellow tails and bills.

The golden pheasants' diet consists mainly of grain, leaves, and invertebrates; they feed on the ground but roost in trees at night. Although the birds are able to fly, their flight is quite awkward and they generally spend more time on the ground.

Commonly found today in aviaries and zoos, golden pheasants were kept in captivity as early as 1740. They are claimed to be the first species of pheasant brought to North America, and there is evidence that George Washington kept them at Mount Vernon. They are hardy, breed readily, and are compatible with other bird species (though, interestingly, not with other kinds of pheasants), making them a great choice for the novice caretaker.

The cover image is from Dover's *Animals*. The cover font is Adobe ITC Garamond; the text font is Adobe Minion Pro; and the heading font is Adobe Myriad Pro Condensed.